THE
ETHNIC FACTOR

How America's Minorities
Decide Elections

BY

MARK R. LEVY

AND

MICHAEL S. KRAMER

Simon and Schuster
New York

*For our parents
and grandparents
and
Dee and Millie*

AUTHORS' NOTE

This book was conceived by Michael S. Kramer of the Institute of American Research at Columbus, Ohio. Mr. Kramer approached Mark R. Levy, then manager of the Election Unit at NBC News, and suggested pooling the resources of the Institute with those of NBC to study ethnic voting behavior in the United States. The Institute contracted with the National Broadcasting Company for use of its computer-tape archives and provided its analytical expertise and staff, under the direction of Mr. Kramer and Arthur Klebanoff. Mr. Levy and Mr. Kramer collaborated in writing the manuscript, with Mr. Klebanoff aiding Mr. Kramer in developing the analytical conclusions and predictions in Chapter 8.

Many people aided the authors with invaluable advice and inspiration over many years. We thank them all, and particularly: Richard M. Scammon, Father Andrew Greeley, Oliver Quayle, Louis Harris, I. A. Lewis, Bert Ivry, Andrew Tremko, Judith Herman, Father S. M. Tomasi, Salvatore LaGumina, Father Joseph Fitzpatrick, Laurel Kovacik, Walter Gellhorn, Nathan Glazer, John Buell, Robert Miller, Tom Plate, Jack Kroll, William Lilley, John William Ward, Earl Latham, Benjamin Ziegler, Eric Foner, and George Kateb.

Our very special thanks to William H. Simon and Dorothea Jean Lynch.

Lastly, most importantly, the debt owed Stephen J. Kovacik, Jr., President of the Institute of American Research, cannot be exaggerated. His commitment to this project never faltered, and he insisted on conducting the most far-reaching accumulation and analysis of ethnic voting data ever undertaken. There would be no book without him.

M. R. L.
M. S. K.

New York City
Columbus Day, 1971

CONTENTS

1

The Ethnic Factor

This book is about clout. Not the kind of clout dispensed daily a generation ago by Joe DiMaggio and Jackie Robinson, but political clout, political power, and how it is and can be wielded by some 65 million Americans termed collectively the ethnics. In this estimate we include the hyphenated Americans, who automatically come to mind, and also the black and Spanish-speaking Americans, for they too are ethnics, outsiders in their own land. Interestingly, although perhaps inevitably, it is the black American who is showing the way politically. His success has been substantial, and our overriding hope is that his lead will be followed by the other ethnic Americans so that they too may fully realize their potential political power and may utilize that power constructively. So, after all, this book *is* about Joe DiMaggio and Jackie Robinson and millions of their ethnic brothers who, while they would probably prefer to be similarly immortalized in baseball's Hall of Fame, deserve, at the very least, to be recognized in American politics and to understand the power which is theirs for the taking.

Although never comprehending the exact extent of the ethnic dynamic, most good (read "successful") politicians have known —perhaps only intuitively, as is often the case with this peculiar breed—the importance of appealing to ethnic pride, the value in

spurring the same buoyancy all men feel when they are identified
and congratulated, regardless of the reason. Thus, New York's
most celebrated mayor, Jimmy "the Hat" Walker, would often
begin a speech with numerous "city comparisons." New York, he
would tell his audience, had more Irish than Dublin, more Jews
than Jerusalem, more Italians than Rome, and so on, his examples confined only by his geographical recollection on that
day. And even though the ethnics were supposedly hard at the
business of burying past associations in the quick-paced effort to
become American, these friendly recitals were always well received, and often rewarded with votes. The "city comparison"
formula became ritual and would no doubt flourish today but for
the fact that the practice has been co-opted for Rheingold Beer
television commercials—commercial co-optation having become
a successful formula all its own.

Of course, there was (and is) more to it than the chance for a
laugh, or the hope of a WASP candidate to carpetbag on a shared
ethnic memory.

The balanced ticket became a normal expression of American
politics, saw the election of many ethnics during the New Deal,
and is still widely employed by both major parties. Even before
the advent of the ethnic candidate, an ethnoreligious influence on
foreign-policy matters was often successfully directed at the
federal government. The swirling controversy surrounding the
1794 Jay Treaty with England witnessed mass Irish opposition,
and later the Irish were largely responsible for defeating a
fisheries treaty with Canada in 1888 and the Anglo-American
Arbitration Treaty of 1897.

German-Americans sought a resolution favorable to their particular "old country" when a dispute arose concerning Pacific
Samoa in 1888, and Polish-Americans were equally effusive in
decrying the Yalta Agreement some sixty years later. Catholic
opinion had a role in keeping the United States from entering the
Spanish Civil War, and Protestant groups forced President Truman to abandon plans to appoint an ambassador to the Vatican.

The catalogue of ethnoreligious "interference" in American
foreign policy is long, and it seems silly at best, and self-serving
at worst, to argue that this activity is somehow less legitimate

than the lobbying efforts of other interest groups. Surely a tight argument can be made for the inverse proposition, that ethnicity allows a group's individual members a greater sense of belonging and a better opportunity to participate.

Classical democratic theory always viewed democracy as a set of institutions which both promoted and depended upon the full rational development of the individual. However, the practical application of such a philosophy falls short of its internally consistent theoretical underpinnings, and democracy by proxy becomes a psychological fraud as the individual who is spoken for by the large pressure group has himself little voice within the rigid group framework. Ambrose Bierce defines politics as "a strife of interests masquerading as a contest of principles," and too often pressure-group politics dissolves into a confrontation of Washington elites; as such it is rarely a source of pride or identity to the local member. The situation becomes absurd. Modern-day pluralists never ask if the A.M.A. is representative of the real opinion within the medical profession, nor do they ask whether that organization encourages or even allows its members to begin to develop their own thinking on issues of importance. Many pluralists accept or even delight in the fact that most doctors do not wish to participate directly in politics, and they then add the crucial thought that, if doctors (or whoever) find their organization unsatisfactory, they can join another. This imagined ability to move among organizations constitutes their new concept of freedom, and such logical posturing flies in the face of the ethnic experience. For these are the very people who have always been denied freedom of movement, and it seems eminently reasonable to allow their interest group to be their common heritage—a proposition, we would add, which allows all in the family to participate, and not merely the breadwinner who might happen to be a doctor or a union member or an Elk. Ours is a pluralist society and the manifestation of that pluralism should be left to personal preference.

But few have seen fit to leave it at that, and ethnic pluralism especially has long borne the brunt of "disunity" criticism. Regardless of the "regardless" legislation (". . . regardless of race, color, creed, or national origin"), the call to forget one's

ethnic roots has echoed for some while. Teddy Roosevelt put it
most bluntly: "We have no room for any people who do not act
and vote simply as Americans and nothing else." But such
rhetoric was soon considered insufficient, as it had been earlier
when the Know-Nothings elevated nativism to the status of a
political party. In recent years there has emerged a never-ending
effort to create and preserve an elusive body of thought and
action, and then to characterize those traits sloppily, without
acknowledging the definitional problems, as "American." Indeed,
an entire ethic has been invented to prove that the ethnics are
no longer ethnic, and the social scientist has given us the Big Lie
of assimilation. A Melting Pot has been decreed, its machinations
have been charted, the end results have been prescribed.
America has been explained.

Our efforts have proven to us, persuasively, that the hyphenated Americans do vote as ethnic blocs, and that, at least, political assimilation has not occurred. We are not sociologists, and we
admit that the case for cultural assimilation has not been dis-
proved by our work. Nevertheless, to the generations of "lookers
back" yet to come we can only hope for an imagination which
will challenge the American hypothesis anew. For if psephology
(the study of voting behavior) transcends its own internal,
political relevance, the American hypothesis of the Melting Pot
just ain't so. Past national affiliations speak eloquently at the polls
and retain their complex interrelationships. The suspicion of this
fact is one of those "feelings" most astute politicians have long
shared. Those who have doubted the persistence of political
ethnicity are herewith forewarned: the knish and the pizza
survive—and not merely as edible ethnic delicacies.

Lost in the shuffle of this political knowledge have been the
ethnics themselves. They have retained their ethnic identity while
being implored not to do so, and in the confusion they have
never known their collective political power—which is considerable. It is for them and for those who must deal with this reality,
that this book is written.

Of the conclusions our research has dictated, a few deserve
mention here. But first understand our basic psephological assumption—one that is congruent with the politician's prime con-

cern—*only votes count.* Only one kind of person counts on election day, and that person is someone who shows up at the polls. Demographers are interested in all people, their numbers, locale and characteristics. Political analysts, of necessity, are interested in voters, a group more elusive than one might think. In any given election, some set of people will become voters. The trick is to properly characterize that set. Election laws provide one barrier. Those under eighteen, or noncitizens, or those not satisfying residency requirements, are, of course, outside the potential-voter pool. Also, age characteristics and geographical mobility vary within and among ethnic groups. Equal total populations of Jews and Mexican-Americans, for example, yield vastly different potential-voter totals.

The difference between potential voters and actual voters in any given election can change the outcome. Voter rolls are like a giant inventory; new voters register (with no consistent pattern of interest) as old voters die or move or fail to keep their registration active. This flow of voters on and off the enrollment books can affect as much as 30 percent of the electorate in any given year, and accordingly, we have chosen throughout to distinguish our demographic information from our political analysis.

When we speak of a group *voting* in a given way, we mean just that; our *precinct returns* suggest whatever conclusion we have drawn. There is no better source of information about voters than the way they vote. (And the only consistent data on the way voters vote are canvasses at the local, precinct, level.) To be sure, there is a sociology of voting, a concern for why people vote as they do. It is a worthwhile inquiry, and one that we hope will be aided by our study. But our concern here is to demonstrate, and in a fashion we believe to be more exhaustive and compelling than our predecessors, how certain ethnically homogeneous groups vote. If we have been successful, the question, "How do America's minorities vote?" will have been answered.

EVERY VOTE COUNTS; SOME ETHNIC VOTES COUNT MORE

Each voter is still legally limited to vote but once in an election. In some sense then, each vote counts, and no vote contributes to victory or defeat more than any other. However, certain votes, and particularly those which can be influenced in blocs, have the effect of counting for more than their numbers in closely contested elections.

Ethnic voters as a general rule move in blocs. Most simply put, the Republican ethnic strategy is to break up the Democratic bloc vote. Thus far the strategy has failed. Each instance of a Democratic candidate who loses statewide without bloc ethnic support highlights a contest where proper attention to ethnic voters would have avoided defeat. We have noted these elections, and have indicated how much better the Democrat would have had to do with the ethnic voters to have won. We have also indicated where extraordinary bloc support provided a greater plurality than the candidate's overall statewide victory margin. In each instance the particular ethnic group had at some time in the past, or could reasonably at some time in the future, meet the performance levels cited. The narrow margin of past defeat is the lesson of future victory.

In the course of dealing with six groups, we will occasionally speculate about apparently contradictory election outcomes; New Jersey, for example, may have been "won" or "lost" too many times in one election for some readers' tastes. The purpose of including the effect of voter switches in each ethnic group on the outcome of one election is to show the delicate interaction of currently competing ethnic group interests, and to warn the budding strategist that the reaction to even well-focused ethnic-oriented activity may not be desirable. A politician is worried about one plurality—the difference between his total and that of his opponent. We are concerned with the ethnic groups' contribution to that plurality and the manner in which the clever politician can work changes in that factor.

TWO-TO-ONE DEMOCRATIC IS NOT "EMERGING REPUBLICAN"

A candidate who maintains a two-to-one margin over his opponent within a given group may be losing ground, but can hardly be said to be losing out. White Catholic ethnics no longer produce unanimous Democratic votes. With a dynamic favoring the Republicans, many commentators confidently predict Republican majorities. But consistent Republican majorities were nothing more than a prediction a decade ago, and will be nothing more than a prediction a decade from now. The Slavs have seen their extraordinary Democratic support fall into the high-60 percent range, but the beneficiary has been George C. Wallace, and the exceptions to substantial Democratic margins are much less persuasive than the rule. The Italians have eroded their Democratic support considerably, yet are no more Republican than in the late years of the Eisenhower Presidency. Even the Irish—the most assimilated ethnics of them all—continue to deliver two thirds of their votes to the Democratic Presidential nominee.

The irony in the still-substantial Democratic margins among white Catholic ethnics is that Republican inroads have been large enough to force a change in Democratic strategies. The difference between winning by four to one and winning by two to one is all too critical to a candidate in a closely contested election. Among white Catholic ethnics, the Democrat used to win by four to one. He doesn't any more, and the Democrat is thus left with two options. Either he can concentrate more attention on frequently neglected Democratic voters, or he can turn to other support groups. The Democrats may find it easier to recruit an Italian whose family is historically Democratic, than to attract an Iowa farmer who has grown up speaking of Democrats in unprintable expletives.

We treat each of our elections as important. Some might quarrel with attributing significance to vote changes that might affect the outcome of one senatorial or gubernatorial election or another, or for that matter an electoral-vote result in one state for the Presidency. But we treat our elections as important, because we think them important. At the same time, we do not contend that one election or even a series of elections is an ultimate experience for American politics. In this regard, our views on the importance of elections are in accord with that of a rookie running back for the Dallas Cowboys, Duane Thomas, who replied, when asked how it felt to be playing in the Super Bowl, the ultimate game, "If it's the ultimate game, how come they're playing it next year?" There will be elections next year and, hopefully, for many years to come. We are viewing a series of elections, and our most certain conclusion is that subsequent elections will force a change in at least the tenor of many of our conclusions. Of course, it is precisely this capacity for change that strengthens the democratic process.

ETHNICS AND THE PRESIDENCY, 1960:
EMERGING DEMOCRATIC BLOCS

John F. Kennedy won the Presidential election of 1960 without unified ethnic support. Kennedy faced an electorate that had given substantial majorities to a Republican in the preceding two Presidential elections, and even the strongest Democratic support groups showed heavy erosion to Eisenhower by 1956. Senator Kennedy did wipe out most of the Eisenhower gains, but without producing stunning pluralities of his own. Kennedy's best white, Catholic performance was with the Slavs, who turned out in decade-high numbers under the tutelage of still-functioning big-city machines. The Slavs produced the kind of margin that over-whelming four-to-one victories are fashioned from, and even Kennedy's own Irish did not do as well by him. The Senator's Irish vote nationwide, and even his Irish vote at home, in Massa-chusetts, trailed his Slavic margins by up to ten percentage points; in fact, Kennedy did as well among Italians as he did among his own.

Kennedy did no better among Jews and blacks than he had done among the white Catholic ethnics. Among Jews, Republican inroads in suburban areas across the country kept overall Kennedy margins down. No area was sacred and this urban-suburban split in the Jewish vote appeared on Kennedy's home turf, as Boston's suburbs gave up to 40 percent of their Jewish vote to Richard M. Nixon. Among blacks, Republican gains in the South offset strong big-city voting for the Democrats in the rest of the country. Southern blacks had not forgotten the civil-rights initiative of the G.O.P. administration, and nationwide, at least one quarter of the black vote remained in the Republican column. But even this Republican vote had become little more than an old dream by the end of the decade.

The most striking Kennedy vote came from the group whose impact on subsequent elections was to be greatly diluted—the Mexican-Americans. Perhaps because of their strong Catholic heritage, perhaps because Senator Lyndon B. Johnson was strongly identified with Mexican-American causes, or perhaps simply because Kennedy-Johnson took the trouble to campaign in their barrios, Mexican-Americans rallied to the Democrats with a most impressive 85 percent vote. Turnout among Mexican-Americans was not particularly high, but was to be the high point for the decade. Mexican-Americans showed the strength of a united bloc in 1960. Their lesson was to be followed, and *overshadowed*, by other groups during the remainder of the decade.

ETHNICS AND THE PRESIDENCY, 1964: UNIFIED DEMOCRATIC BLOCS

Barry Goldwater unified America's minorities. Blacks, Mexican-Americans and Jews voted almost unanimously for Lyndon Johnson in 1964. Some commentators have a habit of dismissing the 1964 contest as "aberrant" and thus not instructive for future political developments. But each time a voter enters a voting booth he tells the careful spectator something about himself, even if all his votes go to one candidate. The lesson of black and Mexican-American voting in 1964 is in the numbers. Blacks turned out in record numbers, though gains in turnout were much more striking in the South than in the North. The black vote set the stage for serious federal intervention in the registration process and laid the groundwork for a quiet revolution in Southern politics. In direct contrast, the Mexican-American vote showed the signs of turnout decline, which four years later would leave the Chicano voter virtually powerless in the Presidential process.

White Catholic ethnics were generally stronger for Johnson than they had been for Kennedy, yet some racially troubled cities showed inklings of a conservative sentiment that would be nurtured during the next six years. The Irish actually gave a shade more of their vote to L.B.J. than they had given to their fellow Irishman John Kennedy. The Irish voted pretty much like the rest of us—large Johnson pluralities with limited, mostly inconsequential, signs of backlash. The Slavs, as in 1960, were once again more Democratic than the Irish. Goldwater gains over 1960 were rare, and when they did surface, they were not of great magnitude. The most consistent Republican gains—and even these were not all that striking—came from the Italians, who had the strongest Republican roots of the Catholics and seemed most sensitive to the quickly changing demographics of the central city.

ETHNICS AND THE PRESIDENCY, 1968:
ERODING WHITE CATHOLIC BLOC

The black, Chicano and Jewish voters, unified in the 1964 Presidential election, again produced nearly unanimous votes for the Democrat in 1968. The surge in Southern-black political participation continued at an increased pace, and blacks provided most of the Democratic votes in the Deep South. Northern blacks failed to follow the Southern example. Registration among blacks declined in the nation's cities, and the decline in the number of blacks on the voter rolls dampened black hopes for local electoral gains. Chicano voters continued their extraordinary support levels for Presidential Democrats and at least in Texas, where turnout stayed close to the 1960 mark, Chicanos had some measurable effect on the outcome. In other parts of the country, Chicano turnout failed to break the slide begun in 1964. Just at the time when Chicano spokesmen were raising their strongest call for Mexican-American unity, Chicano voters were at an all-time low on the nation's voter lists. The Jewish voter performed in 1968 as he did in 1964. Turnout was high (as it consistently is among Jews), and the Democratic percentages were impressively high. The urban-suburban split, wiped out in the Johnson landslide of 1964, failed to reappear in 1968. Another Republican opportunity had been lost.

In 1968 Richard M. Nixon and George C. Wallace together managed to break up the Democratic bloc vote among white Catholic voters. The Irish and Slavs held strongest for the Democrats, and cast nearly two thirds of their ballots for Hubert H.

Humphrey. Wallace inroads among the Irish were minimal and Republican inroads were unconvincing. Regardless of their growing predilection for Republicans at state and local levels, the Irish, at least in 1968, were very much Presidential Democrats. The Slavic vote showed little movement to Nixon in 1968, but flirtations with the Wallace candidacy did reduce Democratic percentages compared to 1964. The Wallace percentage among Slavs was half again as high as his percentage in the states in which Slavs live, but still rarely exceeded 15 percent. As in 1964, Republican inroads were most pronounced among Italians, whose Democratic percentages fell into the low fifties (still a majority). When Richard Nixon carried New York's Italians in 1968, it was the first instance of a Presidential Republican carrying any one of the six ethnic groups, in any one of the fifty states. The Republican inroads were real, but so was the remaining Democratic plurality.

ETHNICS AND THEIR OWN: A GOOD TEST OF ASSIMILATION

The Irish and the Mexican-Americans do not have very good records of supporting their own for elective office; the blacks, Jews, Italians and Slavs generally do support their own. The Irish are the closest example to an assimilated ethnic group. It seems to make little difference to an Irish voter that a candidate is Irish, even if he happens to be a Democrat. A good number of nearly radical Irish Democrats (Paul O'Dwyer and Joseph Duffey among them) have found that it doesn't help much to be Irish among the Irish if your political philosophy is out of sorts with the mainstream. Independent Mexican-American candidates have discovered that ethnic identification alone will not siphon off many votes from the Democrats, and even Chicano incumbents cannot assume united Mexican-American support.

Blacks and Jews are not in the least embarrassed about voting for their own, and both groups increasingly have the opportunity to display that inclination. For blacks, this has meant an increasing attraction, particularly in the South, to independent black candidates who face two major-party white candidates. Soon, an independent black candidate in nearly any Southern state will be able to count on unified black support, and the effect of this development on Southern politics should be dramatic. The independent black candidate cannot win without white support, but either major-party candidate is a virtually certain winner with black aid. A time of bargaining from strength has arrived for Southern blacks.

Jews, of course, do not have the numbers to bargain as effectively as blacks. However, Jewish candidacies are a growing phenomenon, and Jews occasionally have to choose one of two or even three Jews running for a single office. A liberal Jewish candidate running against a middle-of-the-road Republican will receive unanimous Jewish support. However, the Jewish vote begins to split with the absence of a dynamic Jewish personality (as with Abraham D. Beame for mayor of New York in 1965, or Arthur J. Goldberg for New York governor in 1970), or with the presence of a liberal Republican (as in the 1970 New York senatorial contest); these Jewish candidates have received no more, and often less support among Jews than the typical Democratic candidate.

Slavs and Italians are not as likely to have the opportunity to vote for their own, but generally make the most of the opportunity when it does arise. Most Slavic candidacies have involved mayoral contests in cities with increasing black populations, and often the Slav is pitted against a black candidate. In such instances, most Slavic voters support their own against black candidates and we suspect most other ethnics would do the same.

Italians apparently will vote for the Italian, no matter who is in the race, as the Republicans learned in Massachusetts when they ran John A. Volpe for governor. But following their party preference, Italian Democrats, even if they happen to run against Volpe, tend to unify the Italian vote behind their candidacies. A first-time Presidential candidacy by either an Italian or a Slav will certainly find favor with the brethren.

WHITE CATHOLIC ETHNICS: STILL LIBERAL

Much has been made of American racism, and with good reason. Unfortunately, however, the term has been debased in the political rhetoric of the sixties. While Catholic ethnics have had a good number of influential politicians, and some of their own clergy label them as racist, it is a label that has been misapplied, according to our analysis of hundreds of elections.

Slavic voters are convincing in their liberalism. Democrats of even the most liberal persuasion enlist their strong support; Republicans who make inroads among Slavs are from the liberal wing of the party; conservative Republicans again and again fail to make decent runs among Slavic voters.

The Irish move to the political center much as the majority of the American electorate and will have nothing to do with extremely liberal candidacies, even if promoted by their own. At the same time, Irish voters have shown almost as little interest in George Wallace as the Jews have shown, and they have demonstrated a corresponding disinterest in most conservative Republican candidacies. The Irish of Massachusetts managed a very respectable vote for a black man running for the United States Senate, and the impressive Irish vote for Conservative James L. Buckley in the 1970 New York senatorial election is attributable as much to Buckley's Irish Catholicism as it is to any conservative drift among the Irish.

Italians are the least convincing white Catholic liberals, but their overall voting behavior hardly suggests a conservative outlook. Italians continue to be attracted to national Democratic economic policies, and reflect this sentiment in large votes for Kennedy and Johnson, and at least a plurality performance for Humphrey. At the statewide level, Republican candidates do increasingly well among Italian voters, but once again the liberal Republicans (as long as they are not too liberal) pull bigger votes than their conservative counterparts. There is still something about a conservative Republican that strikes fear in the heart of an Italian union member.

JEWS, BLACKS AND MEXICAN-AMERICANS: DEMOCRATIC UNANIMITY WITH COMPLICATIONS

Politicians must worry even about unified voting blocs. Voter groups can hardly be more committed to a single Presidential party than are the Jews, blacks and Mexican-Americans. In 1960 the Democratic percentages among these groups were high, but not overpowering. However, the 1964 election brought with it a unanimity of sentiment that carried intact through the neck and neck contest of 1968. The challenges to Democratic supremacy among Jews, blacks and Chicanos come not from the Republicans but from two frequently overlooked political phenomena: turnout and third-party candidacies.

Of course, among Jews, turnout is not an issue. Jews vote and probably always will. Among blacks, however, turnout is extremely important and as with many other racial issues, splits North and South. Northern black turnout, once nearly the equivalent of white participation, now substantially lags behind white turnout rates in the large urban centers. At the same time Southern black turnout is growing quickly and thereby reversing the traditional weak-sister role of Southern black politics. The weak sister has moved north.

Among Chicanos the absence of turnout is the key to their still-potential impact on Presidential politics and there has been a steady decline in Mexican-American political participation through the 1960s. For the Democrats to benefit from Mexican-American support, the Chicanos will have to vote, and someone will have to register them.

Third-party candidacies present the only formidable threat to the nearly unanimous Democratic Presidential vote among Jews, blacks and Mexican-Americans. All three groups have shown interest in the independent candidacies of "their own" at local levels. The black experience has been particularly impressive, with bloc votes for independent black candidates in many Southern senatorial and gubernatorial elections. Local successes of third-party Mexican-American candidates in the San Antonio, Texas, area suggest that Chicanos may soon be following the black lead. Jews show interest in liberal third-party candidacies even when the candidate is not Jewish.

The entry of serious independent candidates into the 1972 Presidential race can attract substantial numbers of otherwise Democratic voters. The effect of one of these races (and several appear likely) can be devastating to Democratic chances and can assure Republican victory in 1972.

We have chosen to treat each of six ethnic groups in separate chapters. A demographic description precedes the political analysis. Presidential elections are considered as a unit, and state and local contests are grouped thematically to highlight the most salient features of each group's political behavior. We have used tables and graphs where we felt them illustrative, have frequently supplemented the analysis with historical material, and have reported unique campaign circumstances where we felt them to be particularly relevant.

Chapter 8 is an independent attempt to analyze the significance of our findings in the earlier chapters for winning the Presidency in 1972.

More than the others, the black chapter is often historical. The blacks today are the most visible ethnic group, and they provide overwhelming proof of a basic thesis common to all ethnics, but at this time understood best by the blacks: ethnics count electorally, and they should welcome their good fortune and get on with the business of exploiting their potential power.

An increasing black success, and final acceptance of the electoral process as the best way to better their American position, should be emulated, rather than feared, by the other ethnics in the United States. An unhappy, frightened majority has largely succeeded in focusing on the blacks as the embodiment of all that is wrong with America. But the enemy common to all ethnics is not one of their own groups, but rather the system de Tocqueville long ago declared could easily result in a tyranny of the majority. To properly focus on this fact, to move away from the myth of black takeover and thereby allow the other ethnics to follow the black example, it is immediately necessary to understand some of black political history and to feel (as deeply as it is possible for a nonblack to feel) the frustration and setback which has led to the current black era of political action.

Established American power (however defined) has consistently announced a commitment to compromise, but has nevertheless been grossly derelict in its responsibility to America's minorities. In a nation which responds first to the language of the ballot, the American ethnics have been sadly unaware of their potential political power. For many reasons, only one being a long-perceived history of repression, the blacks are showing the way to effective minority use of political muscle. The next few years will witness a continued political activity on their part. The years following—or, hopefully, the same years—must see the other ethnics (Northern city-bound blacks included), take the cue and begin the climb to political power.

Although far from its own goals, the black use of electoral power is the example all ethnics should soon be following. For all of those minority Americans, and for a nation too long out of step with the needs of many forgotten citizens, the sooner the better.

If the ethnics fail this challenge, others will surely seize the power, rush into the vacuum; and we will be left to wonder at what might have been and to echo King Henry of Navarre:

Hang yourself brave Crillon . . .
We fought at Arques and you were not there!

2

The Blacks:[1]
Overcoming in a New Way

In the early spring of 1971 the Black Congressional Caucus
met with President Nixon at the White House. For over a year
this group of thirteen black Democratic Congressmen had tried in
vain to meet with Mr. Nixon in order to offer themselves as the
"elected and legitimate representatives of 25 million American
Negroes." Ostensibly the President's reluctance to meet with the
thirteen stemmed from a desire to see Representatives in their
"Congressional" capacity only, and not as the self-proclaimed
leadership of an ethnic group. Despite this official reasoning,
relations between the Chief Executive and the Black Caucus had
been strained for some while. In a game clearly political in nature
the rhetoric and events occupying those months are perhaps
better indices of why the White House welcome mat had been
withdrawn. Only two months earlier, on January 22, the Black

[1] More than a hundred years ago, in the months following the Dred Scott
decision, a Negro convention in Philadelphia urged Negroes to abandon
the word *colored* and the words *Afric* and *African*. In their place, those in
attendance recommended using the phrase "oppressed Americans." It did
not work. *Negro* and *colored* remained until recently and, while the black
nationalists often use *Afro-American*, the press, the politicians and Negroes
themselves seem happy with *black* today.

Caucus had boycotted the President's State of the Union address decrying Mr. Nixon's "consistent refusal to hear the pleas of black Americans." The President was charged with "pitting the rural areas against the cities, the rich against the poor, black against white and young against old."[2] "You have failed," they wrote, "to give the moral leadership necessary to guide and unify this nation in time of crisis."

Nevertheless, in the wake of this attack, or perhaps because of it, Mr. Nixon finally met with the Black Caucus in March. Perhaps the President's relative civility at that meeting is attributable to his recollection of two other Presidential conferences with black leaders, both considered by all parties to have been disastrous at the time.

In 1862 Abraham Lincoln, the same man who a year later would issue the Emancipation Proclamation (and wipe out memory of this unfortunate event), met with black leaders at the White House and, in a statement understandably condemned by his visitors, urged blacks to emigrate to Africa and Central America. "But for your race among us," the President observed, "there would be no war."

And in 1913, fifty years after Lincoln's proclamation, Woodrow Wilson granted an audience to the great black civil-rights champion William M. Trotter, Harvard's first black Phi Beta Kappa graduate. The meeting quickly became famous for this exchange:

> MR. TROTTER: Mr. President, we are here to renew our protest against the segregation of colored employees in the departments of the National Government.
>
> PRESIDENT WILSON: The white people of the country, as well as I, wish to see the colored people progress and admire the progress they have already made. There is, however, a great prejudice against colored people . . . It will take a hundred years to eradicate this prejudice, and we must deal with it as practical men.

---

[2] In 1971, William Waller, a white, evidently followed the Caucus' rhetoric as he appealed for black support in his successful bid for the Democratic gubernatorial nomination in Mississippi. A political advertisement declared that Waller had "not tried to pit black against white, rich against poor, young against old."

MR. TROTTER: It is not in accord with the known facts to claim that the segregation was started because of race friction of white and colored [federal] clerks. For fifty years white and colored have been working together in peace and harmony and friendliness.

PRESIDENT WILSON: If this organization is ever to have another hearing before me it must have another spokesman. Your manner offends me . . . your tone, with its background of passion.

Six years after the Wilson-Trotter dialogue infuriated the black community, the nation was embroiled in the "Red Summer" race riots. The worst, in Chicago (which had experienced an immigration of sixty thousand black Southerners since 1910),[3] began when an eighteen-year-old black, Eugene Williams, drifted across an imaginary line separating black and white swimmers at the 29th Street beach. White rock throwers caused Williams to lose hold of the railroad tie he had clung to, and he drowned. Soon after, blacks mobbed a policeman who refused to arrest the whites responsible. Rumors swept the city, and after a crowd of Italians killed Jim Lovings, the first black they saw, thirty-eight more Chicagoans died. According to the report of the commission appointed to investigate the tragedy, one thousand were left homeless and 537 were injured. (Less than fifty years later a similar riot, in the same city, would result in another commission, this one headed by Judge Otto Kerner.)

Frustration had been mounting throughout the country as a black people, after having sent its sons into battle to make the world "safe for democracy" in the "war to end all wars," saw a war-weary nation return to its segregationist ways. Indeed, the "Red Summer" had been envisioned at least as a possibility by the other great black activist of the day, W. E. B. Du Bois.[4]

---

[3] The movement to the North had been encouraged by a Chicago committee headed by Robert S. Abbott, the black publisher of the Chicago *Defender*. Total black migration to the North during the period 1900–1910 was 207,000. The following ten years saw the figure doubled for that decade to 412,000.

[4] Trotter and Du Bois considered Booker T. Washington the great "accommodationist" of the era. In what has been labeled the "Atlanta Compromise," Washington, who founded Tuskegee Institute in 1881, said that blacks had erred by rushing into politics during Reconstruction, and he urged a reconciliation with Southern whites. Washington's entire tone was

Writing as editor in chief of the N.A.A.C.P.'s official journal, *The Crisis*, Du Bois urged blacks to reach for their freedom, and he added:

> We *return* [from the war].
> We *return from fighting*.
> We *return fighting*.

Of course, even the right to go to war in the first place had to be won by the blacks. They had been excluded from the Army as early as the first American conflict. Five months after Bunker Hill, on November 12, 1775, in a proclamation designed to win Southern support for the Continental Army, General Washington forbade "further Negro participation" in the War for Independence.

Unfortunately for Washington, his influence did not extend to the enemy, and two weeks later Lord John Dunmore stunned the Colonies with his own proclamation freeing all Negroes "able and willing to bear [British] arms." "Be not then, ye Negroes,

---

a reversal of Frederick Douglass' more militant stance, articulated consistently during the half century before Washington's ascendancy in 1895, upon Douglass' death. Douglass had urged blacks to "agitate," and he observed: "If there is no struggle, there is no progress—power concedes nothing without a demand. It never has and it never will." Impatient with Washington, more comfortable with Douglass, Du Bois (Harvard's first black Ph.D.) demanded, in his 1903 book, *The Souls of Black Folk*, the right to vote, civic equality, and education of black youth according to their ability. Two years later he and Trotter founded the Niagara Movement at Niagara Falls, asserting: "We claim for ourselves every single right that belongs to a freeborn American, political, civil and social; and until we get these rights, we will never cease to protest and assail the ears of America." The Movement lasted only three years. But the murderous attacks on defenseless blacks by white mobs in Lincoln's home town, Springfield, Illinois, in 1908 inspired concerned liberals, black and white, to call for action on February 12, 1909, the centennial of Lincoln's birth. Meetings were held throughout the country, and in 1910 the National Association for the Advancement of Colored People was formed. (Trotter, who was suspicious of whites, refused to join. With the exception of Du Bois, all the officers were white.) A highlight of that meeting was the proof by Cornell Professor Burt G. Wilder that the white man's brain is not superior to that of the black. The theory of black physiological inferiority was widely held. One of its early adherents was Thomas Jefferson. The National Negro Business League too was founded at this time, and it also was conspicuous for the whites involved, notably steel magnate Andrew Carnegie.

tempted by this proclamation to ruin yourselves," cried the *Virginia Gazette*. Ignoring the plea, five hundred Negroes quickly joined Dunmore on his ship, the *Fowey*, and hundreds more were captured in the attempt. This was enough for Washington, and he announced to the Congress on December 31 that he had "reconsidered" and had given permission for "their being reinstated."

It seems unlikely that Richard Nixon in 1971 consulted such poignant history before meeting with the Black Caucus. Rather, the holding of the session is in itself significant, because it illustrates a powerful new political fact, obviously well understood by the President and destined to be well understood by many very soon: Blacks count politically, and they will count more in the years to come.

It also appears unlikely that the President's rejection of the Black Caucus' demands (including an increase to $6,400 for a family of four in Congressman John Conyers' 1966 House bill calling for a federally guaranteed annual income, and a request for 1.1 million jobs immediately) is responsible for an increasing black political awareness. The "deep disappointment" of the Caucus was a foregone conclusion. And surely the breakneck movement since that meeting was contemplated well before the Caucus graded Mr. Nixon's March performance.

Finally understanding the electoral power he can potentially wield in this country, the black politician is in the midst of a fascinating attempt to forge an activist bloc and realize that potential. Leery of being used at election time by the major parties, the black leadership is struggling to mobilize its constituency effectively, to organize and hold blacks together in order to deal in the political power which is the currency of this nation. Accordingly, black leaders everywhere, wanting first to create a force to be reckoned with, echo Georgia legislator Julian Bond's warning that the black man has "no permanent friends, no permanent enemies, just permanent interests."[5] Within the feasi-

---

[5] Bond, like the Reverend Henry M. Turner almost a century before, was at first prevented from taking his seat in the Georgia House of Representatives, but a series of court decisions established his seating. Turner was not so lucky; he never sat in the legislature. In 1896, twenty years after his

bility of translating this statement into political power, and the intelligent targeting of that power if the enterprise is initially successful, lies the political question of our time. The job will not be easy. But if the experience of the great protest marches of the 1960s proves analogous to the emerging political mobilization of the 1970s, success is only a matter of time. And no time is being lost. The pace of political activity is increasing noticeably on a number of fronts.

Three months after the abortive Black Caucus meeting with President Nixon, the thirteen Congressmen raised $250,000 at a Washington dinner and began preparations for staffing the Caucus full time. The message of black political power was getting through. Every major 1972 Democratic Presidential contender appeared at the dinner (along with three black officials of the Nixon administration) and major corporations including A&P, General Motors, Gulf Oil, and the R. J. Reynolds Tobacco Company purchased tables at $2,400 each.[6]

Criticism of the President has not ceased; it is even coming strongly from quarters generally known for their moderate positions. The new Executive Director of the National Urban League (long a "safe" black organization by white standards), thirty-five-year-old Vernon E. Jordan, has accused the Nixon administration of combining "elements of high purpose with an apparent neglect of the deepest needs of poor people and minority groups."[7] The Executive Director of the N.A.A.C.P., Roy Wilkins, also has had harsh words for the President. On June 11, 1971, he answered a

exclusion, Turner, concluding from his bitter experience that "there is no manhood future in the United States for the Negro," launched a "Back to Africa" movement.

[6] The Black Caucus idea is spreading. Many similar groups have appeared in state legislatures throughout the country, and there is also a "National Black Caucus of Local Elected Officials," headed by Highland Park (Michigan) Mayor Richard B. Blackwell.

[7] During the same address to the League's Sixty-first Annual Conference, Jordan also attacked an administration figure who, in view of his comments regarding black leaders, could only be Vice-President Agnew: "Black people are concerned too, at the way in which minor figures, endowed with only symbolic powers, have gratuitously insulted their leadership and, by implication, all black people. To mistake the legitimate and just demands of an oppressed people as 'complaining and carping' is to betray an insensitivity and callousness unworthy of high office."

reporter's question at the organization's sixty-second Annual Convention by saying that Mr. Nixon was "95 percent antiblack." But the dilemma of the moderate black leadership in trying to move with the times while retaining the traditional cautious stance, was dramatically illustrated as Wilkins quickly tempered his remark by giving qualified praise to the President's Family Assistance Plan. A month later Wilkins was still searching for his formula as he first said, "If he [the President] turns loose with some jobs, he'll do all right with the brothers," and then, explaining that his role was to aid blacks as best he could, added, "I make do with Republicans—even though half of them are stupid." He deprived that remark of a large headline when he defined Republican "stupidity" as the characteristic of being "too rigid in their philosophy." The old-line black leadership was wrestling with its identity and seeking to maintain its influence, even though the new militants were deeply involved in the electoral process—a concern even the old-timers could perceive as perfectly legitimate.

In the meantime those younger black leaders were moving quickly. Although too possessed to look back, they managed to retain an appreciation for past successes and therefore felt more keenly the need for new approaches.

Thirty years before, the Civil Rights March, and even the threat of such an undertaking, was enough to change government policy.[8] In 1941, after witnessing President Franklin D. Roosevelt's quick desegregation of federal departments following his threat of a "March on Washington" by a hundred thousand blacks, A. Philip Randolph commented on the successful tactic in words reminiscent of Frederick Douglass: "The threat of the march on Washington proved one thing: the Negro gets only what he has the power to take . . . we have the masses on the street behind us and that gives us the power to make conferences produce something."

Of course, the threat tactic worked only for a short time. Soon blacks were actually boycotting stores in Harlem and buses in

[8] The march and boycott activity that would consume the middle years of the century came a hundred years after Henry Highland Garnett called for a black general "strike," at the Negro Convention of 1843.

Montgomery. In the Alabama city, black solidarity was phenomenal.[9] Fewer than a dozen blacks rode Montgomery buses on
December 5, 1956, less than twenty-four hours after forty thousand copies of the "Call to Boycott" had been illegally mimeo-
graphed in the Administration Building of Alabama State College.

Other boycotts throughout the South shared these years with
white attempts to curtail the activity. Violence was common. But,
as so often happens, a more comic incident eloquently revealed
the irony and pathos of that era: blacks dropped five thousand
copies of the United States Constitution on Jackson, Mississippi,
and (appropriately for that time) a disc jockey, Allen English,
announced selection of Chicago for a retaliatory bombardment of
twenty-five thousand Confederate flags.

The voter-registration demonstrations of the early 1960s became as outdated as the boycotts of the 1950s.[10] Explained black
San Francisco Supervisor Terry François in 1971: "The law of
diminishing returns set in with demonstrations. At first, you
could get press coverage with a small demonstration, then you
needed a couple of hundred people, then thousands . . . that
sort of activity is nonexistent now."

So today, we have black entry into electoral politics. Although
surely the inevitable result of voter registration, this new and

[9] The humiliation blacks felt daily can perhaps best be gleaned from
these Alabama bus regulations, as reprinted in the Baltimore *Afro-American*
on March 3, 1956:

1. Enter bus from rear door.
2. If driver speaks, answer "yes, sir and no, sir."
3. Fill up seats from rear.
4. If all seats are taken, colored must stand up and allow white riders to
   sit.
5. If anyone calls you names, or epithets, you must keep quiet or get
   off the bus.

The Montgomery bus boycott began after Rosa Parks was arrested for
violating Number 4 above; she refused to give her seat to a white woman.
(It is interesting to note that black leaders had planned the action for
months. They had almost put the boycott into effect earlier, over a similar
incident, but the black woman was an unwed mother, and wary of any
complication, they waited.)

[10] Voter-education projects are more prominent than ever and are the
vehicle being used to ensure a black representation sufficient to determine
election results.

ethnically distinguishable black characteristic still seems almost unbelievable. That out of years of oppression and still more years of protest, the wrenching history of black self-discovery should lead to the electoral process as the best hope for black equality and power is simply incredible—and lucky for the United States.[11]

The importance of the phenomenon is proven by the unanimity with which black leaders are encouraging this thrust into the electoral arena. Perhaps Jesse Jackson put it best: "If you're in a car that is headed over a cliff, you can't have any control over it from the trunk. You better get up in the front seat and help drive it."

Blacks may not be driving—yet—but their progress is staggering. A side benefit of the new electoral thrust is explained by Terry Francois: "The very fact that they [black officials] are elected eliminates the nagging question of by what right do black leaders presume to lead." In 1967, when the first Black Power conference was held, blacks accounted for fewer than 480 of the 522,000 public officials in the United States. Today, according to the Joint Center for Political Studies, 1,860 blacks hold public office. Among them are thirteen Congressmen, one United States Senator, eighty-one mayors (including Kenneth A. Gibson of Newark, New Jersey, and Richard Hatcher of Gary, Indiana) and the Sheriff of Lowndes County, Alabama, where in 1965 not a single black was registered to vote.

The new electoral emphasis is reaching across all factions of the black community. In Harlem there is even an insurgent "Malcolm X Democrats Club" trying to oust the entrenched Democratic leadership.

Most far-reaching of all these electoral efforts is the very serious possibility of an independent black Presidential candidacy in 1972. (The implications of such a move, disastrous to the Democrats, are discussed in Chapter 8.) Despite disclaimers (which are politically understandable utterances), this "Third Force" effort was discussed in depth at a meeting in Chicago called by

---

[11] "Lucky" because James Baldwin is undoubtedly correct when he observes: "The Negroes of this country may never be able to rise to power, but they are very well placed indeed to precipitate chaos and ring down the curtain on the American Dream."

Jesse Jackson, and held in the home of black millionaire Dr.
T. R. M. Howard, an Eisenhower supporter in 1956 who inspired
the black G.O.P. activity of that year through Task Force '56.
Among those attending on the seventh day of May, 1971, were
Mervyn Dymally, a powerful black California state legislator,
Cleveland Mayor Carl Stokes, Manhattan Borough President
Percy E. Sutton, and John Cashin of Alabama. (Congressman
Ronald V. Dellums and Los Angeles City Councilman Tom Brad-
ley couldn't make it.) Another businessman present (besides
Howard, who reportedly pledged ten thousand dollars) was Al
Bell of Memphis, Tennessee, Executive Vice-President of Stax
Records. Speculation concerning the decisions reached at that
meeting has been heightened by Congressman John Conyers'
withdrawal of both an early endorsement and his acceptance of a
campaign post, with Democratic Presidential aspirant Senator
George McGovern of South Dakota.

Whether an independent black Presidential candidacy materializes in 1972, at some later date, or not at all is not the crucial
question. What is significant is that such an effort *can* be taken
seriously in 1971 and *can,* if implemented, virtually eliminate all
possibility of Democratic victory—in 1972 or any other year.

Along with the other advances in black electoral activity, the
fact of the possibilities of an independent black Presidential
candidacy clearly demonstrates that black politics is on the move,
and that American politics will never be quite the same.

BLACKS: FACTS AND FIGURES

For the past fifteen years, the problems of Black America have
been the number-one domestic issue. It is not surprising, then,
that when the U.S. Census Bureau released its 1970 statistics on
Black America, the numbers made front-page news. The Census
found that there are 22.7 million blacks, or 11.2 percent of the
total United States population. By November, 1972, one of every
eight Americans will be black.

By region, a very slight majority of blacks still live in the
South. Of the 102 counties where blacks are in the majority, all
are below the Mason-Dixon line. This historic Black Belt of

counties stretches from Waller County in east Texas through Louisiana, Mississippi, Alabama, Georgia and North and South Carolina, to Dinwiddie County in "southside" Virginia. The Black Belt represents a tremendous potential for black electoral power. Greene County, Alabama, for example, recently became the first county to be governed completely by blacks, and in all of Alabama there are now 105 black elected officials, more than in any other state except Michigan and New York.

Between 1940 and 1970, more than four million blacks left the South, mostly for big cities in the Northeast and Midwest.[12] Forty percent of blacks now live in those regions. One out of twelve blacks lives in the West, particularly in California.

CHART 1:   WHERE BLACKS LIVE

State	Black Population	Percent of Total
New York	2,166,933	11.9
Illinois	1,425,674	12.8
Texas	1,419,677	12.7
California	1,400,143	7.0
Georgia	1,190,779	25.9
North Carolina	1,137,664	22.4
Louisiana	1,088,734	29.9
Florida	1,049,578	15.5
Pennsylvania	1,016,514	8.0
Michigan	991,066	11.2
Ohio	970,477	9.1
Alabama	908,247	26.4
Virginia	865,388	18.6
Mississippi	815,770	36.8
South Carolina	789,041	30.5

SOURCE: 1970 Census.

One third of the nation's blacks live in fifteen cities. Sixteen cities—including Washington, Newark, Atlanta, Gary, East St. Louis, Illinois, and Compton, California—are more than half

[12] Migration from the South appears to be slowing, however. According to the Census, an average of 150,000 blacks moved out of the South every year during the 1950s, but only 90,000 blacks migrated yearly during the 1960s. A substantial part of the increased black population in the cities is now attributable to the natural growth of population.

black. Fourteen others—including Baltimore, New Orleans, Detroit, St. Louis, Birmingham, Savannah, Richmond, and Jackson, Mississippi—have black populations in excess of forty percent. New York City has the greatest number of blacks, 1.7 million. It is interesting to note that the cities one normally thinks of as being heavily black—New York, Chicago and Los Angeles—are not on the list of "most-black" cities.

CHART 2: BLACKS IN CITIES

City	Black Percent of Total Population
Washington, D.C.	71
Newark	54
Gary, Indiana	53
Atlanta	51
Baltimore	46
New Orleans	45
Detroit	44
Wilmington, Delaware	44
Birmingham, Alabama	42
Richmond	42
St. Louis	41
Memphis	39

SOURCE: 1970 Census.

The number of blacks living in the suburbs increased during the past ten years. From 1960 to 1970, three quarters of a million blacks moved out of the inner cities, and now about 2.6 million live in the suburbs. Some became suburbanites in name only as the black ghettos expanded over arbitrary city limits. Some went to black enclaves which had existed for many years, and others integrated previously all-white neighborhoods. While relatively few blacks were leaving the cities, whites poured out by the millions. During the sixties, 12.5 million whites moved to the suburbs while, on balance, the percentage of blacks in the suburbs remained constant at less than five.

By most measures, blacks are very much at the bottom of the heap. The average black family earns only $6,279 a year compared to an average white family's income of $10,236. More than one out of every four black families live below the poverty level, and in 1970, for the first time in a decade, the number of poverty-level blacks increased. About 17 percent of all blacks are on welfare, although in absolute numbers more whites than blacks get welfare money. Black unemployment, of course, is a serious problem. Twice as many blacks as whites are out of work, and for black teen-agers the rate is even higher.

The U.S. Census Bureau reports that the combined total of business receipts of black and Spanish-speaking Americans constitutes less than one percent of the overall total of the United States. Black and Hispanic-American businesses had receipts totaling $10.6 billion in 1969. The combined receipts of all American businesses were $1,498 billion in 1967, the last year in which statistics were collected.

Still, there are some hopeful signs. One out of every five big-city black families now earns at least $10,000 a year—twice the figure in 1960.[13] Young blacks appear to be catching up on the education front. Between 1960 and 1968, the percentage of blacks completing high school jumped from 43 to 61, and the number of blacks in college rose by half. The age distribution among blacks should accentuate these positive trends. As a group, blacks are quite young; their median age is only twenty-one, compared to twenty-nine for the total United States population. There are more young blacks, and if these younger blacks can begin to succeed the overall proportion of successful blacks will increase.

The demographic profile of Black America points up the two sources of black political power: big cities and the South. It also hints at some difficulties. Many of the social indices—low income, poor education, unemployment—associated with blacks also make for low levels of political participation. The Census Bureau found that in the 1968 election 13 percent fewer eligible blacks than whites voted, and a Columbia University Public Health study found that only 43 percent of New York City's blacks vote

[13] These better-off blacks still retain a high degree of identification with the Democratic party. A survey done by the University of Connecticut's Institute of Urban Research found, for instance, that 83 percent of blacks with blue-collar jobs said they were Democrats, and 79 percent or only 4 percent fewer white-collar blacks favored the Democrats.

regularly. Black turnout should increase as blacks become better educated and earn more money. The problem for the foreseeable future remains how to overcome this tendency toward nonvoting and how to maximize the advantages which come from concentrated numbers.

PRESIDENTIAL POLITICS

By the end of the 1960s, black voters were firmly in the Democratic Presidential coalition. The Republican party had squandered its opportunity to win black voters early in the decade, yet fluctuating black turnouts came to mean that not every Republican loss was a Democratic gain. And by the end of the decade the threat of an independent black Presidential candidacy left a large question mark over the victory chances of the 1972 Democratic nominee. Black Presidential politics had come a long way.

Until 1934 the black vote in the United States was decidedly Republican. Those blacks who voted did so for the G.O.P. with the same single-mindedness as Southern whites went for the Democrats, and for precisely the same reason—the Civil War. The G.O.P. was the party of Lincoln, and with the exception of his successor, Andrew Johnson, who vetoed a bill providing for black suffrage in the District of Columbia (Congress overrode the veto), the Republicans, perhaps by design, perhaps not, aided the black advance with popular executive orders and selective federal appointments during the succeeding twenty years. In 1871 President Ulysses S. Grant issued a proclamation against the Ku Klux Klan, and six years later Frederick Douglass, often called the "greatest Negro," was appointed Marshal of the District of Columbia by Rutherford B. Hayes. In 1881 President James A. Garfield appointed Blanche Kelso Bruce of Mississippi, the first black to serve a full term in the United States Senate (1874–1881), to the post of Register of the Treasury. And the 1884 G.O.P. national convention that nominated James G. Blaine had a black presiding officer for the first time, John Roy Lynch.

Blacks, of course, enjoyed their political heyday during the

Reconstruction period,[14] and although the era was destined to be short-lived, blacks came out of the nineteenth century firmly in the Republican camp. They remained there thirty-four years longer, despite the disfranchisement statues[15] passed by the Southern states after President Hayes removed the last federal troops from the South in 1877. Louisiana demonstrated the devastating effect these laws had on black electoral participation. In 1896, 130,344 blacks were registered in Louisiana, but only 5,320 were on the rolls in 1900, a decline of 96 percent. The repressive Louisiana legislation, and companion measures throughout the South and in Oklahoma, were all passed during the Republican administrations of Presidents William McKinley, Theodore Roosevelt and William Howard Taft.

The black switch to the Democrats began tentatively in 1928. Two years later Herbert C. Hoover nominated Judge John J. Parker of North Carolina to the United States Supreme Court, and the N.A.A.C.P. led the opposition that successfully blocked

[14] Twenty-two blacks (two Senators and twenty Congressmen) were sent to the Congress by Southern states during and after Reconstruction. All were Republican. The last of this group, George H. White of North Carolina, predicted when he left the Congress in 1901 that the blacks would rise again and that blacks would one day return to the Congress. His prophecy (at that time a prayer) would take twenty-seven years to fulfill. In 1928 Republican Oscar DePriest of Chicago was seated, the first black Congressman since White, and the first ever from a Northern state. In 1934, DePriest lost to another black, Arthur Mitchell, who thereby became the first black Democratic Congressman.

[15] These measures were mostly in the form of poll taxes and discriminatory literacy tests. Of course some whites who might be barred by the standards were given an "out" in the form of a Grandfather Clause, which provided that

> No person who was on January 1, 1867 or . . .
> prior thereto, entitled to vote . . .
> and no son or grandson of any such person . . .
> shall be denied the right to vote . . .
> by reason of his failure to possess the educational
> or property qualifications.

(Since blacks were not voting in January, 1867—the first Military Reconstruction Act providing for their voting having been passed in March of that year—only whites profited from the clause.) This particular form of suppression was eventually declared unconstitutional by the Supreme Court in 1915.

the appointment. Still, in 1932 Hoover managed to capture a majority of the black votes, as was traditional. But by 1934 the move to the Democrats was complete. The reason for this change, like the reason for most changes of that time, was largely economic. The blacks who had suffered most from the Depression thought they were helped most by the New Deal and particularly by the W.P.A.

With the jarring black crossover to the Democrats, the importance of the black vote in future elections became glaringly apparent. The next two Presidential contests, in 1936 and 1940, also produced overwhelming black majorities for Roosevelt. Three weeks before the latter election the President had announced the appointment of Benjamin O. Davis as the first black general in the history of the United States Army.[16]

Nevertheless, black movement back to the G.O.P. was indicated in the subsequent off-year elections,[17] and decisive Republican inroads in the black vote were predicted for 1944 by numerous commentators. Heartened by the voting evidence since Roosevelt's 1940 electoral execution of Wendell L. Willkie, and spurred by the anti–fourth-term stands of two Negro organizations, the Chicago Citizens Committee of One Thousand and the National Negro Council, the Republicans waged a vigorous attempt to recapture the black vote in 1944. The G.O.P. sought to link the President with Rankin, Bilbo and other Negro-hating New Deal Democrats. John E. Rankin of Mississippi particularly was remembered in newspaper ads as having declared representative government to be "trembling in the balance" when the Senate

[16] F.D.R. also brought William H. Hastie (now Federal Circuit Court of Appeals Judge), Ralph J. Bunche (former United Nations Undersecretary General) and Robert C. Weaver (Lyndon Johnson's Secretary of Housing and Urban Development) into his administration.

[17] Taken as most significant were these races: In the Harlem areas of New York's 21st Congressional District, Republican William S. Bennet ran ahead of James H. Torrens, Tammany leader of the 23rd Assembly District. In the 1943 Kentucky gubernatorial election the victor, Republican Simeon E. Willis credited the win to black support. Also significant for the black G.O.P. vote were a special 1944 election in the largely black 2nd Congressional District in Philadelphia and the 1943 Baltimore mayoral victory of Republican Theodore R. McKeldin.

passed a bill permitting servicemen to vote in primary and general elections without paying poll taxes. He wondered whether the next move would be to "abolish the Congress."

The Republican nominee, New York Governor Thomas E. Dewey, strongly endorsed a permanent Fair Employment Practices Commission (for blacks, the burning issue of the day), but his support appeared hypocritical, since he had opposed a bill to create a similar body for New York State. (Interestingly, Dewey signed an identical measure one year later, in 1945.)

For their part, the Democrats relied heavily on the unions, and specifically on the C.I.O.'s Political Action Committee. P.A.C. enjoyed great credibility among blacks for its work in defeating some of the most rabid antiblack Congressmen of the day: Joe Starnes, Cotton Ed Smith and Martin Dies. Its work for Roosevelt in 1944 was equally significant.

Circumstances seemed to be favoring the President as his personal intervention in a Philadelphia transit strike, which had been called because of the upgrading of black workers, received wide attention and was hailed by black leaders. Desegregation of the armed forces, long among the most important black demands, would have to wait for President Truman in 1948. Nevertheless, in three very visible acts, F.D.R. desegregated federal departments (yielding to A. Philip Randolph's march threats), abolished segregation in the transportation and recreation facilities of Army posts, and directed the WAVES and SPARs to accept black women.

When the rhetoricians fell silent and the people spoke, Roosevelt had once more received great black support in every section of the country. Most importantly, blacks provided a significant margin in seven states: Pennsylvania, Maryland, Michigan, Missouri, New York, Illinois and New Jersey.

The black political future was arriving. Seven months before that 1944 contest, the Supreme Court, in *Smith v. Allwright*, removed the last bar to black primary voting. New black registration began immediately, and in the one-year period between 1946 and 1947 total black enrollment doubled.

In 1948, President Truman issued the immensely popular

(among blacks) proclamation desegregating the armed forces,[18] and in the close Presidential race of that year, 68 percent of his 115-electoral-vote margin came in three states, Ohio, Illinois and California. All were carried on the strength of overwhelming black support for the Democratic ticket.

Governor Adlai E. Stevenson, the 1952 Democratic Presidential nominee, had fought for an Illinois F.E.P.C. and had sent troops promptly to Cicero in the summer of 1951 when rioting erupted there. Nevertheless the selection of Alabama Senator John J. Sparkman as his running mate was seen by some Negroes as assuring a black return to the G.O.P.

The Republicans, however, were doing little to exploit the opportunity. The G.O.P. old guard went down to defeat at the Chicago convention; but, to Negroes, Senator Robert A. Taft's position on the crucial F.E.P.C. question was better than General Eisenhower's and Senator Nixon's. The Ohioan had at least favored a noncompulsory federal agency to "persuade" labor unions to cease discrimination, while Eisenhower appeared to favor leaving the matter to the states, and Nixon had voted, as late as June, 1952, against permitting even Senate discussion of the Ives-Humphrey F.E.P.C. bill. By the end of the campaign some black leaders echoed Birmingham *World* editor Emory Johnson, who felt that as between the two Vice-Presidential nominees Sparkman was the "lesser of two evils." Still others, notably Francis B. Glover, editor of the San Francisco *Sun-Reporter,* interpreted the switch from the Democrats of such rabid anti-civil-rights personalities as Texas Governor Allan Shivers to mean that Southerners felt no particular security with Sparkman on the Democratic ticket.

On November 4 black turnout was high, despite continued predictions of low Negro participation because of Sparkman, and the Democrats captured a sizable majority of the black vote.

By 1956 great waves of Negroes had moved out of the South,

---

[18] As with F.D.R.'s earlier order desegregating federal departments following A. Philip Randolph's threat of a march on Washington by a hundred thousand Negroes, Truman's proclamation came on the heels of Randolph's declaration to a Senate committee that he would advocate black draft resistance if the Army remained Jim Crow any longer.

and throughout the nation assumed a new militancy. The N.A.A.C.P. achieved a record membership of 350,000 and three blacks sitting in the House of Representatives were wielding their seniority effectively: Charles C. Diggs, Jr., of Michigan, William J. Dawson of Chicago, and Adam Clayton Powell of New York.

The Democrats produced a lukewarm civil-rights platform at their national convention, and that fact, together with Eisenhower's general popularity, gave rise to the prediction that the black vote would swing back to the G.O.P. The Republicans organized an expansive campaign called Task Force '56, directed to blacks, and actively toured the country. On October 12, 1956, Congressman Powell endorsed President Eisenhower,[19] and three weeks later the Executive Committee of Negro Ministers (101 in all) took a full-page newspaper ad in Chicago urging blacks to vote the straight Republican ticket.

These efforts were largely responsible for 40 percent of the black vote going to President Eisenhower, a record unequaled by a Republican candidate since that year.

Adlai Stevenson won barely 60 percent of the nationwide black vote in 1956, but even when John F. Kennedy brought that total to 75 percent in 1960, there remained signs of Republican opportunity in black voting patterns. One important indicator was Kennedy's rather poor run with Southern blacks in that year. In Arkansas, he took only five out of every eight votes cast in predominantly black precincts. Not surprisingly, among black voters of Little Rock, Kennedy barely managed to win half the vote. Undoubtedly the blacks of that city remembered that a Republican President had sent troops to Central High School in

[19] Earlier, in the wake of the Supreme Court's order desegregating the schools, Powell had attached a rider to the Federal Aid to Education Bill denying federal funds to schools failing to desegregate in accordance with the Court's ruling. Shortly afterward, from the pulpit of his Abyssinian Baptist Church in Harlem, the Congressman called for a "Day of Prayer" on March 28 and a one-hour national work stoppage to dramatize the Negro's plight. This challenge was opposed by most black church leaders. Powell also urged a third party if Eisenhower and Stevenson did not change their middle-of-the-road positions regarding enforcement of the 1954 Court decree. Later, at a Jefferson–Jackson Day dinner, Stevenson foresaw desegregation bringing "the dawn of the day of full democracy," but Powell backed Ike.

1957 to support the nine black youngsters who were trying to enroll. Nixon was part of that Republican administration, and although he personally had little to do with the school desegregation effort, blacks gave him their votes. (They would not do so again in 1968.)

Kennedy's poorest showing with Southern blacks came in Georgia, where he won only 46 percent of the black vote. In some black precincts of Atlanta, Nixon won more than 60 percent. It appeared Atlanta's blacks were particularly sensitive to the ties between Kennedy and the white segregationist leadership of the local Democratic party, and several important local black ministers refused, on religious grounds, to endorse Kennedy.

Kennedy's vote also fell off in some black precincts of New York City. The Senator won better than 80 percent of the vote in Harlem, but his share in the St. Albans section of Queens was fifteen points off the Harlem mark. St. Albans blacks, it should be noted, are more likely to own their own homes and less likely to be subject to the organizational efforts of a Harlem-style, apartment-house–based Democratic machine. These upwardly mobile blacks were attracted to Eisenhower's moderate Republicanism, and they felt a similar pull to Nixon. Even in his home state, Massachusetts, Kennedy won only 58 percent of the black vote, whereas in 1958, when he ran for the Senate, he won more than 80 percent of the black ballots. During the Eisenhower years, Republicans devoted considerable time to organizing black precincts. In 1960, they ran the first black for statewide office, Edward W. Brooke. Brooke lost his contest for Secretary of State, but his presence on the G.O.P. line combined with the G.O.P.'s organizational efforts to pull black voters away from the Democrats and Kennedy.

Yet, despite these signs of Republican opportunity with black voters, Negroes still provided decisive pluralities for Kennedy in seven states. In Illinois, for instance, where Kennedy won by only 9,000 votes, black precincts gave him a plurality of a quarter million. In Missouri, where Kennedy edged Nixon by 10,000 votes, blacks gave the Massachusetts Senator a margin of more than 80,000. In New Jersey, Kennedy won 70,000 more black votes than Nixon, while he carried the state by only 22,000 votes in all. In Michigan, Kennedy came out of black precincts leading by nearly a quarter million votes and he won statewide by only 66,000.

Nearly a million and a half blacks were registered in the South by 1960, and that too made a difference for Kennedy. In Texas, for example, Kennedy's statewide margin was only 46,000, but he received a black plurality of 150,000 votes. In South Carolina, Kennedy's plurality was less than 10,000, while beating Nixon in black precincts by nearly 40,000. And in North Carolina, black voters gave Kennedy 36,000 votes more than his statewide plurality.

A Republican potential existed among black voters in 1960. But neither Nixon nor most local G.O.P. leaders knew how to use the opportunity.[20] Countering this Republican inclination among some blacks was the economic downturn of 1957–1958, for which Eisenhower and the Republicans were blamed. In eight states, including Illinois, Missouri and South Carolina, Richard Nixon's 1960 vote represented the greatest number of black ballots any Republican candidate would win in the next ten years.

The 1964 Presidential election provided an impressive example of the capacity of the black voter to respond in large and nearly unanimous numbers to (or more likely, against) a particular politician. Arizona's Senator Barry Goldwater, the G.O.P. standard-bearer, had voted against the historic Civil Rights Act of 1964 and was anathema to black voters. Lyndon B. Johnson won more than 97 percent of the black vote. Nowhere did Johnson's statewide share of the black vote fall below 95 percent. In the black districts of California, Missouri and Illinois, for example, Johnson beat Goldwater by ratios of almost 50 to one. Turnout in black precincts soared as unions and civil-rights groups poured in workers and money. The U.S. Census found that 72 percent of eligible blacks voted in the North and 44 percent of blacks over

[20] Democrats, on the other hand, did know how to win black support. In one of the most famous events of the 1960 campaign, John Kennedy telephoned Mrs. Martin Luther King, Jr., to express concern for her husband, who was in a Georgia prison, following a sit-in demonstration. This incident received wide attention in the black community and is credited, in part, with producing Kennedy's strong black vote.

twenty-one voted in the South. For Northern blacks, the turnout rate nearly equaled white performance, while the Southern black turnout trailed white turnout by fifteen points.

Goldwater's candidacy eradicated the Republican potential visible in the 1960 Nixon vote. In Atlanta the same black precincts which gave a majority to Nixon in 1960 voted 97 percent for Johnson. Little Rock's blacks voted better than 90 percent for L.B.J. Boston's black voters, who had snubbed J.F.K., gave Johnson 97 percent of their votes, and the middle-class blacks of Queens, too, swung away from Goldwater and voted Democratic by more than nine to one.

The black vote shifted more than any other segment of the electorate in 1964. Johnson's 97 percent represented a 22-point change from 1960, or more than twice the Democratic swing of the population at large. This incredible level of black support may stand for all times as the closest to a unanimous vote cast by any group in American society.

Although it is incontrovertible that Johnson would have defeated Goldwater easily without black support, black votes were critical to L.B.J. in the Southern states that he did carry. In Florida, 98 percent of blacks voted for the President, giving him more than a 150,000-vote plurality over Goldwater, and since Johnson did not carry half the white Florida vote his winning margin came from Florida's black voters. This phenomenon was repeated in Tennessee and Virginia. In Tennessee, which had hosted the first K.K.K. meeting in 1867, 99 percent of the state's blacks cast their ballots for Johnson, giving him a 140,000-vote plurality. Virginia's blacks too voted 99 percent for the President, pushing him ahead of Goldwater by 100,000 votes statewide.

In 1968 Hubert Humphrey learned that a nearly unanimous black vote is not particularly helpful when an inordinate number of black voters fail to turn out. Humphrey almost equaled Lyndon Johnson's black-vote record, winning 94 percent of the vote in predominately black precincts. Nixon won only 5 percent, or one-fifth his vote against Kennedy in 1960. Black fourth-party candidates like Dick Gregory and Eldridge Cleaver won less than one percent of the black vote. But black turnout was down in Northern states where Humphrey had a chance to pick up elec-

CHART 3: BLACK VOTES
PRESIDENT, 1964

	Johnson	Goldwater	Change in G.O.P. Vote from 1960
California	98%	2%	−12%
Florida	98%	2%	−22%
Illinois	98%	2%	−15%
Massachusetts	97%	3%	−39%
Missouri	98%	2%	−16%
New York	97%	3%	−24%
Tennessee	99%	1%	−26%
Virginia	99%	1%	−33%
Nation	97%	3%	−22%

SOURCE: Institute of American Research; NBC News.

toral votes.[21] In Chicago, for instance, the much-vaunted Daley machine failed to deliver its bloc of black votes. Ninety-five percent of Chicago's black votes went to Humphrey, but compared to 1960, 25 percent fewer blacks showed up at the polls. In some black precincts, turnout fell by almost half. If as many blacks had voted in 1968 as in 1960, Humphrey would have picked up 60,000 additional votes and Nixon's statewide margin in Illinois would have been cut in half.

This pattern of high percentage but low turnout was repeated in New Jersey. Humphrey won 89 percent of the black vote, but turnout in black precincts of Essex, Hudson and Camden counties was down by 30 percentage points. In some black precincts only one third as many votes were cast for Humphrey as were cast for Johnson. We estimate that Humphrey lost more than 40,000 votes in New Jersey simply because blacks did not vote, and Nixon carried the state by only 20,000 votes more. And in Missouri, blacks in St. Louis and Kansas City gave Humphrey 96 percent of their votes, but again, not enough black votes were cast to help Humphrey. Turnout was down by 30 percentage points from 1964, and that meant 45,000 fewer votes for Humphrey. The Vice President lost Missouri to Nixon by only 20,000

21 The Census postelection survey reported that 61 percent of voting-age blacks turned out. In 1964, 72 percent had voted.

votes. Even in those states which Humphrey carried easily, black turnout was down. In Philadelphia, despite massive efforts by the local A.F.L.–C.I.O., one quarter fewer blacks voted, and in New York City, black turnout dropped by one third. In Detroit, where blacks have long been the target of U.A.W.-sponsored get-out-the-vote campaigns, the number of black votes in 1968 dropped 35 percentage points.

What happened to the black vote in the North? The main problem in 1968 was organization, or more properly the lack of it. Four years earlier the Democratic big-city bosses and their labor-union allies put on a tremendous show of strength to bring out the black vote for Johnson. Blacks were willing to vote, because they felt Johnson deserved their support. But in 1968 these ingredients were missing or at least mitigated. Humphrey exerted no real emotional appeal for blacks—at least not the way Robert F. Kennedy had—and Nixon didn't seem as hostile to black interests as Goldwater. The urban political machines were fat and inefficient, and white ward healers were no longer welcome in black precincts. The labor unions too neglected black areas, because they were more concerned about stopping defections by their white members to George C. Wallace. And by and large, local black political leaders were not anxious to enroll new voters who might challenge their authority.

In sum, rank-and-file black interest in the 1968 election suggests that many blacks were not willing to go very much out of their way to keep Richard Nixon out of the White House.

But compare what happened in the North with the black vote in the South. According to the Census postelection survey, 51 percent of voting-age blacks in the South cast ballots, a gain of more than 7 percentage points from 1964. This increased black turnout reflected the growing number of blacks who registered to vote, often under the threat of a white sheriff's gun.

Humphrey carried only one state of the old Confederacy, Texas. There were 540,000 blacks registered in Texas, but early polls showed widespread voter apathy in the black community. During the last two weeks of the campaign, party workers went all out to energize the black vote. The results were impressive. In

San Antonio, for instance, the vote in black precincts rose to 105 percent of Johnson's substantial 1964 vote and in Fort Worth black turnout also was higher than four years earlier. Black voters in Dallas and Houston turned out nearly as well as they had in 1964, and in rural Waller County, which is the western buckle of the Black Belt, black turnout was up by a whopping two thirds. Humphrey beat Nixon by more than a quarter million votes in Texas' black precincts, and he went on to carry the state by 40,000 votes.

The magnitude of Humphrey's black vote in the South, and its vital contribution to his total Southern vote suggest why an independent black candidacy can undermine any Democratic chances of carrying Southern states.

In all, about 45 percent of Humphrey's Southern vote came from black precincts. In the five states of the Deep South—Alabama, Georgia, Louisiana, Mississippi and South Carolina— black voters contributed more than 70 percent of the Democratic Presidential vote. In the Border States of Kentucky, Arkansas and Tennessee, Humphrey's white support improved, and blacks accounted for only one third of his losing totals. Black voters in Florida and Virginia contributed approximately 40 percent of Humphrey's vote in those two states.

Democratic politicians understood the enormous potential impact of a well-registered black bloc vote after the black voting performance in the 1964 Presidential election. Certainly Democratic party support for the Voting Rights Act of 1965 was encouraged in part by the extraordinary 1964 participation. The irony of the Democratic effort to enroll black voters lies in the corresponding push of local black leaders for independent black candidacies. There may well be many more black votes to go around, yet many fewer black votes for Democratic candidates.

SOUTHERN BLACKS AND VOTER REGISTRATION

For forty years before Congress passed the Voting Rights Act of 1965, blacks in the South fought for the right to vote and white Southerners fought even harder to keep them from exercising that right. If the score was kept, the whites won. By 1940 only 5 percent of all voting-age blacks were registered to vote.[22] Following the school desegregation decision in 1954, white resistance to black voting stiffened, and many Southern states adopted new restrictions on the vote. The N.A.A.C.P. had been particularly active in the registration drives of those years, and naturally became the object of great harassment. The McCarthy era had recently ended, and it came as no real surprise when much of the Southern anti-N.A.A.C.P. activity involved charges of Communist infiltration of the organization. The South Carolina legislature passed a resolution asking the United States Attorney General to put the N.A.A.C.P. on his controversial "subversive list." Apparently Georgia was not ready to go that far. Attorney General Eugene Cook only asked the state legislature to investigate the N.A.A.C.P. for "possible" subversive influence.[23] In North Carolina Attorney General W. B. Rodman announced that he would ask the courts to fine the organization for failing to register with the state. And in Alabama, after the N.A.A.C.P. began recruiting there, the legislature enacted a bill requiring a fee of one hundred dollars "from any organization soliciting memberships in Wilcox County, and charging a fee of five dollars for every membership gained through solicitation."

On the federal level 96 Southern Congressmen signed a petition declaring the Supreme Court's decision "an abuse of judicial power."

While all of this was happening, two voting-rights laws were passed in 1957 and 1960 giving a new impetus to black registration efforts. Still, at the time of the Kennedy election in 1960, fewer than three out of ten Southern blacks were eligible to vote. The Twenty-fourth Amendment to the Constitution, outlawing the poll tax in national elections, was ratified in 1964. By the midterm elections two years later, an additional 750,000 blacks were registered. In 1965, Martin Luther King led voter-registration

----

[22] Mississippi consistently had the worst record. In 1927 only 840 blacks were registered out of a total black population of 188,074.

[23] Almost two hundred years earlier a passage denouncing the slave trade was stricken from a draft of the Declaration of Independence in deference to the delegates of Georgia and South Carolina.

drives throughout the South, culminating in a violent confrontation at Selma, Alabama. Partly in response to Selma, Congress passed the most sweeping voting-rights law since Reconstruction. The 1965 statute suspended literacy tests, provided federal examiners to register blacks, and ordered the Attorney General to challenge the constitutionality of the poll tax in state and local elections. One year later, the Supreme Court voided the poll tax in all elections, and black registration soared.

CHART 4: BLACK REGISTRATION
IN THE SOUTH, 1940–1971

Year	Estimated Number	Percent of Voting Age Blacks
1940	250,000	5
1947	595,000	12
1952	1,008,614	20
1956	1,238,038	25
1960	1,414,052	28
1964	1,907,279	38
1966	2,657,413	53
1968	3,112,000	62
1970	3,357,000	67

SOURCE: Donald Matthews and James Prothro, *Negroes and the New Southern Politics;* and the Voter Education Project, Atlanta.

By 1970, more than 66 percent of voting-age blacks were registered.[24] On a state-by-state basis, Texas leads with 85 percent of its blacks registered. Tennessee is next with 77 percent on the voter lists. By region the greatest increases in black registration came in the Deep South. In 1964, for example, only 7 percent of voting-age blacks were registered in Mississippi, and only 19 percent in Alabama. In 1970, more than 67 percent of blacks were registered in Mississippi and 64 percent in Alabama, a gain in both states of some 500,000 new black voters.

[24] The 1965 Voting Rights Act also spurred white registration, especially in the Black Belt. In 1964, 68 percent of the South's voting-age whites were registered. By 1970 the number had risen to 83 percent.

CHART 5:   PERCENTAGE OF VOTING-AGE
BLACKS REGISTERED—1964 AND 1970

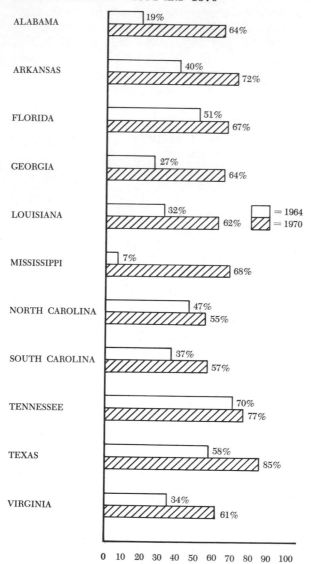

0   10 20 30 40 50 60 70 80 90 100

SOURCE: Southern Regional Council.

The black vote in the South has already produced more than seven hundred black elected officials, ranging from justices of the peace to state legislators, and other Alabama counties, in addition to Lowndes, now have black sheriffs. For the first time since Reconstruction, three blacks sit in the General Assembly of South Carolina, and the lower house of the Georgia legislature has fifteen black members, more than any other state in the nation except Michigan, Maryland and Illinois.

But the importance of the black vote to local politics in the South must be viewed in context. Whites still control most levers of power, particularly in the Deep South. More often than not, a potential black voter faces a choice between two antiblack candidates. Racial attitudes and policies change slowly, but they do change. As more and more blacks register to vote, the power of the black ballot will impress even the most die-hard Southern racists. Already there is a growing list of elections where black votes made a real difference.

BLACKS, SOUTHERN POLITICS, AND THE BALANCE OF POWER

Between 1964 and 1966 the names of more than three quarters of a million Southern blacks were added to the registration books. Some of these first-time voters were the college students who led the sit-in protests of the early sixties. Most were older blacks who had never voted before, because of legal restrictions, ignorance or fear. In 1966 blacks turned out in record numbers for an off-year election. Long lines were reported in nearly all black polling places. The black vote was highly disciplined, picking and choosing among candidates with remarkable skill.

In Virginia, there were two United States Senate contests on the ballot: Democrat William B. Spong, Jr., who had beaten the incumbent A. Willis Robertson in a close primary, faced the Republican mayor of Lynchburg, James Ould, Jr.; and Harry F. Byrd, Jr., who had been appointed to fill his father's unexpired term, was opposed by Republican Lawrence Traylor, a previously unsuccessful Congressional candidate. For years, the Byrd machine ran Virginia with total disregard for the needs of the black community. In the July primary, blacks got their revenge as

Spong, a racial moderate, beat Robertson, the Byrd candidate. In the general election, too, black voters played an important role in Spong's victory. In black precincts of Richmond, Norfolk and Roanoke, Spong won better than 89 percent of the vote. Blacks supplied a cushion of 90,000 votes for Spong, and he coasted to an easy victory over Ould. In contrast, black voters nearly cost "Young Harry" Byrd his Senate seat. Byrd's Republican opponent, Traylor, was no friend of the blacks either, but he did have one unique quality: he wasn't a direct descendant of the much-hated Harry F. Byrd, Sr.[25] Nearly eleven out of every twelve blacks voted for Traylor, a plurality of more than 100,000 votes. Byrd still managed to beat Traylor, but his margin was 70,000 votes smaller than Spong's. More than 80 percent of Virginia's black voters split their ballots in these two Senate contests, an extraordinary show of civic aptitude for a group of new voters.

On the same day that blacks in Virginia were demonstrating their skill at voting, blacks in South Carolina were making an even more dramatic show of their new voting strength. Democrat Ernest F. Hollings, a former governor, was opposed for the Senate by Marshall Parker, a renegade Democrat who had been converted to the G.O.P. by the conservative philosophy of Barry Goldwater. Hollings had run for the Senate four years earlier on a platform of states rights and segregation forever. But in 1966 he changed his tune and began to court black voters. Hollings played up his long-time friendship with Robert Kennedy as proof of his liberal views on race. On election day, Hollings beat Parker by a slim 12,000 votes. Among white voters, Parker led Hollings with 55 percent of the vote. Blacks, however, voted 97 percent for Hollings, and that meant an unbeatable Hollings plurality of more than 65,000 black votes.[26]

---

[25] At the time of the Supreme Court's desegregation ruling in 1954, the elder Byrd had said that interposition was a "perfectly legal means of appeal from the Supreme Court's order . . . if we can organize the Southern states for massive resistance to this order I think the rest of the country will realize that racial integration is not going to be accepted in the South." Byrd's "interposition" talk did not quite lead to a Civil War, as had John Calhoun's a century before.

[26] Not one to forget past debts, or fail to recognize new forces, Fritz Hollings has moved since that election to solidify his hold on South Carolina's

Southern blacks moved off the Democratic line both to punish Democrats with harsh racial stands and to reward Republicans with strong civil-rights records. In the Border State of Kentucky, black voters left the Democratic party, this time to vote for Republican Senator John Sherman Cooper, a former United States ambassador to India. Senator Cooper, a courtly politician who had voted for both the 1964 and 1965 Civil Rights Acts, won 55 percent of the black vote. In some black precincts of Louisville, Cooper beat his conservative Democratic opponent, John Y. Brown, by better than two to one. Blacks accounted for only a fraction of Cooper's 220,000-vote plurality. Still, their vote proved to Kentucky's white politicians that blacks will not always vote for Democrats, particularly when the Republican candidate has a good civil-rights record.

And in Arkansas, which in 1859 had passed a law requiring blacks to choose between exile and enslavement, black voters also moved off the Democratic line for a Republican moderate. Republican Winthrop Rockefeller, brother of Nelson and a racial progressive, was making his second try for the Statehouse. Two years before, Rockefeller lost by only 80,000 votes to archsegregationist Orval Faubus. In that election, more than two thirds of Arkansas's black voters voted against Faubus. But there were not enough blacks registered in 1964 to tip the balance to Rockefeller. By 1966, black registration had doubled and there were 115,000 blacks eligible to vote. Rockefeller's 1966 opponent was "Justice Jim" Johnson, a founder of the White Citizen's Council and a former state court judge. Many political observers sensed a new mood of moderation in Arkansas, but on election day, more than half of the whites voted for Johnson, the racial extremist. In black precincts, though, Rockefeller won 96 percent of the vote,

---

blacks with amazing alacrity. He is now the recognized champion of the hungry American and has sallied even to the Northern urban ghetto in search of this elusive constituency. A media love affair has replaced the expected initial skepticism, and national benefits are now flowing to Hollings as well. To the ticket-balancing devotees of the national Democratic party, anxious to recapture a South that was for so long their exclusive electoral domain, Hollings looms as attractive national political timber, a combination of normally irreconcilable ingredients of political clout—a black-backed white Senator from the Deep South.

and his black plurality put his statewide total ahead of Johnson's by 50,000 votes.

Blacks remained loyal to Rockefeller when he faced a serious challenge in 1968, and they continued loyal when he faced a Democratic racial moderate in 1970. In 1968, Rockefeller was reelected by 30,000 votes. A high turnout and 92 percent of the black vote made the critical difference. When Rockefeller lost to racial moderate Dale Bumpers in 1970, he still managed to poll nearly 90 percent of the vote cast in black precincts. Bumpers won because he received the votes of more than 70 percent of Arkansas's whites.

Arkansas's blacks have proven their sensitivity to the race issue in senatorial contests as well. In 1968, black voters revealed their displeasure with the civil-rights record of Senator J. William Fulbright, by giving one third of their votes to his Republican opponent, Charles Bernard. Fulbright's statewide plurality was the lowest it had ever been.

Black political muscle was evident also in 1968 in North Carolina, where blacks provided the victory margin for Democratic gubernatorial candidate Robert W. Scott. Scott's opponent, Republican Congressman James Gardner had said that the Ku Klux Klan had a perfect right to exist in North Carolina. It was not a statement calculated to win black votes. Scott took 99 percent of the vote in black precincts, and black voters gave him a plurality that was three times his state margin.

The newly registered black voter appears, simply, to be unwilling to vote for segregationist candidates—even if they are Democrats. In 1966, in Georgia, black voters moved from the Democratic line to protest the segregationist policies of the local party. Lester Maddox, who had closed his Atlanta restaurant rather than serve blacks, was the Democratic nominee for governor. He had two opponents: Republican Congressman Howard "Bo" Callaway, a "New Breed" Republican who nevertheless opposed civil-rights legislation with only slightly less vigor than did Maddox, and former Governor Ellis Arnall, a civil-rights liberal who waged a write-in campaign.

Maddox won only 4 percent of the black vote. But this huge desertion from the Democratic camp was only partly a Republican gain. His racial policies notwithstanding, Callaway managed 41 percent of the black vote. The important story involved Arnall; a majority of Georgia's black voters took the trouble to write in his name on the gubernatorial ballot—not an uncomplicated task. This extraordinary, sophisticated performance contained the seeds of independent black candidacies throughout the South.

A similar beginning was made in Alabama in 1968, when black voters decided not to support either segregationist Democrat James Allen or his ultraconservative Republican opponent, Perry Hooper. Instead, nearly 90 percent of Alabama's blacks voted for Robert Schwenn, a young white attorney, who ran as the candidate of the black-liberal National Democratic Party of Alabama. The N.D.P.A. was formed, in part, because George Wallace was running for President on the line of the regular Alabama Democratic party, and a place on the ballot was needed for Humphrey electors.[27] The N.D.P.A. has since grown into the major voice for black Alabamians.

In 1970 the N.D.P.A. chose to pass up an opportunity that might have led to the end of George Wallace's political career. Wallace faced Albert P. Brewer (who had succeeded to the governorship upon the death of Wallace's wife, Lurleen) and five others in the primary. The N.D.P.A. urged its adherents to vote for anyone but Wallace or Brewer in the first primary. As a result Brewer was able to attract no more than 72 percent of the black vote. Twenty-two percent went to Charles Wood, a minor candidate who advertised heavily on television and who had N.D.P.A. support because he was not Wallace or Brewer. Had Wood not pulled the black vote he did, Brewer would have won a majority in the primary. Instead, he had to face Wallace in a runoff, even though he finished first in the field of seven.

The N.D.P.A. now chose to endorse Brewer, since no other non-Wallace choice was available. Brewer profited from the endorsement by blacks (he took 98 percent of their vote, which would have been enough to win outright in the initial primary), but lost

---

[27] An independent black party was not strange in Alabama. Stokely Carmichael and S.N.C.C. organized the Black Panther Party (no relation to today's Panthers) and ran black candidates in Lowndes County in 1966 under that symbol.

to Wallace by 13,000 votes.[28] With Wallace as the Democratic
standard-bearer, the N.D.P.A. ran its own candidate in November, the party's chairman, Dr. John Cashin, a black dentist, who
had led the N.D.P.A.'s credentials fight at the 1968 Democratic
national convention. Cashin managed a respectable 125,000 votes
compared to Wallace's 640,000. Better than 90 percent of Alabama's blacks voted for the independent candidate, a mark of
great solidarity and voting discrimination.

In 1970, national attention focused on the Southern electorate
as politicians and journalists wondered whether Nixon's "Southern strategy" would yield an off-year harvest for the G.O.P. In
the most highly publicized election of the year, Tennessee's
liberal Democratic incumbent, Albert A. Gore, faced Republican
Congressman William E. Brock. The White House (Spiro T.
Agnew in particular) was anxious to defeat Gore because of his
consistent opposition to Nixon's foreign policies and Supreme
Court nominees. Gore, who had a fine civil-rights record, hoped
that moderate and liberal voters in Tennessee would give him the
margin he needed for reelection. Unfortunately for Gore, only
one out of every nine voters in Tennessee was black, and while
96 percent of blacks voted for Gore, Brock took more than
enough of the white vote to win.

Outside of Tennessee, though, there was little to please the
Southern strategists on the White House staff. In J. Strom
Thurmond's home state of South Carolina, Republicans hoped to
pick up the Statehouse with Albert S. Watson, former Democrat
and four-term member of the United States House of Representatives. Watson's Democratic opponent was Lieutenant Governor John C. West, a racial moderate by South Carolina standards. Thirty-two percent of South Carolina's voters had preferred
George Wallace for President two years earlier, and Watson
believed that these Wallace supporters would vote for him. But
Watson's plan overlooked South Carolina's growing black elec-

[28] Some observers believe that the N.D.P.A. wanted Wallace to win so
that the N.D.P.A. might replace the regular Democrats who currently control the party. The fact that N.D.P.A. support of Brewer in the initial primary would have ensured his victory would tend to support this assertion.

torate, and he lost because West won 98 percent of the vote in black precincts of Charleston, Columbia and Georgetown. That black vote added to West's 40 percent of the white vote put him over by 29,000 votes. West's vote reinforced the notion that black voters usually handsomely reward a Democratic racial moderate.

Nixon's Southern strategy fell apart in Florida too, as black voters swamped the G.O.P.'s candidates for senator and governor. In the Senate race, Lawton Chiles, a relatively obscure Democrat from central Florida, beat the state's first Republican Congressman in modern times, William C. Cramer, and his highly organized and well-funded campaign. Underfinanced, Chiles walked the state, while Cramer loudly took credit for the "Rap Brown amendment" to the 1964 Civil Rights Act. That was all Florida's blacks had to hear. On a percentage basis, black turnout equaled white participation, and the vote in black precincts ran 16 to one for Democrat Chiles. More than one half of Florida's whites voted for Cramer. But blacks gave Chiles a lead of more than 100,000 votes, and that was too much for Cramer to overcome. Meanwhile, in the gubernatorial election black voters weren't buying Republican incumbent Claude R. Kirk either. Blacks made up more than three quarters of Democrat Reuben Askew's 240,000-vote plurality over the controversial Republican incumbent.

Black voters in Georgia, who had gone off the Democratic line in 1966 because of Maddox, came back for the Democratic gubernatorial candidacy of Jimmy Carter in 1970. Carter represented a break from the states'-rights tradition. He said Georgia's blacks deserved a better deal and that, if elected, he would see that they got it. Carter's opponent was Hal Suit, a television newsman from Atlanta and a self-styled Taft Republican. Some Atlanta black precincts that Nixon had carried in 1960 went for Suit. But statewide, 72 percent of blacks voted Democratic. Carter's black plurality of 75,000 votes added to his 55 percent of the white vote gave him an easy victory. Carter did not have to deal with a strong independent black candidate, and his racially moderate appeal was quite successful.

In only seven years, black voters have come to play a critical role in Southern politics. In many states they hold the balance of electoral power. In others, they will be in a commanding position soon.[29] Some Republican strategists thought that the more blacks who registered and voted Democratic, the more white voters there would be for the G.O.P. Of course, the Democrats lost some white support as they gained black votes. But the question is one of political balance. Not many white Southerners can be driven from the Democratic party by race alone. Studies by Professors Donald Matthews and James Prothro at the University of North Carolina conclude that it may not be all that difficult for blacks and whites to coexist within the Democratic party. Some hard-core segregationists will not vote for Democratic candidates who attract black votes; but even in the Goldwater election, Matthews and Prothro report, a clear majority of segregationists voted for Lyndon Johnson. Southern whites will stay with the national and local Democratic parties for a number of reasons, two being that it is the party of the "Southern way of life" and the party of jobs and economic prosperity. In the years ahead, Southern politicians will want to consider how to build winning coalitions based on the sophisticated black vote and some portion of the white vote. And they will want to head off the incipient

[29] Of the increasing number of black elected officials in Southern states we believe these men (many of them generally unknown outside their areas) to be among the black leaders who will emerge strongly in this decade:

Mississippi: Charles Evers and State Representative Robert Clark.

Georgia: Atlanta Vice-Mayor Maynard Jackson, Andrew Young, Julian Bond and State Senator Leroy Johnson.

North Carolina: Howard Lee, Mayor of Chapel Hill, is currently running for Congress.

Florida: Neil Butler, Mayor of Gainesville, who was hailed for his calm handling of a student walkout protesting the need for more black teachers and students at the University of Florida.

Alabama: John Cashin and the N.D.P.A. should make great strides in the next few years. They have already elected 109 blacks in Alabama. Cashin is typical of the former civil-rights-movement activists who have been completely converted to electoral politics. And their current views regarding the demonstration tactic they used successfully in past years? Says Cashin: "Confrontations and mass demonstrations are great when there's nothing else to do but that. But you get out there and demonstrate your ass off and all the white folks have to do is pull the blinds and wait until you get tired of doing that."

move to independent black candidacies, for without the black vote, there can be no Democratic coalition in the South.[30]

NORTHERN BLACKS: A POVERTY OF POLITICS

The black voter in the North is taken for granted by most politicians. It is assumed that blacks will vote Democratic and that's all there is to it. But there *is* something more important about the black vote in the North. In 1940, when only 5 percent of voting-age blacks in the South were registered to vote, studies found that 60 percent of Northern blacks voted, a rate equal to white vote participation. Since that time, black registration and turnout has *declined* in the North. In 1972, Southern blacks should far outperform Northern blacks at the polls. In Mississippi more than 67 percent of blacks are registered, but in Brooklyn's Bedford-Stuyvesant less than 35 percent of voting-age blacks are on the voting rolls.

There are several reasons why black voter participation is so dismal in urban centers of the North. Many blacks feel that voting will not make any difference in their lives, and some politicians, both black and white, do not want an untested and potentially uncontrollable bloc of new black voters on the registration rolls. We've already seen how this poverty of politics made things difficult for Hubert Humphrey in 1968. Similarly in the 1968 Ohio senatorial contest, liberal Democrat John J. Gilligan lost by 115,000 votes to conservative Republican William Saxbe, Jr. Black voters let Gilligan down. Only 88 percent of blacks voted for him, while on the same day Humphrey won better than 95 percent in black precincts. Even more important than Gilligan's percentage was the black turnout rate. One quarter fewer blacks voted in 1968 than in 1964. This fall-off cost Gilligan at least 40,000 votes and possibly more. It is doubtful that black votes alone could have changed the outcome of the

[30] The future of Southern black politics clearly lies in coalitions with whites. In the 1971 Mississippi gubernatorial election, black Charles Evers won only 22 percent of the vote, running as an independent. Evers' relatively poor showing proves that in a head-to-head contest with white candidates, black politicians will not fare well. The Southern black future remains bright, however, since they represent the balance of power.

senatorial contest, but if more blacks had been registered and if black turnout had been higher, the election would have been a good deal closer.[31]

In Michigan too, black voters failed to give maximum support to another liberal candidate, Democrat Sander Levin. Levin started the 1970 gubernatorial campaign as a sure loser. But the Democratic party of Michigan rallied behind him and along with the U.A.W. turned Levin into a near-winner. Republican William G. Milliken beat Levin by only 44,000 votes. Ninety-two percent of blacks voted for Levin, but black turnout was off by 10 to 15 percentage points compared to the 1966 election. If the black vote had remained at the 1966 levels, Levin's black vote alone would have cut Milliken's plurality in half.

Maryland lost its liberal Democratic Senator in 1970 almost entirely because blacks did not vote. Joseph D. Tydings was in trouble from the start of his reelection campaign. Heeding polls showing him losing ground because he supported gun laws, Tydings took a harder stand on law and order. He worked for passage of the no-knock provisions of the District of Columbia crime bill, and that act alone turned liberals away from him. The final blow came when *Life* magazine accused Tydings of a conflict of interest.[32] Still the Senator almost won. His Republican opponent, J. Glenn Beall, Jr., beat him by only 25,000 votes. Despite Tydings' work for the District of Columbia crime bill, black voters had nowhere to go and gave him 91 percent of their votes. Again, crucially, turnout in black precincts was down; compared to the 1966 off-year election, 21 percent fewer blacks

[31] Ohio's *black* history is amazingly tortured. In 1807 the state passed the first "Black Laws" in the United States, restricting the rights and movements of black citizens. In 1829 a vicious race war raged in Cincinnati, and 1,100 blacks fled to Canada. The following year saw new enforcement of an old "Black Law" in Cincinnati. Any black person who emigrated to the city had to pay a bond of $500 within thirty days; in effect, the entire black population was being driven out. One wonders if Ohioans recall these actions with pride or would rather point to the fact that in 1855 the first black elected to public office in the United States, John Mercer Langston, became Clerk of Brownhelm Township, Ohio.

[32] According to *Time* magazine, the White House encouraged the mid-campaign Tydings story in *Life* magazine, through the efforts of Charles W. Colson, Special Counsel to the President. (Since Time Inc. owns *Life*, perhaps there is some truth to the report.)

voted. Some said blacks stayed home because they didn't really like Tydings. But black turnout should have been up in Baltimore, where a black was running for Congress. It wasn't. Tydings lost at least 20,000 votes because blacks did not show up at the polls, and with a little more effort in black precincts he might just have beaten Beall.

By and large, black voters in the North uncritically vote Democratic. Republican liberals may try to win black votes and on occasion they will succeed. But the New Deal heritage, reinvigorated by the Goldwater and Nixon elections of the sixties, has welded the black voter in the North permanently to the Democratic party.

Consider the following elections. In 1966, against liberal Democrat Paul H. Douglas, Republican liberal Charles H. Percy won only 11 percent of the black vote in Illinois. In 1968, moderate Republican Charles McC. Mathias of Maryland, who helped write important civil-rights legislation in Congress, won only 14 percent of the black vote against liberal Democrat Daniel Brewster. Even strong Republican vote-getters like Clifford P. Case of New Jersey and Jacob K. Javits of New York have a difficult time cracking the black vote. In 1966, for instance, Case won only 36 percent of the vote in black precincts of New Jersey, and that was a record black Republican vote. Javits too has never done all that well with blacks. In 1968, when he trounced Democrat Paul O'Dwyer, Javits captured only slightly more than a quarter of New York's black vote;[33] in some Harlem precincts blacks voted better than 8 to one for O'Dwyer.

Few Republicans have made substantial inroads with black voters. The list of all the important Northern Republicans who have won 85 percent or more of the black vote since 1960 is a short one indeed: Senator Edward W. Brooke, Mayor John V. Lindsay and Governor Spiro T. Agnew—yes, Spiro T. Agnew.

Senator Brooke is an obvious and easy example. It seems par-

[33] Just how undistinguished a showing this is can be seen in comparison with the 1970 Senate contest. Liberal Republican Charles E. Goodell, who trailed badly in a three-man race against James L. Buckley and Richard L. Ottinger, won 25 percent of the black vote, or just about as many black votes as Javits. Ottinger won 71 percent, and only one of 20 blacks voted for Conservative Buckley.

ticularly fitting that the first black man to sit in the United States Senate since Reconstruction belongs to the party of Lincoln. When Ed Brooke joined the Republican party in the 1950s, many other middle-class blacks like himself were flirting with the party of Eisenhower. During the fifties Brooke worked hard to build a Republican base among Massachusetts blacks. In 1960 he ran for Massachusetts Secretary of State and lost. But in 1962, Brooke won his race for Attorney General, a post he held until he was elected to the Senate in 1966. Obviously, Brooke's success is based not only in the overwhelming support he wins from the 3 percent of Massachusetts' population that is black. He wins because so far he has been able to turn the potential handicap of his blackness into a decisive advantage. During his Senate campaign, for example, Brooke opposed demonstrations and sit-ins as the way to win black rights. Instead, he argued, blacks should follow traditional political and legal paths to redress their grievances. Black-power advocates said Brooke was an Uncle Tom. But white Massachusetts voters applauded his moderation. In a double whammy against both blacks and whites who raised the question of race, Brooke said, "If I am to lose this election because of whites who will hold against me that I am Negro, then I am prepared to lose on this issue. Or if I lose because I refuse to go along with the advocates of black power in the Negro community, then I am prepared to lose because of that, too." On election day, the same Massachusetts blacks who gave Democrat Edward M. Kennedy 95 percent of their vote two years before bolted the Democratic line to give Brooke 90 percent. In white precincts, Brooke won 61 percent of the vote for an easy victory over liberal Democrat Endicott Peabody.

John Lindsay too exerts a special pull on the black voter. But it wasn't always that way. Blacks in New York were slow to realize they had a champion in Lindsay. Despite his outstanding civil-rights record in Congress, when Lindsay first ran for mayor in 1965, he was strongly identified by blacks as a "silk stocking" Republican. (Which he was in one sense—his 17th Congressional District has always been known as the "Silk Stocking District.") Lindsay tried hard to win black votes, and he made some inroads.[34] But on election day, Democrat Abraham D. Beame took 62 percent of the vote in black precincts. To win the election, Lindsay had to overcome a Democratic plurality of more than 45,000 black votes for Beame.

New York's melting pot boiled furiously during the next four years and by 1969 John Lindsay was clearly identified by blacks as their man. But in 1969, Lindsay had another problem with black voters. According to estimates by Arthur Klebanoff, then working in the Lindsay campaign, no more than 40 percent of New York's blacks were registered to vote. To make matters worse for Lindsay, the black registration situation was deteriorating. A major registration drive in 1964 had added more than 100,000 blacks to the rolls. But a similar drive in 1968 added fewer than 20,000 blacks.

Further complicating the picture was New York's election law requiring a voter to vote every two years or lose his registration. Black turnout had not been high in 1967, and it was down more than 25 percent in the Presidential election of 1968.

In all, Klebanoff estimated, close to 100,000 blacks would have to re-register if they wanted to vote for Lindsay. Some efforts were made to register black voters and to increase black turnout. But Lindsay's strategists decided that a campaign focused exclusively on the black community would hurt their man with white voters, and Lindsay concentrated his efforts elsewhere. On election day, blacks gave Lindsay 85 percent of their vote, or more than one quarter of the Mayor's total. But if black registration had been better—say even half of those of voting age, compared to better than 60 percent of whites—Lindsay would have picked up an additional 100,000 to 125,000 votes.

Spiro Agnew's claim to the black vote comes from the 1966 gubernatorial election in Maryland. Agnew's principal opponent was Democrat George P. Mahoney, who campaigned in opposi-

[34] One of Lindsay's black supporters was the Reverend George Lawrence of Brooklyn. Reverend Lawrence often introduced Lindsay to black audiences by saying, "Out in Queens where the white bigots live, they are writing on the walls that Lindsay is a nigger-lover. We're going to vote for Lindsay for mayor, because when they write that he is a nigger-lover, they're telling the truth, every word of it."

tion to a state open-housing law. Agnew had gained some favor
with blacks for his handling of a civil-rights dispute involving an
amusement park in suburban Baltimore. Given a choice between
Mahoney, who campaigned for residential segregation, and
Agnew, who was a moderate Republican, blacks cast more than
85 percent of their votes for Agnew.

Each of these examples—Brooke, Lindsay and Agnew—represents a fairly unique set of political circumstances. Brooke was a
black and could naturally expect substantial black support;
Lindsay went out of his way to help New York's blacks; and
Agnew had the good fortune to be running against a racist. In a
sense, they just prove the rule: *any* Republican will have a very
hard time winning black votes.

BLACKS AND JEWS

During a New Left convention in 1967, black militants demanded that a resolution be passed condemning Israel as an
imperialist aggressor in the Middle East. One year later, at the
height of the school decentralization controversy in New York
City, an apparently anti-Semitic poem by a black writer was read
over local radio. In 1971 three Jewish principals in New York
were forced out of their jobs by black parents. These are just three
of the more publicized examples of what many people consider a
growing anti-Semitism among blacks. Today there is a major rift
in the long-standing alliance between Jews and blacks. But if the
pollsters are to be believed, most accounts exaggerate the difficulties. A Louis Harris survey taken in 1969 showed a high level
of regard for Jews among blacks. Blacks said that Jews are more
than twice as likely as other whites to favor open-housing laws,
and a majority of blacks thought that, of all whites, Jews were
most likely to support black rights in general. Many blacks do
hold traditional anti-Jewish stereotypes, though. Three quarters
of blacks interviewed by Harris said most slum landlords are Jews,
and 71 percent of blacks said that, given a choice between money
and people, Jews will always choose the money. But most blacks,
Harris discovered, do not single out Jews for criticism because

they are Jews. Rather, blacks react against Jews because they are white and are in positions of authority over blacks.

Do these black attitudes carry over to the ballot box? In Illinois, Jewish liberal Democrat Samuel H. Shapiro won 93 percent of the black vote when he ran for governor in 1968. Shapiro endorsed a state open-housing law, while his opponent, conservative Republican Richard B. Ogilvie, sidestepped the controversial issue. Black support wasn't enough to elect Shapiro, but his 93 percent was among the highest black percentages for any Illinois Democrat in the sixties.

Pennsylvania's black voters had no trouble at all voting for Milton Shapp in either of his contests for the governorship. Even though nearly five out of every six blacks voted for Shapp, he lost to Republican Raymond P. Shafer in 1966. In 1970, when Shapp beat Republican Raymond J. Broderick, blacks gave him better than 80 percent of their votes. Both times, Shapp's black vote was just about equal to the average over the decade for Democratic candidates in Pennsylvania.

There is little variation from this pattern in either the Maryland gubernatorial or the Ohio senatorial election of 1970. Democratic Governor Marvin Mandel coasted to an easy win over Spiro Agnew's former staff aide, C. Stanley Blair. Eighty-eight percent of Maryland's statewide black vote went for Mandel, and in some black precincts of Baltimore and Prince Georges County Mandel ran even stronger.[35] In Ohio, liberal Democrat Howard Metzenbaum lost a relatively close contest to conservative Republican Robert A. Taft, Jr. But black voters supported Metzenbaum with better than 90 percent of their votes, a ten-year record for statewide Democratic candidates in Ohio.

If black anti-Semitism appears in any vote, it should be in New York. In 1970, Democrat Arthur J. Goldberg faced Nelson A. Rockefeller in the gubernatorial election. Rockefeller had won a

---

[35] Curiously, the most Republican precinct in the sample of blacks in Maryland was in Cambridge on the Eastern Shore. We checked and found that the polling place had been partly destroyed in the riots following Rap Brown's 1968 appearance in Cambridge. Maybe the Republican vote represented a black reaction *for* "law and order" or *against* the local white Democratic power structure.

third of the black vote against Democrat Frank D. O'Connor in 1966, when blacks shied away from O'Connor because of his lukewarm support for the Civilian Review Board. But in 1970, Rockefeller's black support fell to only 21 percent. Rockefeller had moved to the right and Goldberg was helped in black precincts by his black running mate for Lieutenant Governor, State Senator Basil A. Paterson. Goldberg won a greater percentage of the black vote than any other Democrat running for statewide office since Robert F. Kennedy.

These elections demonstrate clearly that blacks are not anti-Jewish in their voting. Rather, blacks are strongly attracted to the liberal political orientation of most Jewish Democrats, and that outweighs any ill-feeling which may exist between blacks and Jews.

THE INEXORABLE METROPOLITAN PARADIGM

The 1970 Census shows that 23 percent of the people living in America's central cities are black. The number of urban blacks increased by 3.4 million in the last decade, while the white population decreased by 2.5 million. Six cities already have black majorities, and many others are well on their way. Black mayors should follow closely behind black majorities. But you don't have to have a black voting majority to elect a black mayor. In 1965, in Cleveland, Carl Stokes came within one percentage point of becoming mayor. At the time of the election, fewer than one third of Cleveland's voters were black. To win, Stokes needed white votes. As expected, he ran extremely well in Cleveland's black precincts; blacks accounted for 97 percent of his total vote. But Stokes won only 6,000 white votes, and that wasn't enough.

Stokes ran again two years later and during those two years, the deck had been shuffled in his favor. The Ford Foundation had sponsored a vote drive among blacks, pushing their numbers to 40 percent of the total electorate, and an efficient black organization had been built as well. On primary day, black turnout averaged fifteen points higher than white, and Stokes won more than 96 percent of the vote in black precincts. In white neighborhoods, Stokes took 12 to 15 percent of the vote. Combined with his solid black base, these white votes put Stokes ahead of incumbent Mayor Ralph S. Locher by 18,000 votes. In the general election, Stokes faced Seth Taft, of the famous Ohio political family. The primary-election pattern repeated itself. Black turnout rose even higher than it had been in the primary, and Stokes won nearly every black vote cast. In white precincts, Stokes's percentage was up too, largely because he was the official Democratic candidate. The combination of black and white votes was good for a narrow, two-thousand-vote margin over Taft.[36]

The year 1967 also saw the first black elected mayor of Gary, Indiana—a "company town" (U.S. Steel) of 175,000 people, with a murder rate twice New York City's. Richard Hatcher swept into office on the Stokes formula. Half of Gary's residents are black, but white voters outregistered blacks by two or three thousand. It was a bitter electoral contest. The local white Democratic organization refused to support Hatcher and backed Republican Joseph Radigan instead. Tensions rose in the racially polarized community and the Indiana National Guard was called out to prevent possible violence. Fortunately, election day passed without serious trouble. More than 80 percent of Gary's voters went to the polls. In the predominantly white neighborhoods of Glen Park and Miller, Radigan won more than 90 percent of the vote. However, in predominantly black precincts, Hatcher took better than 93 percent. This black support, coupled with the 4,000 white votes he did manage to win, gave Hatcher the victory.

By 1971, a majority of Gary's voters were black. The Lake County Democratic machine still had not made peace with

---

[36] In 1969, also, Stokes coupled a substantial black vote with white votes to defeat Ralph Perk. In black precincts, Stokes won better than 95 percent of the vote, and in white neighborhoods he picked up 15 to 20 percent. In 1971, Stokes decided not to run for re-election in the Democratic primary. Carney won 94 percent of the black primary vote. However, in the three-man general election, Stokes tried to swing the black vote behind independent black candidate Arnold Pinkney and failed. Democrat Carney took 20 percent of the black vote, Republican Ralph Perk won only 3 percent, and 77 percent of blacks voted as Stokes asked for Pinkney. However a united black vote, say 95 or 96 percent, for Pinkney would have put him over.

Hatcher and decided to run its own black candidate in the May primary. But Gary's black voters were not about to desert Hatcher simply because his main opponent, Dr. Alexander Williams, was black. On election day, Hatcher won sixteen times more black votes than Williams. Gary's white voters swallowed hard and voted for Williams, because if Williams was black, at least he was *their* black man. Nevertheless, Williams' white voters were outnumbered, and Hatcher won a clear decision, taking 60 percent of the total vote.

The 1967 Stokes-Hatcher model also explains what happened in the 1970 Newark mayoral election. Fifty-four percent of Newark's residents are black, but blacks account for less than half of the registered voters. In the May election, Kenneth A. Gibson, a black highway engineer, won 43 percent of the total vote, or more than twice as many ballots as incumbent Mayor Hugh J. Addonizio, who ran second. There were also two other blacks in the contest besides Gibson, but together they won only 4 percent of the vote. Newark's black community had decided that Gibson had the best chance to win and they rallied behind him. More than five out of every six votes in the black Central and South wards went for Gibson, while Mayor Addonizio won a surprising 8 percent of the black vote.

If Gibson had taken all the black vote, and if he had improved on his white showing of 7 or 8 percent, he might have been elected without a runoff. But Gibson failed to win a majority, and he and Addonizio faced each other in a second go-round. Gibson won the runoff with 56 percent of the vote and 96 percent of Newark's black ballots. Still, Gibson needed white votes and he got one out of every six, enough for victory. Apparently, Gibson won these all-important white votes because some Newarkers could not bring themselves to vote for Addonizio, who was then under federal indictment for extortion and tax irregularities. (He has since been convicted.)

In the years ahead, cities like Atlanta, Philadelphia and Baltimore will reach the point where a black can make a serious run for mayor. In each of these cities the experience of Cleveland, Gary and Newark will be repeated. Black candidates will try to mobilize the black community, register blacks to vote, and get them to the polls on election day. But black votes won't be enough until blacks make up a substantial majority of the electorate. Until then, black candidates will need white support.

The problem then becomes whether a black politician is a *black* politician or a black *politician* (as Richard Scammon put it). If he sees himself solely as a black candidate, he will not attract many white votes. But if he follows the examples of Stokes, Hatcher and Gibson, and runs as the "candidate of all the people," he will stand a very good chance of winning.

Of course, if a black politician does not depend on white votes for election, his range of rhetoric and policy choices is greatly expanded. Not all black politicians seek a constituency that extends outside the black ghetto. The most important group of ghetto-based black officeholders is the Black Caucus. All but three of the thirteen black Congressmen who make up the Caucus represent districts that are overwhelmingly black. Some caucus members—Robert Nix of Philadelphia and Ralph H. Metcalfe and George W. Collins of Chicago, for instance—are political moderates. They came up through the ranks of strong, white-dominated Democratic machines and they are not about to rock the boat. Often they soft-pedal the question of race altogether. Others in the Black Caucus—Charles C. Diggs, Jr., of Detroit and Augustus F. Hawkins of Los Angeles, for example—have been around Congress for several terms and are regarded as competent, but quiet, liberals. The real attention-getters in the Black Caucus are militants like Shirley Chisholm of Brooklyn, Ronald Others in the Black Caucus—Charles C. Diggs, Jr., of Detroit and William L. Clay of St. Louis. Mrs. Chisholm has made a reputation for herself as a combative champion of women's rights. Dellums recently held his own hearings on United States war crimes in Indochina (conducted in the House Office Building, but not sanctioned by the Democratic leadership). Conyers is active in the "third force" and its Presidential plans. And Clay, who cut his political teeth organizing sit-in demonstrations for CORE, is also a strong critic of the war in Vietnam. Each of these Congressmen comes from a "safe" district, and unless the boundaries are changed or they decide to seek another office, they will be around for a long time. In 1972, an additional three or four blacks will be elected to Congress, among them the first black Congressman from the South in many years—undoubtedly from a new district in downtown Houston with a population 50 percent black.[37]

BLACK AMERICANS: A CODA

Over the past dozen years, the black revolution has been the single most important force moving and shaping American society. It has changed the way Americans think about themselves—and the rest of the world. It has caused severe stresses in our ways of life and violence in our streets. Electoral inroads are coming with great frequency and blacks, both North and South, believe that black power is theirs for the taking. The political fact is clear: black Americans are finally using the electoral process as the way to equality in the United States. Their success has been meteoric, but a great deal remains undone.

Martin Luther King's exclamation at the success of the Montgomery boycott he led a decade and a half ago serves equally to summarize the state of black politics today:

> Lord we aint what we wanna be,
> but thank God we aint what we was.

[37] Texas politicians apparently agree that the occupant will be either State Senator Barbara Jordan or State Representative Curtis Graves.

3

Chicanos and Puerto Ricans: If They Vote, They Count

"We're not doing so well. We want parity of attention," said Martin Castillo, the first chairman of the Cabinet Committee on Opportunity for Spanish-speaking Americans and then the highest-ranking Mexican-American in the Nixon administration. Castillo's complaint came during a meeting at the White House between Vice-President Agnew and eleven Spanish-speaking government officials. Agnew listened to the bureaucrats, agreed that too few federal policymakers came from Spanish-American backgrounds, and promised to prod official Washington into action. A few months later Castillo resigned; his job was left vacant for seven months. In August of 1971, the President appointed Henry Ramirez, a former migrant worker and aide to the U.S. Civil Rights Commission, to fill the vacancy. White House press releases incorrectly claimed that Ramirez was the first Hispano-American to serve on the President's staff, and Press Secretary Ronald Ziegler let it be known that the President felt that the Cabinet should be more responsive to Spanish-American needs. (Although the law required such meetings, the previous chairman and the Cabinet had never met.) The ballyhoo surrounding the Ramirez appointment was a clear sign that the Presidential election campaign was only months away. Once again politicians were rediscovering America's "second-largest minority group."[1]

Little public attention had been paid to Spanish-Americans during the decade of the sixties. The grape boycott of Cesar Chavez and his United Farm Workers was a liberal "cause" for a time. The Young Lords attracted some attention, when, in the name of Puerto Rican power, they "liberated" an East Harlem church. And Reies Lopez Tijerina made news, when, in a dispute over old land rights, he and his band of followers had a shoot-out at a New Mexico courthouse.[2] But by and large, Chicanos and Puerto Ricans were a forgotten minority.

If the general public wasn't concerned about Spanish-Americans, then the politicians didn't care very much about them either. Chicano votes were important in some states of the Southwest, but not all that important, and in New York City Puerto Rican prospects were headlined by *The New York Times* as "10% of the Population, 0% of Political Power." Even today, only six members of Congress are Spanish-speaking Americans, and in Los Angeles, which has more Chicanos than all but three Mexican cities, not a single Chicano is on the City Council.[3] Spanish-

---

[1] Spanish-Americans are not really the second largest ethnic group. There are, for instance, more Americans of German and Irish ancestry. What people who use the sobriquet usually mean is that Spanish-Americans comprise the second-largest nonwhite minority.

[2] Tijerina, Chavez and Denver's "Corky" Gonzales are the country's three most prominent Chicano leaders. Tijerina is a former Pentecostal preacher. His land-right cause appears to have little chance of success, since today only 2 percent of the hundred million acres covered by the 1848 Treaty of Guadalupe Hidalgo belongs to direct heirs to land guaranteed to the defeated Mexicans after the Mexican-American War. The other, spiritual aspect of Chicano ties to America involves a growing Chicano identification with the concept of "Aztlan." In Uto-Aztecan mythology Aztlan is the ancestral home, and it stretches from Mexico to Nebraska. The "new" Chicano believes ever more strongly that he belongs here—that he is not merely a visitor to be welcomed only to work in the *gringo*'s fields. These Chicanos are activists, and for them Tio Taco (the stereotype of the motionless, docile Mexican under a sombrero) is dead.

[3] The six Spanish-American members of Congress are Senator Joseph M. Montoya, of New Mexico, and Congressmen Eligio de la Garza, of Texas; Henry B. Gonzalez, also of Texas; Manuel Lujan, Jr., of New Mexico; Edward R. Roybal, of California; and Herman Badillo, of New York. All but Lujan are Democrats.

speaking Americans may be at the political takeoff point that blacks reached fifteen or twenty years ago. They have the numbers to play an important political role. But to date, they haven't shown the desire or the ability to translate those numbers into vote power.

THE SPANISH-AMERICAN VISTA

Spanish-speaking Americans are one of this country's largest ethnic groups. According to a U.S. Census survey, 9.2 million Americans, or 4.5 percent of the total population, identify themselves as being of Spanish origin. Of these 9.2 million, some 5.1 million are of Mexican ancestry and 1.5 million have family ties to Puerto Rico.[4]

Mexican-Americans and Puerto Ricans occupy a unique place in America's immigrant history. Neither group had to come very far to become Americans. The Mexican-Americans actually lived in Santa Fe before the first settlement at Jamestown and they somewhat reluctantly became citizens after the Mexican War of 1846–48 when the border of the United States was moved south to include territory which had belonged to Mexico.[5] Puerto Ricans also became Americans through Manifest Destiny; the United States took control of Puerto Rico following the Spanish-American War and granted citizenship to the natives. Still, both Chicanos and Puerto Ricans are immigrants in one sense: their language and culture sets them off from the rest of American society. Only one quarter of Mexican-Americans claim English as their mother tongue; even fewer Puerto Ricans (about 15 percent) learn to speak English as their first language.

Eighty percent of Chicanos and Puerto Ricans live in cities. About one in four lives in or near New York or Los Angeles. There are more than one million Puerto Ricans in New York City,

---

[4] In addition there are approximately 600,000 Americans of Cuban or other Central and South American heritage, and 1.6 million whom the Census classifies as "other Spanish."

[5] An interesting use of this history is exhibited when it is suggested that Chicanos can learn from the black political example. Said one Chicano leader seeking to distinguish his people from the blacks, "We didn't come here, we started here."

and there are large Puerto Rican settlements within commuting distance—in nearby New Jersey and Connecticut. Los Angeles has a Mexican-American population of one million, and in all California Chicanos number 2.6 million. The next-largest number of Mexican-Americans is in Texas, followed by New Mexico, Arizona and Colorado. And more than 400,000 Chicanos and Puerto Ricans live in the greater Chicago–Gary area, where they work in the heavy industries.

One demographic factor which limits the political clout of Chicanos and Puerto Ricans now, but which may make them a force in the future, is their relative youthfulness. Half of the Chicanos and nearly as many of the Puerto Ricans in percentage of their own total are less than eighteen years old. In fact, 30 percent of Chicanos and Puerto Ricans are less than ten years old. In the overall population of the United States, half are less than thirty years of age, and 20 percent are less than ten years old.

On most social indices, Spanish-Americans rank quite low, although they may be better off than blacks. The average Puerto Rican family had an annual income in 1970 of $5,975, or only three-fifths the median United States family income. Chicano families earned more, about $7,117 a year. More than one third of Puerto Ricans had annual family incomes of under $4,000, and three out of ten Mexican-American families earned less than $4,000. The Puerto Rican and Chicano middle classes are relatively small; just about one in five Puerto Rican families and only one in four Chicano families makes more than $7,500 a year. Most Spanish-Americans work in either blue-collar or service-industry jobs, and less than one out of five Puerto Rican or Chicano men are white-collar workers. More Spanish-speaking women hold white-collar jobs, but most of them work in low-level, nonprestigious employment. The Spanish-American rate of unemployment is high, about one and two thirds greater than the national average. The educational level of Chicanos and Puerto Ricans thirty-five years old or older lags seriously behind the national average as well. In a nation where most people are high-school graduates, older Chicanos and Puerto Ricans have, on the average, less than eight years of formal schooling. The record is somewhat better for younger Spanish-Americans, however; Mexican-Americans between twenty-five and thirty-four have been to school for an average of eleven years, and for Puerto Ricans the figure is close to ten years. This increasing educational attainment undoubtedly will have a positive effect on Spanish-American political strength. In New York City, for instance, the Puerto Rican turnout rate is the lowest for any group. A Columbia University Public Health survey found that only 30 percent of Puerto Ricans without a high-school diploma say they almost always vote, while among those Puerto Ricans with a high-school education those who almost always vote constitute 37 percent—not high, but certainly an improvement.

All these factors—language difficulties, poor-paying jobs, and low levels of education—add to a culture of poverty which discourages Spanish-American electoral participation.

PRESIDENTIAL POLITICS

Recently, the League of United Latin American Citizens and the Mexican-American Bar Association of California issued a white paper entitled, "The Electoral College and the Mexican-American: An Analysis of the Mexican-American Impact on the 1972 Presidential Election." The document argued that a shift in Mexican-American voting patterns could alter the outcome of the upcoming Presidential election in three states of the Southwest, and in Illinois. Like similar documents put out by other ethnic groups, this one somewhat overstated the case. There are two sides to the Spanish-speaking Presidential vote: high percentages for the Democratic candidate, yet generally declining turnouts.

In 1960, John Kennedy won 85 percent of the Chicano vote and better than three quarters of the Puerto Rican vote. "Viva Kennedy" organizations sprang up throughout the Southwest as Kennedy sought to woo Spanish-Americans, and the Chicano vote was vital for Kennedy in two states, New Mexico and Texas. In New Mexico, Kennedy needed Chicano votes to win; he did not receive 50 percent of the "Anglo" vote. Seventy percent of the Chicano vote went for Kennedy, a 20,000-vote plurality, and the Senator carried New Mexico by only 2,000 votes. In Texas,

Chicano votes also made the difference, as the ticket was significantly aided by Texan Lyndon Johnson, a long-time friend of the Chicanos. Kennedy-Johnson did not win a majority in "Anglo" precincts, but in Chicano neighborhoods the ticket took a remarkable 91 percent of the vote (a 200,000-vote Chicano plurality as Kennedy-Johnson carried Texas by fewer than 50,000 votes).

Puerto Rican voters in Spanish Harlem and the South Bronx voted for Kennedy three to one over Nixon, for a Kennedy Puerto Rican plurality of at least 125,000. (J.F.K. carried New York by 384,000 votes.) In three states, Arizona, California and Colorado, Kennedy lost to Nixon by margins of 35,000 to 71,000 votes. Kennedy won substantial Chicano pluralities over Nixon in those states and at least 75 percent of the Chicano vote, but not enough Chicanos had registered (and voted) to tip the balance in Kennedy's favor.

While the 1960 election revealed the potential for Spanish-American Democratic pluralities, the 1964 election showed the beginnings of a profound weakness in the Spanish-American vote, a disintegrating turnout. Lyndon Johnson won 90 percent of the Chicano vote and 86 percent of the Puerto Rican vote, while carrying all the Spanish-American states but Arizona, the home of his G.O.P. opponent, Barry Goldwater. But the turnout in Chicano and Puerto Rican precincts dropped from 1960. In some Chicano precincts of New Mexico, for example, nearly 15 percent fewer voters turned out.

The drop-off in Chicano votes saved Goldwater in Arizona. The Senator carried his state by only 5,000 votes, while Johnson won 86 percent of the vote in Chicano precincts. In some Chicano sections of Tucson and Phoenix the vote was off by one third, and that was lucky for Goldwater. Had Chicano turnout equaled its 1960 mark, L.B.J. would have had a victory in Goldwater's backyard.

Only in New York City did Spanish-American turnout hold up. A large-scale voter-registration drive had added many new Puerto Rican names to the voter rolls, and Robert Kennedy, a particular favorite of Puerto Rican voters, was running for the

Senate. The turnout in most Puerto Rican precincts nearly equaled the 1960 vote, and in some Puerto Rican neighborhoods it exceeded that showing by half. By running very hard, the Puerto Rican vote was able to stand still.

The pattern of shrinking Spanish-American electoral participation continued in the Presidential election of 1968, while the Democratic percentage remained strong. Hubert Humphrey received 87 percent of the Chicano vote and 83 percent of the Puerto Rican. Richard Nixon took 10 percent of the Chicano vote and 15 percent of the Puerto Rican vote, while less than 2 percent of Chicanos and Puerto Ricans voted for George Wallace. Yet turnout for both groups reached its low for the decade. In Chicano precincts of Arizona, for example, there were one third fewer votes than in 1960, and in some precincts of Colorado the number of voters dropped nearly as much. (The Vice-President's percentages in those two states were 81 and 75 respectively.) Puerto Ricans in New York City cast less than half the number of ballots that they had cast in 1960, but Humphrey carried 83 percent of the votes cast. Humphrey won six out of every seven votes cast in the Chicano precincts of California, but turnout was off by one sixth compared to 1960.

Texas was a glittering exception to the rule of Chicano turnout decline in 1968. Following the abolition of the poll tax in 1966, the Texas A.F.L.–C.I.O. and other liberal groups had registered many thousands of Mexican-American voters. In the election of 1968, contrary to the national trend for Spanish-American voters, turnout in Texas rose by more than twenty points from 1960. Ninety-three percent of the Chicano vote went for Humphrey, and he beat Nixon by more than 300,000 votes in Chicano areas alone. Humphrey carried Texas by only 39,000 votes.

Although Nixon's overall Chicano percentage fell 5 points from 1960, he did make one substantial gain. In New Mexico, Nixon won almost four out of every ten votes cast in Chicano precincts—a good showing that came on the coattails of incumbent Republican Governor David F. Cargo, a popular figure with New Mexico's Chicano voters. Nixon's inroads with the New Mexican Chicanos helped him carry the state as Humphrey came out of

Chicano precincts leading Nixon by only 10,000 votes, a margin which the former Vice-President quickly overcame in "Anglo" precincts of Albuquerque. During the 1960s, the Spanish-American vote lost ground, although its Democratic affiliation held firm. At a time when black voters in the South were making great strides toward equality at the ballot box, Spanish-Americans, both Chicanos and Puerto Ricans, were voting less. With only a handful of notable exceptions, there were fewer Chicano and Puerto Rican Presidential voters by decade's end—a decline which inevitably meant shrinking Democratic pluralities.

CHICANO CANDIDATES, THIRD PARTIES AND "LIBERAL" STRATEGIES

Southern blacks will go out of their way to vote for black candidates, even if it means voting a third-party line. Blacks use the ballot to reward candidates, Democrats and Republicans alike, who hold moderate racial views. The Chicano voter fails to show this same degree of political sophistication; Chicanos do not display interest in third-party candidacies, even when fostered by their own. In addition, the Chicanos have failed to make effective use of split-ticket voting.

First, a mixed bag. In 1970, in New Mexico, Chicano voters cast critical ballots for Joseph M. Montoya, the only Mexican-American in the Senate. Montoya's Republican opponent was Anderson Carter, an unsuccessful former senatorial candidate and a conservative. Montoya, who had been in public life for thirty-five years, expected to win an easy victory. Registered Democrats outnumber Republicans two to one in New Mexico, and Montoya had strong support from the local A.F.L.–C.I.O. and other liberal groups. Carter, who waged an aggressive and well-financed campaign, said that Montoya was one of those "ultraliberals" that Spiro Agnew wanted defeated. Carter lost, but by only 16,000 votes.[6] Chicano votes made the difference for

[6] In 1964, when Montoya was first elected to the Senate, he beat Republican Edwin Mecham by 31,000 votes and won 74 percent of the Chicano vote.

Montoya. Turnout in Chicano precincts was strong for an off-year election, and Montoya won better than 77 percent of the Chicano vote, a respectable but not overwhelming performance. Carter garnered 21 percent, and William Higgs, the candidate of the People's Constitutional Party, a Chicano group, polled just about 2 percent of the Chicano vote.[7] Montoya's 77 percent equaled L.B.J.'s record Chicano vote in 1964 and gave Montoya a plurality of more than 25,000 votes. Since the Senator won only 47 percent of the "Anglo" vote, his statewide margin of 16,000 came from his fellow Chicanos.

Now the more typical case. The Chicano vote failed a fellow Chicano in a race for the governorship of New Mexico in 1968. Democrat Fabian Chavez, Jr., was opposed by the Republican incumbent David Cargo and by Jose Maestas, the P.C.P. nominee replacing Reies Tijerina, who had been ruled off the ballot because of a felony conviction. Chicano voters found themselves in a difficult position. On the one hand, Chavez was one of their own; but so was Maestas, and he was associated with the heroic Tijerina. Cargo too was not at all unpopular among the Chicanos; his wife was a Spanish-American, and during his first term in office he appointed many Chicanos to state jobs.

A year before the election, Cargo had sent special state police to put down a disturbance caused by Tijerina's land-grant-claims group, and no one knew how this would affect the Governor's standing in the Chicano community. Chicano turnout was light for a Presidential year, with some precincts casting one third fewer votes than in 1960. Cargo won by 3,000 votes as the Chicano community split 67 percent for Chavez, 33 percent for Cargo, and less than one percent for Maestas.

New Mexico's Chicanos had stayed with the two major parties in overwhelming numbers and Cargo's Chicano showing was only 5 percentage points from its record high in 1966. Chavez won only 46 percent of the "Anglo" vote, and he needed more than his 17,000-vote Chicano plurality to win. The combination of

[7] The P.C.P. nominee for governor, Wilfredo Sedillo, ran even worse in Chicano precincts, winning less than one percent. Sixty-nine percent of the Chicano vote went to Democrat Wayne King, and 30 percent to Republican Peter Domenici.

low turnout and Cargo's relatively strong performance in Chicano precincts spelled defeat for Chavez.

Chicano voters again let down a Mexican-American candidate in the 1970 gubernatorial election in Arizona. Democrat Raul Castro (a former United States Ambassador to El Salvador and no relation to the Cuban Castro), ran against two-term Republican incumbent Jack Williams, a conservative, heavily financed by the state's Goldwaterites. Castro had won the Democratic nomination in an upset, and he had little organization or financial backing. In the fall election campaign, Castro stressed his Mexican ancestry in an attempt to stir up support among Arizona's Chicanos, who make up 15 percent of the state's population. He need not have bothered. For although drawing nearly 90 percent of the Chicano vote for a plurality of 35,000, Castro lost to Williams by 7,000 ballots. Turnout in Chicano precincts was low, approximately half of those registered, compared to a statewide turnout of nearly 70 percent. If fewer than 10,000 more Chicanos had voted, Castro could have become Arizona's first major Mexican-American officeholder.

The way Chicanos treat "their own" running as Democrats looks spectacular, compared with Chicano support of Chicanos on third-party lines. Chicano voters showed little interest in the candidates of the People's Constitutional Party as William Higgs (who considered Montoya a "Tio Tomas") captured less than 2 percent of the Chicano vote in New Mexico's 1970 senatorial contest while his gubernatorial running mate, Wilfredo Sedillo, did only half as well (thus paralleling the nearly nonexistent vote for Jose Maestas for governor in 1968). Other electoral contests are similarly instructive. In California's 1970 gubernatorial contest, Ricardo Romo, a United Farm Worker organizer, ran on the Peace and Freedom Party ticket. Romo had traveled extensively throughout California on behalf of Chicano unity, and he expected to run well in Chicano precincts. But Romo's organizing skills did not bring him an electoral payoff. Liberal Democrat Jesse Unruh won nearly five out of every six votes cast in Chicano precincts, incumbent Governor Ronald Reagan took 16 percent, and Romo received the support of less than 2 percent of his fellow Mexican-Americans.

It was much the same story in Colorado,[8] where Albert Garrule ran for governor as the candidate of the Raza Unida, or United Race, party. Garrule, a twenty-seven-year-old community organizer, said he wasn't bothered by Colorado's law which requires governors to be thirty years old, since he did not expect to win. Instead Garrule claimed he was running only to increase the political awareness of Colorado's Mexican-Americans. Given the election results, his success was questionable. The real contest was between two-term incumbent Republican John Love and Democrat Mark Hogan, the Lieutenant Governor. Love beat Hogan by nearly 50,000 votes, with Garrule managing 12,000, or less than 2 percent. In Chicano precincts, Democrat Hogan captured better than two thirds of the vote, Love took a respectable 23 percent, and Garrule won only one out of every twelve Chicano votes.

Chicano voters are wedded to the two major parties, and particularly to the Democrats. In fact, Chicanos are so strongly tied to the Democratic party in some states that often they vote blindly Democratic when there is good reason not to.

By failing to vote off the Democratic line for either governor or senator in Texas in 1966, the Chicano vote squandered the impact liberal strategists had sought. In the senatorial contest, archconservative Republican John G. Tower, who had been elected in 1961 to fill L.B.J.'s seat, was opposed by Democrat Waggoner Carr, an equally conservative Democrat, who was then the Texas Attorney General. In the gubernatorial election, two-term incumbent Democrat John B. Connally was opposed by conservative Republican T. E. Kennerly. Texas liberals, including the state A.F.L.–C.I.O. and many black and Chicano organizations, were displeased with the Connally Democrats for running two conservatives. Carr, for example, opposed repeal of Section 14b of the Taft-Hartley Act, and Connally had snubbed Chicano farm workers when they marched on the state capitol demanding a minimum wage of $1.25 an hour.[9] The "liberal" strategy called

[8] In addition to New Mexico, these two states, California and Colorado, are bilingual; their constitutions require state laws to be published both in English and in Spanish.

[9] Ironically, Connally owed his first election as governor to Chicano votes. In the 1962 election, Connally did not win a majority of the votes in Texas'

for a protest vote against the Democrats, and *for* the Republican candidates. Most Chicano voters did not get the message. In the Senate election, Democrat Carr won 82 percent of the Chicano vote, or only 10 percent less than Texas Democrats usually won from Chicanos; and Connally won 90 percent of the Mexican-American vote—just about as well as he always did. Carr lost to Tower by nearly 200,000 votes statewide, and Connally beat Kennerly by more than 669,000.

Four years later, Chicanos reinforced their consistent, undeviating support of Democratic candidacies with their behavior in the Texas race for the United States Senate. The liberal-conservative split in the Texas Democratic party reappeared with a vengeance in the primary campaign. Incumbent Senator Ralph Yarborough, leader of the party's liberal wing, was challenged by Lloyd Bentsen, Jr., a conservative millionaire who was backed by the Connally forces. Bentsen took the standard conservative line, attacking Yarborough for voting against Nixon's Supreme Court nominees and for "compulsive spending of taxpayers' money." Yarborough emphasized his powerful committee positions— chairman of the Senate Labor Committee and an important member of the Appropriations Committee—and said he could do more for Texas in Washington. Yarborough was counting on a strong grass-roots campaign to win him renomination and he expected Texas' Chicano voters to help him as they had done in the past. Although he lost the primary by 89,000 votes, Chicano voters gave the Senator solid support. Yarborough won more than 80 percent of the vote in Chicano precincts and the turnout was high. In some precincts, the Chicano primary vote was nearly equal to the 1968 Presidential totals, an extremely impressive performance for a primary election. Yarborough lost not because Chicanos let him down, but because he won far less than half of the "Anglo" vote.

After the divisive primary, some political observers wondered whether the Democrats would unite in time for the general elec-

---

"Anglo" precincts; but he did win 93 percent of the Chicano vote, for a margin of nearly 150,000 votes over Republican Jack Cox.

tion. Bentsen had a tough opponent in George Bush, a "New Breed" Republican, and some pro-Yarborough forces, most notably the Texas Teamsters union, endorsed the G.O.P. Congressman. If the Chicanos had lost a good friend in Yarborough, they did not hold a grudge against Bentsen, and he beat Bush statewide, but by only 155,000 votes. Chicano turnout was strong, and almost 83 percent favored the conservative Bentsen. That Chicano support resulted in a Chicano plurality of 185,000 votes—Bentsen's victory margin and then some.

On balance, Chicano voters seem to lack the political acuity which marks the Southern black voter. Years of political neglect have made the Chicano voter apathetic. Even when a Chicano politician stands on the verge of a political triumph, Chicano voter response is often lackadaisical. Further, Chicano voters are generally disinterested in attempts to create third-party movements that would speak directly to their needs or force the powers that be into dealing with Chicano problems. No third-party Chicano candidate has done well with his own people, and Chicano voters appear little interested in ideology. They are, almost without exception, straight Democratic party voters. The Chicano vote of the Southwest has a long way to go before it can claim to be a powerful, informed and influential voting bloc.[10]

SPANISH-AMERICANS, LAW AND ORDER, AND BLACK CANDIDATES

A study by the U.C.L.A. task force on Mexican-Americans found a high degree of prejudice among Chicanos toward blacks, and a survey of Puerto Ricans in Connecticut reported that more

[10] The most impressive Chicano political organization is in Texas, where La Raza Unida (United Race party) won a series of elections in 1970 in Crystal City, Carizzo Springs and Cortulla, all farm towns southwest of San Antonio, with large immigrant worker populations. La Raza was born in 1967, after a 400-mile march to Austin (the state capital) to demonstrate for a minimum wage of $1.25. The party is headed by José Abgel Gutierrez, who was also elected chairman of the Crystal City Board of Education. San Antonio itself appears ripe for Chicano political activity. Its official population is 41 percent Chicano (with over 50 percent believed to be Chicano).

than a third of Puerto Ricans thought relations between the races are getting worse. Newspaper accounts frequently report conflicts between Spanish-Americans and blacks for control of local antipoverty agencies, and New York's Mayor Lindsay, for example, recently appointed a high-level panel charged with "cooling" tensions between blacks and Puerto Ricans in the Bronx. Chicanos and Puerto Ricans may be at the bottom of the social heap, but they are most anxious to differentiate themselves from blacks.[11] This is not surprising when it is remembered that Spanish-Americans and blacks often compete for the same low-paying jobs and the same miserable housing. Tension and conflict are inevitable.

The strains in Spanish-American and black relations carry over into electoral politics.

In Los Angeles in 1969 Thomas Bradley, a black former policeman, faced incumbent Mayor Samuel W. Yorty and twelve other candidates in a nonpartisan primary. In Mexican-American precincts, Bradley won more than 43 percent of the vote, while Yorty took 30 percent, with the rest scattered. Bradley's Chicano vote was low compared to the nearly unanimous support he received in black precincts. One reason for the relatively weak showing was the campaign that Yorty waged, courting the Chicano voter. The Mayor never missed an opportunity to address Chicano groups, and he spoke to them in fluent Spanish. But another reason was also telling: Bradley was black. Since Bradley had not won a citywide majority, he had to face a runoff against Yorty. In that campaign, Yorty hit hard at Bradley for being weak on "law and order," and Bradley chose not to cite his own outstanding record as a policeman. Yorty campaigned hard in Mexican-American neighborhoods, reminded them of past favors, and hinted that Chicanos were "different" from blacks. The Mayor won the runoff with 53 percent of the vote; Chicano turnout rose 20 percentage points, and Yorty won 56 percent of the Chicano ballots.

One year later, Los Angeles' Chicano voters again shortchanged a black candidate—this time a successful one. In the

[11] Ninety percent of Puerto Rican marriage license applicants in New York City, for instance, say on the official forms that they are "white."

election for State Superintendent of Public Instruction, Wilson Riles, a moderate black, opposed incumbent Max Rafferty, an ultraconservative. Riles ran an easygoing campaign and was not mouse-trapped into taking the wrong side of the social issue. He beat Rafferty three to one statewide, but in Chicano precincts, won only 59 percent of the vote. There was little reason for the Mexican-Americans to vote for Rafferty; he had not asked for their support, and his right-wing philosophy certainly had little promise in it for the impoverished Chicanos. The most likely reason that 41 percent of the Chicanos voted for Rafferty was that his opponent was black.

New York's Puerto Ricans seem less sensitive to black candidacies and the law-and-order issue than are Los Angeles' Chicanos. In 1966, New York's voters were asked to approve a plan for a civilian watchdog panel which would oversee the actions of the city's police. Liberal organizations, blacks, and many prominent politicians supported the Civilian Review Board proposal. Conservatives, the police, and veterans groups opposed the board, saying it would shackle the police and send the crime rate spiraling upward. By a ratio of two to one, New Yorkers turned down the Review Board. But not New York's Puerto Ricans. Even though most Puerto Ricans live in high-crime-rate areas and even though they were far more likely than most New Yorkers to be victims of crime, the Puerto Ricans also knew what was meant by the phrase "police brutality." They wanted the police regulated. In Puerto Rican precincts, the vote was 70 percent in favor of the Review Board. Undoubtedly crime in the streets is a concern in the Puerto Rican community, but so are the actions of the city's police.

Four years later, Puerto Ricans rallied to support the first major black candidacy in New York in some time. Basil A. Paterson, a black state senator from Harlem, was running in the 1970 Democratic primary for lieutenant governor against Jerome Ambro, an Italian public official from suburban Long Island. Paterson was the choice of the Democratic party convention, and the chief issue in the primary was Paterson's color. Ambro said the Democrats were looking for trouble in November if they ran a black for lieutenant governor, but Paterson still won the primary handily. In Puerto Rican precincts he took an astounding 91 percent of the vote, there being little desire on the part of Puerto Rican voters to deny Paterson a place on the ticket because he was black.

THE PUERTO RICANS OF NEW YORK

New York City's Puerto Ricans do not yet play a major role in city or state politics. They could. Most Puerto Ricans are concentrated in only a handful of neighborhoods, and these neighborhoods could form the base for Puerto Rican political organization. There are no longer any legal obstacles to an enlarged Puerto Rican franchise; the literacy test was wiped off the books by 1970 amendments to the Voting Rights Act. Puerto Ricans are just beginning to become involved in antipoverty politics. They are waging political warfare against blacks for control of the local O.E.O. agencies, and some good may come from these tension-filled racial confrontations. The in-fighting for federal money and jobs might teach Puerto Ricans the same political skills that the political clubhouses provided for earlier waves of immigrants. Puerto Rican political power is possible, but for the time being, at least, no more than potential.

There are more than one million Puerto Ricans in New York City. That's more than in San Juan. Many came to New York shortly after the Second World War and settled in the run-down neighborhoods of East Harlem and the South Bronx, while others chose the fringes of the black ghetto of Bedford-Stuyvesant in Brooklyn. Even though Puerto Ricans make up more than 10 percent of the city's population and are concentrated geographically, they are dramatically underrepresented in terms of elected officials. There are no Puerto Ricans currently serving on the city council and only four are members of the state legislature. New York City has a Puerto Rican Congressman, Herman Badillo, but he was not elected until 1970.

Informed estimates place the number of Puerto Ricans now registered to vote at between 100,000 and 120,000, only 4 percent of total registrants. Still, every vote counts in an election, and sometimes Puerto Rican votes take on a greater significance.

Consider the 1965 Democratic primary for mayor in which City Council President Paul Screvane lost the nomination to City Comptroller Abraham D. Beame. In Puerto Rican precincts, Screvane won nearly 60 percent of the vote, Beame trailed with less than one quarter, and liberals Paul O'Dwyer and Congressman William F. Ryan together won 18 percent. Puerto Rican voters made up about 7 percent of the primary vote, which meant Screvane came out of Puerto Rican neighborhoods leading Beame by nearly 20,000 votes. A stronger Puerto Rican turnout effort by Screvane would have won the primary for him.

Even with their low participation rate, however, Puerto Rican voters nearly made the difference in the 1965 primary for Comptroller. Orin Lehman, who was running on Screvane's slate, won nearly five out of every eight votes cast in Puerto Rican precincts, while Mario Procaccino, who won the nomination over Lehman, took less than one quarter. Puerto Rican voters gave liberal Lehman a plurality of more than 20,000 votes over Procaccino, and Procaccino won the nomination by only 7,000 votes citywide. If 20,000 more votes had been cast in Puerto Rican precincts, Lehman would have defeated Procaccino.

In the 1965 general election, the Puerto Rican turnout was the lowest of any group in the city. Only 63 percent of registered Puerto Ricans cast ballots, compared to more than 75 percent of all registered New Yorkers. Two thirds of the Puerto Rican vote went to Democrat Beame. But Republican John Lindsay, who had already developed a reputation as a champion of the city's minority groups, won 30 percent, and Conservative William F. Buckley, who was running as a lark, took only 3 percent of the Puerto Rican vote. Beame did not run as well in Puerto Rican neighborhoods as either of the Democratic nominees for Council President or Comptroller. Lindsay managed to shave between 10,000 and 15,000 votes from Beame's Puerto Rican performance.

In 1969, New York's Puerto Rican community had a chance to make political history, yet failed to mobilize its resources. Herman Badillo became the first Puerto Rican to run for mayor of New York, and he would have won the Democratic nomination if more Puerto Ricans had supported him. In the Democratic primary, Badillo tried to put together a coalition of Puerto

Ricans, blacks, liberals and reformers. His two main opponents
were former Mayor Robert F. Wagner and City Comptroller
Mario Procaccino. Badillo ran third, behind Procaccino and
Wagner, but succeeded in building at least part of his coalition.
Badillo won substantial Jewish support. Turnout in Puerto Rican
precincts rose slightly to just about the citywide average, and
Badillo won 71 percent of their votes—unimpressive indeed
when compared with Paterson's showing a year later. Procaccino's stress on law and order was less important to Puerto Rican
voters than Badillo's ethnic heritage, and the Comptroller won
only 11 percent of the Puerto Rican vote. Wagner took 14 percent, and liberal Congressman James H. Scheuer and novelist
Norman Mailer together won only 4 percent.

Badillo's 71 percent was good for a plurality over Procaccino of
more than 30,000 votes in Puerto Rican precincts. But Badillo lost
by 40,000 votes citywide. If Badillo had won 90-plus percent of
the Puerto Rican vote—a not altogether unreasonable possibility,
given the symbolic importance of a first-time Puerto Rican mayoral candidacy—Badillo would have edged Procaccino. New
York's Puerto Ricans and perhaps Badillo himself were asleep at
the switch.

Either a slight increase in Puerto Rican turnout or a larger
percentage of the Puerto Rican vote would have done wonders
for Badillo's paper-thin margin in a Congressional primary the
following year. Badillo was to become the first Puerto Rican
member of Congress, representing the Triborough District which
includes parts of the South Bronx, East Harlem and the Astoria
section of Queens. Political commentators said the district was
created especially for Badillo, but Badillo was unhappy with the
boundaries, because many areas of heavy Puerto Rican population
were excluded and some heavily Italian neighborhoods drawn in.
In fact, only 30 percent of the district's registered voters are
Puerto Rican.

In the June primary, Badillo had five opponents for the nomination: Peter Vallone, an Italian lawyer from Queens; the Reverend Louis Gigante, also Italian and a long-time community
activist in the Puerto Rican neighborhood of Hunts Point; Ramon
Velez, the Puerto Rican director of the Hunts Point O.E.O.

agency; Dennis Coleman, a black former state senator; and Joseph Loubriel, also Puerto Rican and a political unknown. Badillo barely won the primary with less than a 600-vote margin over Vallone. Voting irregularities were charged by Vallone, and it took a decision of the state's highest court to declare Badillo the winner. Because there were three Puerto Rican candidates, the vote in Puerto Rican precincts was split. Badillo won about half, for a Puerto Rican plurality of about 3,000 over Vallone; Velez, who was the Puerto Rican antipoverty boss, and the Reverend Gigante each took about 15 percent. The rest of the votes were divided among the other three candidates. Despite the presence of three Puerto Rican contestants, only one third of registered Puerto Ricans voted in the primary.

The same low levels of Puerto Rican participation detrimental to Badillo created serious problems for Mayor Lindsay in the 1969 general election. Early soundings indicated that Lindsay could expect to run significantly stronger with Puerto Rican voters than he had done four years earlier. His administration had been openly favorable to Puerto Rican interests, and that meant votes. But in a city whose eligible voters are 60 percent registered only 30 percent of New York's voting-age Puerto Ricans were enrolled—and the figure would have undoubtedly been lower but for a major registration drive spearheaded by Robert Kennedy in 1964 that added some 50,000 Puerto Rican names to the voting lists. (A similar drive in 1968 netted only 5,000 new Puerto Rican registrants.)

Further compounding Lindsay's difficulties was the low turnout in Puerto Rican neighborhoods for the Presidential election of 1968. Less than half of those Puerto Ricans who voted in 1964 voted in 1968. In order to retain voting eligibility under New York law, a registrant must vote at least once every two years. Since many Puerto Ricans who were on the books in 1964 did not vote in either 1966 or 1968 they were no longer eligible; some 20,000 Puerto Ricans fell into this category. Lindsay wanted their votes, but felt that an all-out drive to re-register them might further provoke the white middle-class and working-class New Yorkers who already thought Lindsay was paying too much attention to the poor.

When a *Daily News* poll showed that he could expect up to 80 percent of the Puerto Rican vote, Lindsay eased off in Puerto Rican neighborhoods to concentrate on "swing" districts. On election day, Puerto Rican voters did not vote for Lindsay in the expected numbers, and the Mayor won only 63 percent of the vote in predominantly Puerto Rican precincts. (Compare that with the 85 percent that Lindsay won in black neighborhoods.) Procaccino took slightly more than one quarter of the Puerto Rican vote and Republican John J. Marchi the rest. Lindsay won a 40,000-vote plurality in Puerto Rican precincts, but he could have done better. Some Puerto Ricans voted for conservative Procaccino simply because he was on the Democratic line, and others may have voted against Lindsay because they felt he hadn't done anything for Puerto Ricans—lately. If Lindsay had run as well with Puerto Ricans as he did with blacks, his margin over Procaccino would have been 40,000 votes higher.

In statewide elections, New York's Puerto Rican voters are strong Democrats, occasionally moving slightly to G.O.P. liberals. The decade record for Democrats among Puerto Ricans was set by Robert Kennedy. In 1964, Kennedy, who had a sympathetic understanding of the Puerto Rican people, beat moderate Republican Kenneth B. Keating and won 82 percent of the vote in Puerto Rican precincts.[12] Four years later, the Puerto Rican Democratic vote dropped to a smaller, but still impressive 71 percent for Paul O'Dwyer. His opponent in the Senate election, incumbent Jacob Javits, won better than 26 percent of the Puerto Rican vote. Only 2 percent went to Conservative James Buckley. The Democratic share of the Puerto Rican vote fell again in 1970, but liberal Democrat Richard Ottinger still won a very respectable 70 percent. Republican-Liberal Charles Goodell ran almost as well with Puerto Rican voters as Javits had done, taking 22 percent; and once again, Puerto Rican voters were not attracted

---

[12] Chicano voters too were strongly attracted to Kennedy. In the 1968 Presidential primary in California, Kennedy won 81 percent of the Chicano vote. Senator Eugene McCarthy trailed with 15 percent, and the "Lynch slate" of Johnson-Humphrey supporters picked up only 4 percent. Turnout was relatively heavy for a primary, largely because California's Chicanos were brought to the polls by Cesar Chavez' farm workers.

to James Buckley as he captured only one out of every fourteen votes cast in Puerto Rican precincts.

In the 1970 gubernatorial election, incumbent Republican Nelson Rockefeller set a record for Puerto Rican votes for the G.O.P., although this performance was only a shade higher than earlier liberal Republican showings. Rockefeller worked hard, handed out campaign flyers picturing himself and the Puerto Rican Miss Universe, and campaigned in Spanish through the barrio. The Governor did not come anywhere near winning a majority of the Puerto Rican vote, but he did receive 28 percent, and that set the record. Seventy-one percent of the Puerto Rican vote went to Democrat Arthur Goldberg and less than 2 percent to Conservative Paul Adams.

CHICANOS AND PUERTO RICANS:
A POLITICAL OVERVIEW

The 1960s witnessed the beginnings of a new militancy on the part of Spanish-Americans. For the first time, Chicanos and Puerto Ricans were seeking redress of their grievances in a loud voice.[13] But, by and large, Spanish-Americans did not choose to make their demands known through the ballot box. The number of Chicano and Puerto Rican voters fell as the number of demonstrations, marches and strikes increased. Spanish-Americans have not yet shown any real sophistication in the use of the ballot. In virtually every state where there is a substantial Spanish-American vote, the Democratic percentage of that vote has remained constant for years. Chicano and Puerto Rican voters do not go out of their way to support Spanish-American candidates, and they have had little success in organizing their own third parties. The Spanish-American voter has been neglected by both major

---

[13] With the Spanish-speaking people needing to unify for political action more than ever, a particularly disturbing development has been the recent rift between Chicanos and Puerto Ricans concerning the staffing of the Cabinet Committee on Opportunity for Spanish-Speaking People. The new chairman, Henry Ramirez, a Mexican-American, has replaced two Puerto Rican staff members, explaining that the services of one, a consultant, were no longer required and that the other's position, that of Congressional liaison, demanded that Ramirez appoint his "own man."

political parties. The Republicans in New Mexico have shown it is possible for the G.O.P. to win Chicano votes, but their interest and success have not been repeated elsewhere. So few Spanish-Americans are registered voters that the first party which shows enough interest to sign them up to vote may gain a considerable electoral windfall.[14]

The future of the Spanish-American vote lies in registration and turnout. With increasing levels of income, education, and job opportunities, Spanish-Americans will move into a position where voting will be a more meaningful part of their lives. For the moment at least, Spanish-Americans do not have real electoral power, and they are collectively one of the best-kept political secrets in the United States. Chicano and Puerto Rican electoral strength is potentially very large, but still largely potential.

[14] There is every reason to believe that the Republicans could do well with the Spanish-speaking people if they were willing to exert the effort. Robert Gnaizea of the California Rural Legal Assistance group echoes Spanish-American feelings on this subject as his ethnic group casts about for aid: "If Richard Nixon were to espouse a position sympathetic to our needs and desires and implement it with some real programs—if he were to recognize our demand that there be some parity between the population of Mexican-Americans and the ratio of jobs available to them—then I'll bet he would get at least 50 percent of the Chicano vote." The Republicans, of course, can always use 50 percent of the Chicano vote, or any other vote, for that matter. Richard Nixon apparently understands the opportunity. He has recently appointed Philip V. Sanchez to head the Office of Economic Opportunity, Mrs. Romana Banuelos as Treasurer of the United States, and Antonio V. Rodriguez to the White House recruiting staff. In addition, there are already 35 "Latins" in policy-level and supergrade classifications—those paying above 25 thousand dollars annually—according to the administration. The President has also ordered the federal government to hire more Spanish-speaking citizens, to a level commensurate with their percentage of the nation's population—or at least 7 percent.

4

The Jews: Forever Liberal
Wherever They Are

Shortly after the mid-term elections of 1970, a student from the
Jewish Theological Seminary, in New York, visited the offices of
the NBC News Election Unit. The young rabbi had worked in
the senatorial campaign of Conservative James L. Buckley and
now wanted to see the special precinct returns which would
prove that Buckley had won because of Jewish voters. In fact, he
asked, wasn't it true that Jews everywhere were voting far less
Democratic?

Twenty-five years ago or even a dozen years ago, his questions
would have been laughable. Everyone "knows" that Jews are the
most liberal voters in the country and are among the strongest
supporters of the Democratic party. A 1968 survey mirrored
many others when it reported that 49 percent of Jews considered
themselves liberal compared to only 20 percent of the national
electorate. Nevertheless, some people believe America's politics
are changing. And, as has been said on many occasions (most
recently by the General Council of the Anti-Defamation
League), the Jew is like everyone else, only a little more so.
Today, Jewish Americans live in unparalleled prosperity and
acceptance, yet there is a vague uneasiness in some parts of the

Jewish community. There is talk of rising anti-Semitism among blacks, of a new, combative Jew born in the Six-Day War, and of the young Jews who reject traditional concerns for revolutionary pursuits and populate the ranks of the Jewish Defense League.

These fears and anxieties have contributed to a new "conventional wisdom," which is illustrated by the student from the Jewish Theological Seminary. But like much of what passes for common sense in politics, this easy rhetoric needs closer scrutiny.

A DEMOGRAPHIC PORTRAIT

In the Old Testament (Numbers 1:2) the Jewish people are commanded to "Take ye the sum of all the congregation of the children of Israel, by their families, by their fathers' houses, according to the number of names." And they've been doing it ever since. No other ethnic minority in America is more interested in finding out about itself than the Jews. The Bible notwithstanding, the picture is incomplete. Tiny Jewish communities such as those in Charleston, West Virginia, and Des Moines, Iowa, have been surveyed in detail by local Jewish organizations, but no one knows for sure how many Jews live in New York City, where, as the saying goes, there may be nearly as many Jews as in all of Israel.[1] According to the most widely accepted estimates there are approximately six million American Jews, or 2.9 percent of the United States population, down from the 1920s when Jews were 3.7 percent of the total.

Experts in Jewish demography believe that in the years ahead Jews will increasingly disperse throughout the nation. At this moment approximately two thirds live in New England and in

[1] One estimate, by the Federation of Jewish Philanthropies, places the Jewish population of New York City at 2.1 million. However, the *American Jewish Yearbook, 1963* shows a total Jewish population of 1.8 million for the five boroughs of New York. In 1954 an attempt was made to estimate the Jewish population by figuring how many children were absent from school on the holy day of Yom Kippur. Undoubtedly, the resulting figure of 2.3 million is too high. The number of Jewish children in heavily Jewish neighborhoods was most certainly inflated by Christian students who were kept home too on the poorly attended school day. (In New York, on a Jewish holiday, everyone's a Jew, and especially schoolchildren.)

the Middle Atlantic states. Sizable Jewish populations are also found on the Pacific coast, particularly in California, and in the Midwest, especially in Illinois and Ohio.

CHART 1:   WHERE JEWS LIVE

State	Jewish Population	Percent of State Population
New York	2,522,000	14
California	693,000	4
Pennsylvania	444,000	4
Illinois	283,000	3
Massachusetts	260,000	5
Florida	189,000	3
Maryland	177,000	5
Ohio	161,000	2

SOURCE: *American Jewish Yearbook, 1970.*

Nearly all Jews live in or around big cities; most still within the city limits. But an ever-increasing number are leaving older Jewish neighborhoods for new sections of town or even the suburbs—some because they are receiving a higher income and some, apparently, because blacks move in.

As long ago as 1930, in New York, the fabled immigrant ghetto of the Lower East Side had passed its peak; only one out of every six New York City Jews lived in Manhattan. Nearly one half lived in Brooklyn, about one third in the Bronx, and fewer than one out of every twenty Jews lived in Queens. The Jewish areas had changed again one generation later. Old Jewish neighborhoods like the Grand Concourse in the Bronx and Brownsville in Brooklyn had become run-down at the heels, and blacks and Puerto Ricans were moving in. By 1957 the number of Jews in Queens had quadrupled from the 1930 figure; there were one quarter fewer Jews in the Bronx, and the Jewish population of Brooklyn had declined slightly. The trend is continuing, and by 1975 Queens, "the borough of homes," will be the residence of one quarter of New York City's Jews.

CHART 2:   JEWISH POPULATION DISTRIBUTION
IN NEW YORK CITY 1923–1975

	1923	1930	1957	1975 (estimated)
Manhattan	37.4%	16.3%	16.0%	15.1%
Bronx	20.3%	32.1%	23.3%	21.1%
Brooklyn	39.3%	46.6%	40.3%	38.6%
Queens	2.7%	4.8%	20.0%	24.8%
Staten Island	0.2%	0.2%	0.3%	0.4%

SOURCE: Federation of Jewish Philanthropies of New York.

Those who can do so are moving farther—to the suburbs.
Upper-middle-class Long Island communities like Great Neck
and Hempstead, and wealthy Westchester villages such as Scars-
dale and Mamaroneck have many more Jewish residents than
they had a few years ago. And by 1975, two out of every ten New
York area Jews will live in the New York suburbs, with another
one out of ten living in nearby New Jersey and Connecticut.

CHART 3:   JEWISH POPULATION
DISTRIBUTION IN GREATER NEW
YORK CITY AREA

	1957	1975 (estimated)
New York City	81.9%	78.5%
Nassau County	12.8%	14.6%
Suffolk County	0.8%	1.2%
Westchester County	4.5%	5.7%

SOURCE: Federation of Jewish Philanthropies of
New York.

The trend to the suburbs is not limited to New York. In Chicago, Jews have left the old West Side neighborhoods for the
apartment buildings and small houses of West Rogers Park, and
more than one quarter of all of Chicago's Jews now live outside
the city in the $70,000 "ranches" of Highland Park, the garden
apartments of Skokie, and the split-levels of Buffalo Grove. The
once heavily Jewish Dexter section of Detroit became increasingly
black, and most Jews left for the North West Section, while others

moved to the quiet suburbs of Oak Park and Huntington Woods. Another demographic factor with political impact is the decline in foreign-born Jews.[2] (Jewish immigration to the United States dropped off sharply after the 1920s.) The vast majority of America's Jews are now native-born. According to a survey by the Columbia University School of Public Health, foreign-born Jews in New York City favor the Democratic party slightly more than native-born Jews. In fact, a native-born Jew with a high-school education is six times more likely to be a Republican than a foreign-born Jew without a high-school diploma. (Of course, these Jews are still 7 to 1 Democratic.) The Public Health Survey also showed that foreign-born Jews are a little less likely to vote than their native-born counterparts. As the Jewish population becomes almost entirely native-born or even second- or third-generation American, the turnout rate among Jews, which is already the highest of any ethnic group, should increase, and the number of Jews who strongly prefer the Democratic party will probably decline slightly—but that difference will be negligible.

CHART 4:   NEW YORK JEWS PARTY PREFERENCE

	Democrats	Republicans	Independent	"Almost always vote?"
Native-born Jews	75%	6%	19%	79%
Foreign-born Jews	77%	2%	21%	70%
All New Yorkers	65%	19%	16%	59%

SOURCE: Columbia University Public Health Survey.

In a society which prides itself on being middle-class, America's Jews are solidly middle-class; and many are upper-middle-class and even wealthier. In 1965, for example, nearly half of all Jewish families had annual incomes between $7,000 and $15,000, while in the same year, only slightly more than one quarter of all American families were making that money. The

[2] According to the U.S. Census the highest percentage of foreign-born Jews (one third) is in Dade County, Florida. It was these Miami Beach Jews—many of them retired people living on Social Security—who, among all Jews in the nation, most strongly and uniformly opposed Barry Goldwater in 1964.

number of Jews in white-collar jobs is two or three times the national average, and only about one fifth of Jews work in blue-collar jobs; thus, despite a long-standing Jewish interest in the labor movement, only about 10 percent of Jews belong to unions.[3] If income and occupation alone determined political preference, then Jews, who are nearly as well-to-do as upper-class Protestants, should be Republicans. But Jews remain Democrats. Income, education and occupation have little impact on Jewish loyalty to the party of Al Smith and F.D.R. Survey after survey comes up with returns similar to these from Connecticut, which reveal across-the-board income identification with the Democratic party.

CHART 5: POLITICAL PARTY PREFERENCE
CONNECTICUT JEWS

	Percent Democrats	Percent Republicans	Percent Independents
All Jews	81	8	11
White-Collar	81	8	11
Blue-Collar	83	7	10

SOURCE: Institute for Urban Research, University of Connecticut at Storrs.

Most Jews are well educated, hold good jobs, and live in comfortable homes. The lower-class militants of the Jewish Defense League may get the headlines, but they simply are not the typical Jewish voter.

PRESIDENTIAL POLITICS

Oddly enough, it was the French Revolution that brought American Jewry into politics. While Napoleon's armies freed Jews as they conquered, the French Republic was supported in America by the Jeffersonians and condemned by the Federalists. In the years following it was therefore not surprising to find Jews

[3] The Jews stand out on the education scale as well. Although only 3 percent of the United States population, the proportion of Jews in college is twice the national average and three times the national average in graduate and professional schools.

working in the Jefferson political clubs. In New York the Tammany Society was founded in 1794, and three years later a Jew, Solomon Simson, became its president.[4]

The Federalist party died with its opposition to the War of 1812 but, in its last gasp at the Hartford Convention in 1815, the party managed to pass a resolution urging a Constitutional amendment to prohibit naturalized citizens from serving in the Congress. Any Jews not siding with the Jeffersonian Republicans at this point moved over quickly.

America's Jews remained with the party of Jefferson (soon to be called the Democrats) from its founder's own election to the Presidency in 1800 through the election of James K. Polk forty-four years later.

Large-scale German-Jewish immigration occurred in the twelve years preceding the Civil War, and with the new immigrants came a new political liberalism. Millard Fillmore's Whig administration had concluded an anti-Semitic commercial treaty with Switzerland (allowing Swiss cantons to expel American Jews in accordance with their law), and when a Jewish delegation failed to persuade President Buchanan to renegotiate the agreement, Jews began straying from the Democrats—and immediately encountered Lincoln's Republicans.

During the Civil War, General Grant issued the infamous Order No. 11 giving all Jews in Tennessee twenty-four hours to leave the area. President Lincoln quashed the order when he learned of it, General Grant apologized for having issued it when he ran for President in 1868, and the Jews stayed with the Republicans. (Grant quickly offered his friend Joseph Seligman the Cabinet position of Secretary of the Treasury, but the proposal was rejected.)

---

[4] The largest Jewish colony of the day was not in New York, but in Charleston, South Carolina, and following Jefferson was the rule there as well. In the years preceding Independence, America's Jews were denied the right to vote in all of the colonies except South Carolina, whose liberal Charter had been written by the great English philosopher John Locke in 1663. Elsewhere voting restrictions were gradually removed with Jefferson's "Act to Disestablish the Anglican Church in Virginia" paving the way to Jewish suffrage in the new states. The last disability, however, in New Hampshire, was not removed until 1876.

By 1890 America's Jewish population had increased threefold to 900,000. The G.O.P. continued its domination of the Jewish vote during this era as a succession of Republican Presidents sought to intercede in behalf of Jews being persecuted throughout Europe.[5]

Two million Jews arrived in the United States between 1896 and the First World War. Some became Democrats during this period, but the majority were Republicans and with the exception of Woodrow Wilson in 1916, continued to vote for the Republican Presidential candidate until 1928.

Of all the Republican Presidents of these years, Jews reserved a special affection for Teddy Roosevelt. This "special relationship" is traceable to 1895, when T.R., as New York's Police Commissioner, assigned only Jewish patrolmen to guard the German anti-Semite Hermann Ahlwardt when he visited the city. After his election, Roosevelt became the first President to welcome the United States Rabbinical Conference to the White House and he even predicted the election of a Jewish President of the United States. Roosevelt was careful to continue Presidential interest in the plight of European Jewry throughout his incumbency.

Roosevelt's successor, William Howard Taft, had indicated during his 1908 campaign that he would renegotiate a discriminatory Russian trade treaty, but he did not do so after his election. Jewish protest was widespread, and a rally in Carnegie Hall was addressed by the up-and-coming governor of New Jersey, Woodrow Wilson. By 1916, when Wilson was running for his second Presidential term, Jewish support for his Democratic candidacy was strong and enthusiastic, despite the constant disclaimers, by Jews, that there was a Jewish "bloc" vote in the first place.

[5] President Rutherford B. Hayes warned Rumania in 1879 that the United States was concerned about Jews in foreign countries; in 1882 Chester Alan Arthur urged the Russian government to end the pogroms and President Benjamin Harrison sought to follow up on Arthur's initiative through Secretary of State James G. Blaine, the leading Republican of the day. (Domestic Jewish political activity flourished during these years as well. The most powerful of Jewish politicians at this time was "Boss" Abe Ruef, of San Francisco, whose citywide reign ended only when he was convicted of bribery in 1908.)

The 1920 Republican candidate, Senator Warren G. Harding of Ohio, was accused of being anti-Semitic because of his vote against the confirmation of Louis D. Brandeis as Associate Justice of the United States Supreme Court. But it was a Republican year and without Wilson, Jews ended their flirtation with the Democratic party.

Calvin Coolidge carried the Jewish vote in 1924, but Republican fortunes were already changing. For in 1922 (for the first time since the Civil War), more Democratic than Republican Jews were elected to Congress.

Democrat Alfred E. Smith took the Jewish Presidential vote in 1928, and in 1930 six of the eight Jews elected to Congress were Democrats. (Just ten years before, the Jewish Congressional delegation of eleven consisted of ten Republicans and a lone Socialist.) The Jews were returning to the Democratic fold. They have remained there ever since—overwhelmingly.

CHART 6:   JEWISH PRESIDENTIAL VOTE 1940–1968

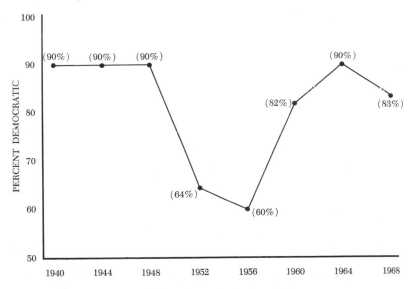

NOTE: 1948 represents the combined Truman (75%)–Wallace (15%) vote.
SOURCE: National Opinion Research Center; Angus Campbell and H. C. Cooper, *Group Differences in Attitudes and Voting;* Institute of American Research; NBC News.

Although declining in the Eisenhower elections, from the uniformly outstanding Franklin Roosevelt performances of 1936, 1940 and 1944, the Jewish Democratic vote rebounded to near–New Deal levels in the decade of the 1960s.

In the closely fought election of 1960, Jewish voters played a significant role in electing the nation's first Catholic President. In New York, where Kennedy carried the state by 384,000 votes, Jewish precincts gave him a plurality of more than 800,000.[6] And in Illinois, where Kennedy barely got by with a 9,000-vote margin, Jewish voters gave him a plurality of more than 55,000 votes. Religion had been on everyone's mind in that campaign, and a definitive study by the Michigan Survey Research Center concluded that Kennedy's Catholicism cost him, on balance, some 1.5 million votes nationwide. Jews, however, seemed pleased to vote for the liberal, urbane Kennedy, and in Jewish neighborhoods the Senator generally did better than Stevenson did in 1956.[7]

At least one variation in the strong Jewish support for Kennedy deserves attention. In state after state, there was an urban-suburban split in the 1960 Jewish Presidential vote. Kennedy had no trouble at all with city Jews, but with their suburban cousins his vote fell substantially. It is wrong to suggest that the Jews of suburbia voted against Kennedy because he was Catholic. Far from it. What is more likely is that the suburban Jew felt the pressures of his higher standard of living and voted more like his upper-middle-class neighbors. We have seen that in general, wealthy Jews still say they identify with the Democratic party. Suburban Jews, at least in 1960, were more willing than city-bound Jews to vote Republican.

In Kennedy's home state of Massachusetts there was a real

6 Kennedy did not win a majority on the Democratic line alone. Four hundred six thousand votes were cast for him on the Liberal party line. Slightly more than half of Kennedy's Liberal-line votes were cast by Jews.

7 Father Andrew Greeley of the National Opinion Research Center reports that in the period 1952 to 1965 there was a tentative, but apparently real increase in anti-Catholic sentiments among Jews. One major exception to this growing anti-Catholicism, Greeley says, comes in response to the question, "Would you vote for a Catholic for President?" In 1952, five out of eight Jews said they would vote for a Catholic candidate; by 1965, nearly seven out of eight said the same.

difference between the Democratic Jewish vote in Boston and that in the surrounding suburbs. Boston has long been a Democratic stronghold, and the Irish political machine which ran the city was noted for its power to deliver votes. The historic antagonism between the Boston Irish political machine and other ethnic groups, including the Jews, failed to hurt Kennedy. While the Senator carried Boston with nearly 80 percent of the vote, he actually ran 4 to 5 percent stronger in the Jewish precincts of Dorchester and Mattapan. But in the suburbs of Brookline and Newton, Jewish voters behaved very much like their upper-middle-class neighbors and Kennedy's vote dropped to less than two thirds of his showing in Boston.

CHART 7: MASSACHUSETTS
JEWISH VOTE FOR
JOHN KENNEDY

All Jews	70%
Boston	79%
Boston Suburbs	49%

SOURCE: Institute of American Research; NBC News.

The pattern was repeated in Michigan. Approximately half of Detroit's Jews live in the neighborhood known as the North West, and in these middle-income precincts, Kennedy won more than three quarters of the vote. However, many of Detroit's younger Jewish families had moved to the suburb of Oak Park by 1960, and Kennedy managed to take only half the votes in this new Jewish area.

CHART 8: MICHIGAN
JEWISH VOTE FOR
JOHN KENNEDY

All Jews	75%
Detroit	78%
Detroit Suburbs	51%

SOURCE: Institute of American Research; NBC News.

Vice President Nixon's home state of California was no different. The Jews who live in the Fairfax section of Los Angeles are
distinctly middle-class, and Stevenson had swept the Fairfax vote
in 1956. In one seven-precinct area, Eisenhower polled only 105
of 1,400 votes cast, and in 1960 Kennedy did at least as well with
these same voters.[8] The Jews who live in Beverly Hills, on the
other hand, are far wealthier. Family incomes in excess of $35,000
are not uncommon, and there is a suburban air to the neighborhood. Among these well-to-do Jews, Kennedy's vote dropped to
three quarters of its total in Fairfax.

CHART 9: LOS ANGELES
JEWISH PRESIDENTIAL VOTE,
1960

	Kennedy	Nixon
Fairfax	84%	16%
Beverly Hills	63%	37%

SOURCE: Institute of American Research;
NBC News.

This 1960 Jewish urban-suburban split all but disappeared in
the Johnson landslide of 1964. Jews voted nearly 90 percent for
the President, a showing reminiscent of that for Franklin Roosevelt a generation earlier.

The most striking increase in Jewish Democratic votes came in
the suburbs, and this was consistent with the national trend.
Compared to Nixon in 1960, Goldwater's suburban vote in the
Northeast, for instance, fell off 10 to 30 percentage points. Again,
Jewish suburbanites voted much like their neighbors, going from
12 to 35 points more Democratic. It apparently did not matter in
the slightest that Goldwater had a Jewish grandfather. Jews were

[8] In 1960, there were constant rumors about the alleged anti-Semitism
of both Kennedy and Nixon. Kennedy was not charged with being directly
anti-Semitic, but it was said that when his father, Joseph Kennedy, was
United States Ambassador at London, the elder Kennedy had been sympathetic to the Nazis. Nixon, on the other hand, signed a restrictive covenant
for his home in Washington, D.C. The American Jewish Committee reported
that voters of the Fairfax section in Los Angeles were particularly sensitive
to this alleged anti-Semitism, even though Nixon was never condemned
for his action by any major Jewish organization.

frightened by the darker side of Goldwater's *political* heritage, and they voted accordingly.[9]

CHART 10: VOTE FOR PRESIDENT
JOHNSON IN SELECTED JEWISH
PRECINCTS

		Gain from 1960
Chicago	87%	+13%
Chicago Suburbs	81%	+22%
Boston	93%	+14%
Boston Suburbs	83%	+35%
Cleveland Suburbs	76%	+12%
Cincinnati	65%	+20%

SOURCE: Institute of American Research; NBC News.

The city Democratic vote, which had been quite strong for Kennedy, was even more Democratic in 1964, but the pattern is far from uniform. In Philadelphia, for example, Jewish voters in the somewhat run-down Logan neighborhood went only 2 percent more for Johnson, and in Brownsville, a working-class Jewish neighborhood in Brooklyn, L.B.J. outpolled Kennedy by only 4 percent. The Johnson increase was more dramatic in Brooklyn's Coney Island section, where Jews voted 20 points more against Goldwater. Chicago's pattern was mixed, as well. One definitely lower-middle-class precinct in Ward 50 went 25 points more for Johnson than for Kennedy; two Jewish precincts in a better part of the same ward voted in opposite ways, one showing only a minimal Democratic increase of 2 percent, and the other a jump of nearly 16 points against Goldwater. Of course, Goldwater lost badly even in those precincts where he did nearly as well as Nixon had done in 1960.

The Jewish urban-suburban split failed to reappear in convincing fashion in 1968, so at least as far as this Jewish voting is concerned the 1964 election was not an exception. In Chicago, where Nixon in 1960 had run 15 percentage points better in the

[9] Goldwater was attacked from the Jewish pulpit on numerous occasions. Rabbi Joachim Prinz of Temple B'Nai Abraham in Newark, New Jersey, is reported as having sermonized: "A Jewish vote for Goldwater is a vote for Jewish suicide."

suburbs than in the city, he ran but 6 points better eight years later. In Boston a 30-percentage-point advantage declined to 14 points in 1968. Nixon's vote was off more in the suburbs than in the cities. Jewish suburbanites had started the decade as potential Presidential Republicans, but by its end it was difficult to label them other than Presidential Democrats.

CHART 11: JEWISH VOTE FOR NIXON
1960 AND 1968

	1960	*1968*	*Loss*
Chicago	26%	17%	− 9%
Chicago Suburbs	41%	23%	−18%
Boston	21%	8%	−13%
Boston Suburbs	51%	22%	−29%
New York City	15%	12%	− 3%
New York Suburbs	—	20%	
Cleveland Suburbs	36%	32%	− 4%
Cincinnati	55%	44%	−11%
Nation	18%	15%	− 3%

SOURCE: Institute of American Research; NBC News.

Republican leaders expected to recoup Jewish votes in the 1968 campaign. Many Jews had opposed the renomination of Lyndon Johnson and were not much more favorably inclined toward Hubert Humphrey. (Preconvention polls showed that Jews supported the candidacy of Senator Eugene McCarthy more strongly than any other group.)[10] The Democratic convention in Chicago did little to heal party wounds, and Jews were particularly critical of the behavior of the Chicago police. A survey found that 42 percent of all Jews thought the police were too tough on demonstrators, while only 19 percent of all voters felt the same way; less than 10 percent of Jews thought the police should have been tougher, while three times as many other voters wanted stronger police action.

[10] Curiously, in California, which was the only Presidential primary test of Jewish sentiment, the slate of delegates pledged to Robert Kennedy ran ahead of the McCarthy delegates. According to returns from selected Jewish precincts, the vote was 47 percent Kennedy, 38 percent McCarthy, and 15 percent for the Lynch slate which was originally pledged to President Johnson. Kennedy's appeal was strongest in middle-income Jewish precincts, while McCarthy ran stronger with more wealthy Jews.

Nixon even appeared to be making inroads in the Jewish vote after McCarthy failed to win the Democratic nomination. In late September, Gallup reported that 31 percent of all Jews planned to vote for him, and if the Gallup figures had held up, Nixon would have run better with Jews than Eisenhower had in either election.

But on November 5, Nixon's Jewish support evaporated. Many liberal Jews who sat out the campaign turned out for Humphrey, giving him more than eight out of every ten votes in Jewish precincts.[11] Humphrey's showing was higher than high and only a little less than remarkable, while Nixon ran behind his 1960 vote in every Jewish community.

JEWS, BLACKS, AND LAW AND ORDER

The acid test for Jewish liberalism came with the black-white confrontations of the 1960s. Much has been written about the traumatic effects of the New York City teachers strike in 1968 and about the fears of Jewish shopkeepers who trade in the black ghettos. America's liberal Jews seemed confused when black militants questioned their motives and refused to let them work any longer in the civil-rights movement. New Left and black-militant tracts attacking Israel received widespread attention in the Jewish press, and Jewish radicals walked out of a 1967 New Left coalition conference in Chicago rather than support a black demand for a resolution condemning Israel as an imperialist aggressor in the Middle East.

Still, Jews remain more committed to black rights and economic progress than any other group. During the Presidential campaign of 1968, Oliver Quayle of NBC News asked voters to identify the most important issues. Forty-five percent of all voters said "law and order," while a virtually identical 46 percent of all Jews responded in the same way; America's Jews are just as concerned as the next guy about being mugged. Everyone is afraid of

[11] George Wallace won only about 2 percent of the vote in predominantly Jewish precincts, or just as few votes as he received in most black areas. Jewish distrust of Wallace was overwhelming, and a column in the Boston *Jewish Advocate* had called Wallace an "embryonic Hitler."

crime in the streets, but there is a fundamental difference between the attitudes of most voters and Jews. For in the same poll, only one out of eight Jews thought the government had gone too far in helping blacks achieve social and economic equality, while twice as many voters at large felt the government had done too much for blacks.

Jews had a chance to express their attitudes in the 1966 New York City Civilian Review Board election, that asked voters to approve a review board of civilians to oversee the Police Department's actions. Mayor Lindsay, Senators Javits and Kennedy, various civil-rights and Jewish organizations, and the Liberal party all backed the review board. The Patrolmen's Benevolent Association, the Conservative party and various veterans groups opposed it. By a ratio of nearly two to one, New Yorkers rejected the review board. "It couldn't happen in New York," they said, not with New York's liberal tradition. The lack of Jewish support disturbed them even more. A survey taken for the American Jewish Committee found that 40 percent of the Jews in Brooklyn, for instance, backed the review board, while it received 32 percent of the vote boroughwide.

CHART 12: BROOKLYN
JEWS FAVORING
CIVILIAN REVIEW
BOARD BY OCCUPATION

Clerical	20%
Blue Collar	31%
Business	46%
Professional	63%
All Jews	40%
Citywide vote	37%

SOURCE: American Jewish Committee.

Jews *do*, however, support black candidates in addition to everyman's black man, Senator Edward Brooke of Massachusetts.[12]

---

[12] When Republican Brooke defeated Democrat Endicott Peabody for the U.S. Senate in 1966 by 400,000 votes, he received 55 percent of the vote in

In one of the more remarkable and little-noticed political upsets of 1970, Wilson Riles, a black moderate, beat Max Rafferty, the incumbent California Superintendent of Public Instruction whose superpatriotism and hard line against youthful dissent made him the darling of the Right. In winning the nonpartisan election, Riles became the first black to hold statewide-elective office in California.[13] Jewish precincts which had given more than half their vote to Mayor Yorty in 1969 voted nearly three to one for Riles.

	Riles	Rafferty
Statewide	75%	25%
Los Angeles Jews	73%	27%

A year earlier the absence of unified Jewish support cost Los Angeles the chance to have its first black mayor. Incumbent Sam Yorty, a conservative whose administration was scandal-ridden, faced a nonpartisan primary challenge from thirteen opponents, including Thomas Bradley, a black veteran police officer. In the April Fools' Day primary, Bradley ran far ahead of the field with 42 percent of the vote, as Yorty trailed, a distant second. Since Bradley had not won half the vote, he and the mayor were matched in a runoff, and Bradley needed a substantial portion of white votes to win. (Los Angeles is only 17 percent black.) Yorty, however, set out to keep white votes for Bradley to a minimum. He hinted that Bradley was supported by militants and subversives and he said there would be trouble in the streets if Bradley won.[14] Yorty's appeal worked, and Bradley was narrowly defeated.

Jewish precincts—more than any Republican senatorial candidate had won in a decade.

[13] Riles was helped by the endorsement of S. I. Hayakawa, President of San Francisco State College. He "used" Hayakawa extensively during the campaign in conservative and upper-middle-class areas, the idea being to present Riles (through his association with the man who successfully put down the student strikes at San Francisco State) as a man who would deal firmly with disciplinary problems in education.

[14] "The election of Bradley," Yorty declared, "will make Los Angeles an experimental area for taking over of a city by a combination of bloc voting, black power, left-wing radicals and, if you please, identified Communists."

CHART 13: JEWISH
VOTERS IN THE LOS
ANGELES MAYORAL
ELECTION

	Primary	*Runoff*
Bradley	53%	51%
Yorty	21%	49%
Others	26%	

SOURCE: Institute of American
Research; NBC News.

In the April primary, Bradley had run ahead of Yorty by better than two-and-a-half to one in Jewish neighborhoods and he maintained his Jewish primary support in the general election. However, Yorty's hard-line general election campaign corralled most of the non-Bradley primary vote and most of the turnout increment of the Jewish vote in the general election went to the mayor as well.

Jewish voters are understandably not enchanted with a black candidate who beats a Jewish incumbent in a primary. Maryland's Seventh Congressional District covers western Baltimore and part of suburban Baltimore County. It is 40 percent black, 40 percent Jewish, and the rest white Protestant. For eighteen years, the district had been represented by Sam Friedel, an old-fashioned liberal ward politician of little distinction. But in the 1970 primary, demography caught up with Friedel. He lost by 38 votes to Parren J. Mitchell, a black peace-activist, professor at Morgan State University. Not surprisingly, Mitchell's strength came from black precincts and Friedel's votes from predominantly Jewish areas. (Friedel certainly was not helped by the presence of another Jewish candidate in the race.) In the November election, Mitchell, who was now the official Democratic candidate, faced Peter Parker, a young Presbyterian attorney who had been active in local Republican politics. Large numbers of young people, mostly students at Morgan State and Johns Hopkins, worked for Mitchell because of his opposition to the Vietnam War. But race, and not peace, turned out to be the overriding issue. Jewish voters were angry that one of their own had been beaten in the primary. In past elections, Friedel carried

Jewish precincts with more than 90 percent of the vote, but in 1970, these staunchly Democratic precincts voted Republican two to one. Seventh District Jews voted against the man who beat Sammy Friedel, and then they turned around and voted almost 80 percent for liberal Democratic Senator Joseph Tydings, and more than 90 percent for their coreligionist Governor Marvin Mandel.

Maryland's Jewish voters had also deserted the Democrats in 1966, when a man they perceived as racist won the gubernatorial primary. Democrat George P. Mahoney, a perennial office seeker, won an extremely close Democratic primary on the anti–open-housing slogan, "Your home is your castle—vote to protect it." The Republican candidate was Spiro Agnew, at the time an obscure county official from suburban Baltimore. (Hyman Pressman, City Comptroller of Baltimore, ran as an independent.) Mahoney came on strong with his antiblack rhetoric, counting on the fact that more than 40 percent of Marylanders had supported George Wallace in the Democratic Presidential primary two years before. Agnew took a middle-of-the-road course on open housing and hammered away at the failings of the old-guard Democrats who ran the state under outgoing Governor Millard Tawes. Agnew won by 82,000 votes, Mahoney was a strong second, and Pressman trailed, winning only 90,000 votes statewide.

One key to Agnew's success lay in the predominantly Jewish precincts. Maryland's Jewish voters clearly rejected Mahoney's none-too-covert racial appeals. Some, mostly in Baltimore, could not bring themselves to vote Republican and found a convenient out by voting for Pressman, who certainly was more moderate than Mahoney. Nevertheless, Republican Spiro Agnew, who at

CHART 14: MARYLAND JEWISH VOTERS
1966 GUBERNATORIAL ELECTION

	Baltimore	Suburbs
Agnew (Republican)	45%	77%
Mahoney (Democrat)	21%	15%
Pressman (Independent)	34%	8%

SOURCE: Institute of American Research; NBC News.

the time was universally acknowledged to be the "liberal" candidate, carried the Baltimore Jewish community.

JEWS AND REPUBLICANS: OR IT MATTERS HOW YOU LOSE

If a politician can turn a group normally 6 to 1 against him into a group 2 to 1 against him, he has neutralized one of his opponent's best weapons—the bloc vote. Liberal Republicans break up the Jewish bloc vote. Some examples. Liberal Senator Thomas H. Kuchel of California won about one fifth of the Jewish vote in 1962 against HUAC-boosting Democrat Richard Richards.

Charles Percy lost to Otto Kerner for governor of Illinois in 1964, but set a Republican record among Jewish voters with almost 30 percent of the vote.

Republican Hugh Scott bucked the Goldwater conservatives in 1964 and because of that won more than 40 percent of the Jewish vote in Pennsylvania, against Genevieve Blatt. By 1970, Scott was a leading spokesman for the Nixon administration and he lost one quarter of that Jewish support.

Republican Charles Mathias ran for senator with a good record as a civil-rights moderate. Accordingly he won one third of Jewish votes in Baltimore and the Maryland suburbs against the soon-to-be-indicted Senator Daniel Brewster.

Republican Kenneth Keating fought a losing battle against Robert Kennedy in 1964, but still managed to win a quarter of New York's Jewish votes against the Kennedy magic.[15]

George Romney nearly won a majority of Jewish votes in his race for governor of Michigan in 1966 against Zoltan A. Ferency. On the way, more than a third of the Jewish vote was carried on Romney's coattails for conservative Robert P. Griffin, running for the United States Senate against G. Mennen "Soapy" Williams.

[15] Polls taken early in the campaign showed that Kennedy was doing very badly with Jewish voters. Harry Golden, the Jewish journalist-humorist, was called in to campaign for Kennedy in older, Jewish neighborhoods. Kennedy tried everything to court Jewish votes. He made it a point to be photographed wearing a yarmulke and he even held a curbside news conference during which he exonerated the Jews for the Crucifixion.

Sometimes you don't even have to be all that liberal to win Jewish votes. Ohio's Jews, for instance, tend to vote more Republican. In both 1960 and 1968, President Nixon ran better with Ohio's Jews than anywhere else. In 1960 he won 37 percent of the votes cast in Jewish neighborhoods of Cleveland and Cincinnati, and in 1968 he still took a comfortable third of the Jewish vote. Twice in the past decade, Ohio's Jewish precincts turned in substantial pluralities for moderate Republican Governor James A. Rhodes. And even conservative Senator Robert A. Taft, Jr., won nearly half the votes cast in Jewish precincts despite the Johnson tide of 1964.

Part of the explanation lies in an analysis of the Jewish vote in Cincinnati, where a tradition of Republicanism has existed since the first wave of German immigrants voted there in the 1850s. Apparently some of this Republican tradition has rubbed off on today's Jewish voters in Cincinnati.[16]

CHART 15: REPUBLICAN
VOTE IN CINCINNATI
JEWISH PRECINCTS

1960	Nixon	55%
1964	Taft	53%
1966	Rhodes	75%
1968	Nixon	44%

SOURCE: Institute of American Research; NBC News.

It appears very unlikely that the Republicans will ever break the Democratic grip on the Jewish voter. But in any given close election, it may matter considerably whether a Republican loses the Jewish vote by three to two or by six to one.

John Lindsay became mayor of New York twice because he did a good job losing the Jewish vote. Jewish voters make up one third of the electorate in a general election for mayor. When

---

[16] Massachusetts Jews play a variation of this game, called "Would you rather trust a Brahmin or an Irishman?" In 1960, Republican Leverett Saltonstall, member of an old-line New England family, won 45 percent of the vote in Jewish precincts against Democrat Thomas O'Connor. And in 1962, young Ted Kennedy took an undistinguished two thirds of the Jewish vote against George Lodge, the son of Henry Cabot Lodge.

Lindsay first ran in 1965, he was very much the Republican candidate, with a coalition based largely on traditional Republican voters in conservative sections of the northeast Bronx, Italian areas of Brooklyn, German and Irish neighborhoods in Queens, and just enough nominal Democrats to squeak by. In the city's Jewish neighborhoods, Lindsay won 30 percent of the vote, about half of it coming on the Liberal line. His Democratic opponent, Abraham Beame, a Jew, won a plurality of nearly 600,000 votes among Jewish Democrats. Still, citywide, Lindsay won by slightly more than 100,000 votes. Had the Jewish Beame duplicated the Catholic Kennedy's 1960 showing among Jews he would have become mayor.

A lot happened in New York between Lindsay's first election in 1965 and his second try for office four years later: a civilian review board vote, school decentralization, and the teachers' strike. Jews became the most critical group in the electorate. (Lindsay had lost the Republican primary and was running on the Liberal party line.) Lindsay's campaign strategists figured that the Mayor would do very well with black and Puerto Rican voters and also believed that the conservative and Republican areas which had supported Lindsay in 1965 would go for Democrat Mario Procaccino or regular Republican John Marchi. Lindsay's campaign team set out to find those nominally Democratic voters who were still undecided and who might switch to Lindsay.

A precinct-by-precinct analysis of past* elections was undertaken and votes from the previous five years were rated according to assumptions about the "switchable" voter. It was considered important, for instance, that Paul O'Dwyer had run well in the 1968 senatorial primary, that the Liberal party had shown consistent strength for Lindsay in 1965 and for the Liberal party candidates for governor, and that Lindsay and Herman Badillo had run well in the 1969 primary. Of the city's 5,200 election districts, about one quarter—made up almost exclusively of Manhattan's whites, blacks, or Puerto Ricans—"showed up" as certain for Lindsay. Another one quarter—almost exclusively white Catholic and all outside Manhattan—were considered almost certainly not for the Mayor. The campaign then focused on the remaining half of the districts which were rated neither strongly for Lindsay nor strongly opposed to him. Field canvassers found that these middle-range precincts contained most of New York City's Jewish voters.

Just after the June primary, a poll determined Lindsay's Jewish support to be 35 percent. This was up 5 points from Lindsay's 1965 showing, but Lindsay staffers felt he needed a still greater vote. Lindsay spent more time in temple during the summer of 1969 than an Israel bonds salesman, and he took his lumps, getting hostile receptions in Brooklyn and Queens. Still, he plugged away, moving toward the political center with a get-tough stance on crime and disorder. By election day, a vital change had taken place. Lindsay did not win a plurality in Jewish neighborhoods, but he increased his 1965 share of the Jewish vote by almost half.

CHART 16: JEWISH VOTERS
NEW YORK MAYORAL ELECTION, 1969

	Lindsay	Procaccino	Marchi
All Jews	42%	49%	9%
Wealthy	55%	36%	9%
Middle Class	39%	53%	8%
Working Class	36%	54%	10%

SOURCE: Institute of American Research; NBC News.

Most analyses of the election heralded a new Lindsay coalition of wealthy whites, poor blacks and Puerto Ricans. It is true that Lindsay picked up considerable support from these two ends of the social spectrum, but the real Lindsay victory was forged in the city's switchable Jewish precincts. For John Lindsay it mattered by how much he "lost" the Jewish vote.

A JEW AMONG JEWS

No Jewish mother we know ever wanted her son to be President. Special Assistant to the President, maybe; but President, never. Politics never traditionally played the same role in the Jewish scheme for upward mobility as it did for the Irish. But, alas, the Jewish mother is not what she used to be. Alexander Portnoy is running all over the place. There are currently three Jewish governors (Marvin Mandel of Maryland, Frank Licht of Rhode Island, and Milton Shapp of Pennsylvania), two Jewish Senators (Jacob Javits of New York and Abraham Ribicoff of Connecticut) and twelve Jewish members of the House of Representatives. All but Senator Javits and two Congressmen—Seymour Halpern of New York and Sam Steiger of Arizona—are Democrats. And in 1970 Jewish Democrats narrowly lost the governorship of Michigan (Sander Levin) and United States Senate contests in Arizona (Sam Grossman), New York (Dick Ottinger) and Ohio (Howard Metzenbaum).[17]

Sometimes Mrs. Portnoy herself has a complaint. Even fellow Jews won't always vote for her son. In Illinois, in 1962, Sidney Yates, a Jewish Democratic Congressman from Chicago, ran for the United States Senate against the ever popular Everett Mc-Kinley Dirksen. Yates won three quarters of the Jewish vote, yet that was a drop of from 3 to 15 percentage points from the normal Jewish Democratic vote. In the 1970 Ohio senatorial contest, Howard Metzenbaum won better than 85 percent of the Jewish vote. But Metzenbaum, a Jew, actually ran slightly behind John Gilligan, the successful gubernatorial candidate.[18]

A survey conducted for *The New York Times* by Daniel

[17] One Jew with a super complaint was Arthur Goldberg, who was stung by a WASP in the 1970 New York gubernatorial election. (While the Lowells, the Cabots, the Lodges and perhaps even God might think Nelson Rockefeller a Jew, Jews know that he is a WASP.)

[18] The ill-feeling between Metzenbaum and Ohio's Jewish leaders, most notably Edward Ginsberg, a former president of the United Jewish Appeal, is of long standing, dating back to Mike Sweeney's unsuccessful race for Representative Michael Feighan's 20th Congressional District seat. Gilligan, on the other hand, has been on the best of terms with Ginsberg for some while. The funds raised by Ginsberg were instrumental in Gilligan's 1970 gubernatorial victory, and since that election his influence has ᴜeen felt in the capital, as a former Ginsberg law partner, Jim Friedman, occupies the powerful position of Executive Assistant to the Governor and reportedly controls Ohio patronage. Ginsberg has also opened a branch of his Cleveland law firm in Columbus (the only Cleveland firm with an additional office in the capital) and has further solidified his hold on Ohio's Democratic political structure by taking the state's second-strongest Democratic political leader, Joseph Bartunek, into his firm.

Yankelovich found that Jewish voters of New York are among the most liberal and the most Democratically inclined segment of the electorate. More than three quarters of Jews are registered Democrats, half describe themselves as "liberals," and a shade more than one quarter say they are political "moderates." Of New York voters, the Jews are the most dissatisfied with President Nixon. (Seventy-six percent give him a strongly negative job rating.)

The Democratic nominee for the governorship in 1970, Arthur Goldberg, seemed tailor-made to capitalize on this liberal, Jewish sentiment; and polls showed that Jews considered Goldberg the very model of a successful Jewish public figure. Goldberg's relatively poor showing among Jewish voters was surprising.

Goldberg did win a healthy share of the Jewish vote against long-time Jewish-vote-getter Nelson Rockefeller,[19] but he should have done much better among Jews. His vote in Jewish precincts was off by about one sixth compared to Hubert Humphrey's showing in 1968, and Goldberg even trailed the poor record of another Jew, Robert Morgenthau in 1962. (Rockefeller had alluded to his possibly Jewish ancestry, while Goldberg said he thought ethnic campaigning was "cheap." The Governor had thirty-one nationalities' organizations and perhaps Goldberg would have been wise to follow the Republican's lead.)

The Jewish senatorial candidate, Richard Ottinger, was in trouble with the Jewish vote as soon as he lost the Liberal party's designation to incumbent Senator Charles Goodell. Ottinger lost the election to the Conservative James Buckley[20] while winning 67 percent of the Jewish vote—a not particularly low all-time low for a New York Jewish Democrat.

Senator Goodell won only about one fifth of the Jewish vote, and more than one third of those votes came on the Liberal party

[19] In 1966, Rockefeller did not have a major Jewish opponent and his percentage in Jewish precincts rose to its all-time high of close to one third.

[20] Buckley's Jewish vote of 13 percent equaled the percent of Jews who indicated in a poll that Vice-President Agnew was helping the country. The higher Buckley Jewish vote in the suburbs reflected his general statewide appeal. Buckley had campaigned hard for Jewish votes. Shortly before election day, for instance, his signature appeared on an advertisement in *The New York Times* condemning Russian treatment of Jews.

line. If Ottinger had run on the Liberal line and if he had drawn as many Jewish Liberal voters as Hubert Humphrey, then from Jewish support alone, Ottinger would have beaten Buckley by a hundred thousand votes.

CHART 17: NEW YORK JEWISH VOTERS
1970 SENATORIAL ELECTION

	Buckley	Ottinger	Goodell
All Jews	13%	67%	20%
New York City	10%	70%	20%
Suburban	17%	61%	22%

SOURCE: Institute of American Research; NBC News.

It doesn't help a Republican to be a Jew, unless it helps. In 1971, when Richard J. Daley was reelected mayor of Chicago for a fifth term, his opponent was Richard Friedman, a young, articulate Jewish attorney and karate expert. Friedman was endorsed by every major reform group in Chicago, and he ran an energetic, media-oriented campaign. Daley didn't need karate to chop him down. Jewish voters—from the small apartment buildings in Rogers Park to the VanderRohean high-rises on the Lakefront—voted for Daley. In Jewish precincts turnout was the highest anywhere in the city and Richard J. Daley won more than 65 percent of the vote, a decline of 10 percentage points from his vote against a lackluster opponent in 1967, but of course in 1967 Daley did not run against a Jew.

Although some advocates of his invincibility might not believe it, Jacob Javits lost the Jewish vote to Catholic Democrat James Donovan in 1962.[21] Still, Javits ran ahead of Nelson Rockefeller in

[21] The story had been the same six years earlier, when Javits also lost the Jewish vote. Both he and his Democratic opponent, New York Mayor Robert F. Wagner, campaigned hard for Jewish support. The Democrats placed an advertisement in the *Jewish Forward* claiming "A vote for Javits is a vote for Nixon" (the prevalent liberal distrust of Nixon surfacing even then, four years before he would run for President). The *Day Jewish Morning Journal* featured an election-eve rebuttal advertisement reciting Javits' "Historic Services to the State of Israel," and at the eleventh hour Javits appropriated an idea General Eisenhower had used in his 1952 election campaign. "If elected, I will go to Israel," said Javits. He went, and still goes, but in 1956 (as in 1962) a majority of the Jewish vote stayed with his Democratic opponent.

Jewish areas, and with the help of the Liberal party line in 1968, increased his portion of the Jewish vote to 60 percent. (From Jewish voters alone, Javits won more than 650,000 votes of his astounding 1.1 million vote plurality.)

CHART 18:   JEWISH VOTERS, NEW YORK, 1962 AND 1968

1962		1968	
Javits (Republican)	41%	Javits (Republican)	33%
Donovan (Democrat)	47%	O'Dwyer (Democrat)	35%
Donovan (Liberal)	11%	Javits (Liberal)	27%
O'Doherty (Conservative)	1%	Buckley (Conservative)	5%

SOURCE: Institute of American Research; NBC News.

So even though Javits is Jewish, his Republicanism causes problems for New York's Jewish voters. In both 1962 and 1968, heavily Republican Jewish suburbs gave him majority votes, but it took the Liberal party line for Javits to break into traditional Jewish Democratic strongholds in Brooklyn and the Bronx. More than 60 percent of Javits' Liberal-line vote came from predominantly Jewish election districts.[22]

Candidates will continue to make special appeals to Jewish voters. No serious Presidential candidate, for instance, can afford to be considered anti-Israel. But when all is said and done, Jewish voters will still ask, "Which candidate is best for the Jews?" And it is hard to imagine that candidate not being a liberal Democrat.

[22] The Liberal party is usually said to be a very heavily Jewish party. But with the exception of the Javits vote in 1968, most elections show that Jews make up only about one third of Liberal-line *voters*. In 1966, for instance, about 32 percent of the Liberal vote for Franklin D. Roosevelt, Jr., came from Jewish areas and only about 35 percent of Arthur Goldberg's Liberal-line support was Jewish.

5

The Irish: Unethnic

New York was enjoying a beautiful Indian-summer day in early October. John Kennedy had just completed a busy campaign swing through the city and was resting at the nearby, ocean-front house of a friend. But even when a Presidential candidate rests, politicking continues. Visiting Kennedy that day were several New York City political figures, men on whom Kennedy was counting to bring out the vote in a few weeks. One of the local pols present was James Power, whose political career stretched back to the days of Woodrow Wilson, and another was "Little Larry" Murphy, a state legislator from Brooklyn who, a decade later and after twenty-six years in the Assembly, would be defeated by a brash young reformer. Kennedy talked easily with these men. They reminded him of those early days in Boston when, as the grandson of "Honey Fitz," he first ran for office. And Kennedy's visitors found it easy to pass the time with the candidate. They understood each other, because each understood the "rules of the game." They were Irish politicians, that breed of public man to whom ideology is divisive and consensus is what politics is all about. Looking back, years later, one who was there said, "It was my finest day."

Indeed, for many American Irish the Kennedy years collectively were their "finest day." When Kennedy took office, Irish political power appeared to be at its zenith. The President, Speaker of the House, Senate Majority Leader, and Chairman of the Joint Chiefs of Staff were all Irish. So were the mayors of several major cities. Irish control of the Democratic party, it seemed, would last forever. But in fact, in 1960 Irish political power was already on the wane. Gone were the old-line political machines that had been built by Irish politicians of the late nineteenth and early twentieth centuries. The Irish machine in Brooklyn, for example, which had run the borough from the time it was an independent city, lost power within a year of Kennedy's election, and in that same year the Irish politicians of Newark who had controlled the city from their Vailsburg enclave were beaten out by an unlikely coalition of Italians and blacks. Only Mayor Daley of Chicago stood out as the head of a major American city. (Of course, it is the luck of the Irish that "only" is the last word any American politician would use in describing Richard J. Daley.)

The urban political machine faded away with the ending of massive immigration in the 1920s and the institutionalization of public-welfare services. With the passing of the machine came also the end of the Irish political era. Some of the Irish families no longer wanted to make their living in politics. Rather they were attracted to the respectability of corporate life or the civil service. And, in their search for respectability, the Irish ceased being Irish and started acting like WASP Americans. During the 1960s, there were no cries of "Irish Power." The Irish, who had given this country so much of its political style, had become almost indistinguishable from the rest of America.

SOME SOCIAL STATISTICS

Of all the white ethnic groups considered in this book, the Irish have been Americans for the longest period of time. The first major waves of Irish immigrants arrived in the United States in the 1820s, and Irish immigration reached its peak following the Potato Famine of the late 1840s. According to one survey more than three quarters of the Irish are at least third-generation Americans. It is, therefore, relatively difficult to say with great precision much about Irish demographic characteristics or political behavior. But based on the available evidence, it is possible to draw a *relatively* accurate portrait.

There are approximately thirteen million Americans of Irish descent, about 6.5 percent of the total United States population. Two thirds live in the East. There are large numbers of Irish Americans in New York, Massachusetts, Pennsylvania and New Jersey. About one out of every six Irish-Americans lives in the Midwest, with the largest concentration found in Chicago. About one out of every seven Irish lives in the West, most in California. There are relatively few Irish Catholics in the South; Scarlet O'Hara was an Irish Protestant.

By many social measures, the Irish voter is the typical American voter. Like their countrymen, Irishmen are increasingly suburbanites. About 39 percent of the Irish live in the suburbs compared to about 36 percent of all voters. Approximately 37 percent live in the cities; the national electorate is 30 percent city-bound. Thirty-four percent live either in small towns or on farms, while 35 percent of all voters live outside metropolitan areas.

The Irish who live in the suburbs are not all that politically different from the city Irish. The suburbanite may tend to vote slightly more Republican, but a study by Scott Greer found that just about as many suburban Irish as city Irish said they belonged to the Democratic party. The suburban Irish were two and a half times more likely than the city Irish to say they were Republicans, but only 20 percent of the suburban Irish that Greer studied identified with the G.O.P. in the first place.

The average American voter is a high-school graduate and so is the average American Irishman. Most Irish thirty-five years old or over have completed exactly twelve years of schooling. About 12 percent of all Irish over the age of twenty-five have a college degree, compared to 13 percent of the general electorate. It makes some difference in political behavior whether an Irish voter has been to college or not. Father Greeley found that 67 percent of Irish high-school graduates say they belong to the Democratic party, but only 41 percent of Irish who have completed college say they are Democrats. This conforms to the national pattern. Thirty percent of Irish college graduates say they are Republicans and more than one quarter claim to be political independents.

Of all the white Catholic ethnics, the Irish are the most successful. A National Opinion Research Center (NORC) survey found that almost one third of Irish workers hold "prestige" jobs.[1] A very substantial number of Irish are white-collar workers. In one survey of Irish in Connecticut, for example, almost half worked at white-collar jobs. And the U.S. Census Bureau found that almost 30 percent of all Irish held high-level white-collar jobs, compared to only 19 percent of the electorate at large.[2] According to the Census survey in 1969, 45 percent of all American Irish earned between $7,500 and $15,000 a year, a very substantial middle class.

The Irish have made it in American society. There is a large Irish upper-middle and professional class. The Irish are becoming less interested in their ethnic heritage. It is unlikely that they are ashamed of the past; rather, they don't perceive it as particularly relevant. A major part of the Irish experience in America is an attachment to the Democratic party. To the extent that the American Irish turn their backs on their ethnic past, they will drift away from this legacy.

PRESIDENTIAL POLITICS

The Irish can safely be said to be Presidential Democrats. During the last decade, the Democratic share of the Irish vote declined, but the Irish still gave substantial, and sometimes spectacular, majorities to the Democratic Presidential nominees.

In 1960, John F. Kennedy was elected President with 50.1 percent of the major-party vote and 75 percent of the vote of his fellow Irish. Kennedy was a very different kind of Irishman from that represented by Al Smith, the first Irish Catholic to run for

---

[1] "Prestige" jobs are determined by a combination of the Duncan Occupational Scale (using income and education factors) and data developed by the National Opinion Research Center.

[2] Occupation has an impact on Irish political party preference. In Connecticut, for instance, nearly seven out of every eight blue-collar Irish said they preferred the Democratic party, but only five out of eight white-collar Irish said they were Democrats.

the Presidency (in 1928). Kennedy represented the "new Catholic," no longer tied to the immigrant and blue-collar past. Interestingly, his Irish plurality was only a modestly good vote for an Irishman among the Irish. But in the process many middle-class, conservative Catholics returned to the Democratic fold. In his home state Kennedy beat Richard Nixon four to one among the Boston Irish. However, Kennedy's Irish support was not uniform across the board. In some lower-middle-class precincts of Charlestown and Dorchester, he ran up to 10 percentage points better than his citywide Irish average. In middle- and upper-middle-income Irish precincts, on the other hand, Kennedy's vote was 5 or more points under his city figure. Nevertheless, it was among these better-off Irish voters that Kennedy's presence proved to be most important. In 1956, Eisenhower won about one third of the middle-class Irish vote. But Kennedy, in 1960, brought many of these voters back to the Democratic party as he won better than three quarters of their votes.

The pattern was repeated in Chicago. Citywide, Kennedy won 73 percent of the Irish vote. In the working-class Irish precincts "back of the Yards," Kennedy took better than three quarters of the vote. But in the middle-class Irish neighborhood of Gresham, Kennedy's share dropped to only 55 percent. Even though the Senator did not run as well with the Gresham Irish as he did with the working class, he did manage to strip away the Eisenhower Republican inroads of four years earlier.

This class split in the Kennedy vote also appeared in New York state. Generally, New York's Irish identified less with Kennedy, and he won only 60 percent of their votes. But in Irish precincts of Buffalo, Manhattan and the Bronx, where the Irish voters are blue-collar and where the old-line political machines worked hard for Kennedy, he exceeded his New York state average by up to 10 points. Kennedy's total Irish vote was depressed somewhat by his showing in the more middle-income precincts of Boro Park in Brooklyn and Sunnyside in Queens. In those areas, Kennedy's Irish vote dropped 10 percentage points and he ran neck and neck with Nixon. Once again, however, that was an improvement over 1956, as Kennedy recaptured straying middle-class Irish Democrats.

It appears that Kennedy appealed to the Irish for two very different reasons. For the blue-collar Irish, Kennedy's economic liberalism and Roman Catholicism combined to make him a highly attractive candidate. On the other hand, some members of the Irish middle class did not vote for Kennedy *because* they perceived him as liberal. Still others of these conservative Irish voters were swayed to Kennedy because he was a symbol of Catholic success in a WASP world.

The Kennedy myth aside, Lyndon Johnson actually improved slightly on the 1960 Irish vote. Nationwide, in 1964, the President won 78 percent of the vote cast in Irish precincts. Johnson seems to have gained strength from both working-class and middle-income Irish voters. In Massachusetts, Johnson's largest gains came in those better-off precincts of Dorchester and Roxbury, where Kennedy ran behind his statewide Irish average. In some of those precincts, Johnson gained 10 or more percentage points over Kennedy's vote. The working-class Irish of Boston also went slightly more strongly for Johnson. And in New York, where L.B.J. won 64 percent of the Irish vote, the totals in some blue-collar precincts of Buffalo ran better than 80 percent for the President. In middle-class Irish precincts of Brooklyn and Queens, he picked up 2 to 5 percentage points more of the vote than Kennedy, pushing the Goldwater share under half. Only in Chicago did Johnson run behind Kennedy's 1960 showing, and there the drop was small, only about 5 percentage points. Ethnicity may not be important to the Irish generally, but it appears to have been very important to Mayor Daley in 1960 when his party nominated an Irish Catholic for President.

Over all, Irish voters were not attracted to Barry Goldwater. The blue-collar Irish feared that Goldwater would repeal the New Deal and destroy the labor unions. They were not "backlash" voters, but they were strongly Democratic. Those middle-class Irish who had given Nixon a majority of their votes in 1960 turned back to the Democrats by a small margin in 1964. Many middle-class Irish voters, particularly in New York, were not impressed by the domestic policies of the Johnson administration. Nevertheless, on balance, the middle-class Irish stayed marginally Democratic.

The worst year of the decade for the Irish Democratic vote was 1968 and it really wasn't all that bad. According to a postelection survey conducted by the National Opinion Research Center, 64 percent of Irish voters said they cast ballots for Hubert Humphrey. One third said they voted for Richard Nixon, and only 3 percent reported voting for George Wallace. In most states of the Northeast, Nixon led Humphrey among Irish voters. In New York, Nixon won 48 percent, Humphrey 45 percent, and the Alabama Governor had to be content with only 7 percent of the Empire State's Irish vote. In the middle-class neighborhoods of Brooklyn and Queens, Nixon won better than 55 percent of the Irish vote. Only in the Bronx did Humphrey come close to winning a majority. In New Jersey a survey taken during the campaign showed that Nixon would win a slight majority of the Irish vote, that Humphrey would take 45 percent and that Wallace would win only one out of twenty-five Irish ballots. Another survey, in Pennsylvania, confirmed the general trend, but gave Wallace a higher percentage than he achieved in New York. Humphrey and Nixon were running neck and neck, with Wallace getting a substantial 13 percent. In the East, then, there was a significant trend to Nixon among Irish voters. Also interesting is the generally low vote that Wallace received. Irish voters were comfortable with the conservatism of Nixon and, with the exception of Pennsylvania, felt no great need to vote for the more extreme point of view expressed by Wallace and his American Independent Party.

If the NORC national figure of 64 percent for Humphrey is correct, the Vice-President must have improved on his Irish showing in states other than New York, New Jersey and Pennsylvania. It is possible, for example, that Humphrey won upwards of 80 percent of the Irish vote in the Democratic stronghold of Boston. Similarly, the Daley machine in Chicago may have garnered Humphrey as much as 70 percent of the Irish vote.

The 1960s were marked by a slow erosion of the Democratic Irish vote. By the decade's end, though, the Democratic Presidential nominee still won the ballots of almost two thirds of the oldest ethnic group. It appears that today's Irish vote is very much in flux. Irish middle-class voters are increasingly prone to vote Republican, and their ranks are growing. The working-class Irish, however, have not reacted strongly against the black civil-rights revolution, and they remain very much a bedrock Democratic Presidential vote. Political trends are only as good as the most recent election. For the time being, though, the Irish Presidential voter is still a Democrat.

THE IRISH, LIBERAL ISSUES
AND LIBERAL CANDIDATES

Of all the white Catholic ethnics, the Irish are the most "liberal." According to Father Andrew Greeley, a survey taken in 1970 found that Irish Catholics were second only to Jews in favoring racial integration. The Irish scored higher on the pro-integration scale than Northern WASPs. The survey also found that on a scale designed to measure sympathy with student and black militants, Irish college graduates were more favorably disposed to political militancy than any other Catholic group, or even the nation at large. And a NORC survey taken five years ago determined that the American Irish were second only to Jews and blacks in the percentage who were "doves" on the Indochina War. These data suggest that the Irish hold relatively liberal attitudes compared with other white Catholics and, in some cases, white Anglo-Saxon Protestants. Is this a meaningful distinction in terms of voting behavior? How do issues which are "liberal" fare with Irish voters? Do black candidates run well in Irish precincts? Are Irish voters strong supporters of liberal candidates in general?

A Liberal Issue

The 1966 New York City referendum on a civilian review board (to consider citizens' complaints against the city's police) provides an index of liberal attitudes. Citywide the vote was two to one against the review board. According to a survey taken by the American Jewish Committee, Irish Catholics (both on and off the Force) were even more opposed, and they voted seven to one against the review board.

A Black Candidate, Senator Edward Brooke of Massachusetts

In 1966, when Brooke was elected to the Senate, he beat patrician Democrat Endicott Peabody with 61 percent of the vote. Brooke took a moderate racial stance; he said he did not believe that demonstrations and marches were the way for blacks to win their rights. Peabody actually appeared to support black rights more aggressively than Brooke as he stressed the urban-affairs programs that had been enacted during his term as governor. In Irish precincts of Boston, Republican Brooke won only 35 percent of the vote. This produced an Irish plurality of nearly 150,000 votes for Peabody. The Boston Irish are strongly Democratic, so at first glance Brooke's 35 percent seems to be a decent Republican showing. But on the same day, Republican John Volpe, an Italian in a state where the Irish and the Italians have feuded for years, won 46 percent of the Irish vote, or 10 points better than Edward Brooke.[3] Undoubtedly it was because he was a black that Brooke did not run as well with the Irish as Volpe.

Some Liberal Candidates

The 1965 mayoral election in New York City illustrates how difficult it is for a liberal Democrat to run well with the Irish. The Irish vote split just about evenly among liberal Democratic City Comptroller Abraham Beame, liberal Republican Congressman John Lindsay and Conservative William Buckley, the Irish editor of the *National Review*. Democrat Beame led with 37 percent of the vote in Irish precincts, Conservative Buckley was second with 32 percent and Lindsay followed with 31 percent. Most of Beame's Irish plurality came from blue-collar workers who lived in the "machine" Democratic areas of the Bronx and Manhattan. Lindsay and Buckley shared much of the same constituency, the middle-income Irish of Brooklyn and Queens. The Irish who voted for Lindsay did so largely because he was the regular Republican candidate, even if he was something of a liberal,

[3] Volpe's 45 percent of the Irish vote represented a high-water mark for him among the Irish. In three previous elections, the best that the present Secretary of Transportation had done was 40 percent of the Irish vote against another Italian, Democrat Francis X. Bellotti, in 1964.

while those Irish who voted for Buckley were attracted to his conservative personal style. Significantly, two thirds of the Irish vote went to either a Republican or a Conservative. In past years, Democratic mayoral candidates had won up to 60 percent of the Irish vote.

In 1969 the Irish realized that Lindsay was a liberal and they dropped him like a hot potato. The Mayor faced two conservative opponents, Democrat Mario Procaccino and Republican John Marchi. (Lindsay had lost the Republican nomination to Marchi and was running as the Liberal party candidate.) Both Procaccino and Marchi attacked Lindsay for favoring New York's blacks and Puerto Ricans at the expense of the city's other ethnic groups, and both accused Lindsay of being "soft" on crime in the streets. A poll taken almost a year before the election found that only 15 percent of Irish New Yorkers thought Lindsay was doing a good job and well over half thought he was doing a poor job. A late October NBC News poll found that Lindsay could expect 25 percent of the Irish vote, a drop of 6 percentage points from four years earlier. About 28 percent of the Irish voters interviewed said they were going to vote for Procaccino, also a slight decrease compared to the 1965 Beame performance. Republican-Conservative Marchi picked up most of the defecting Irish. According to the survey, Marchi would win a remarkable 47 percent of the Irish vote. Much of his plurality carried over from Buckley four years before. Other Irish may have chosen between Marchi and Procaccino on the basis of Marchi's "cooler," less earthy political style. As with the Massachusetts Irish in the 1964 Volpe-Bellotti gubernatorial race, New York's Irish favored a Republican Italian over a Democratic one.

The 1965 and 1969 New York mayoral elections reveal that liberal candidates have a hard time with Irish voters. The 1965 Democratic mayoral *primary* in New York showed that liberal candidates don't run any better if they *are* Irish. The two Irish candidates in the four-man primary field were Congressman William Fitts Ryan, a liberal reformer from the Upper West Side of Manhattan, and Paul O'Dwyer, the youngest brother of New York's last Irish mayor, William O'Dwyer. Both Ryan and O'Dwyer were well known throughout the city for their espousal of liberal causes. Neither did well with Irish voters. The two regular Democrats in the contest, City Council President Paul Screvane and City Comptroller Abraham Beame together won almost five out of every six votes cast in Irish precincts. Ryan took a meager 11 percent of the Irish vote and O'Dwyer ran even worse with only 7 percent. New York's Irish voters would have little to do with Irish politicians who were outspoken liberals.

Perhaps believing that the luck of the Irish could not desert him so completely a second time, O'Dwyer ran for the United States Senate in 1968. No luck. O'Dwyer faced incumbent Liberal Republican Jacob Javits and Conservative candidate James Buckley. In the minds of the voters, very few issues separated O'Dwyer and Javits. (Of course, Jacob Javits has a flair for separating himself from all politicians regardless of political ideology.) Both Javits and O'Dwyer were liberals, and both were opponents of the Indochina war. Buckley, making his first try for public office, ran a low-budget, low-key campaign. At times it seemed that Buckley, more laconic and less charismatic than his brother William, would do poorly with the Irish. Javits won a landslide victory, but the Irish vote split almost equally among the three candidates. The Republican Senator received 32 percent, and 32 percent also went for O'Dwyer.[4] Buckley won a slight edge in the Irish precincts, taking about 36 percent of the vote or twice his statewide average. Viewed one way, the Irish vote can be said to have gone two to one for liberal candidates. But Buckley's performance should not be taken lightly. He carried the Irish vote and did so at a level twice his statewide percentage.

As political circumstance would have it, 1968 was only a warm-up for Jim Buckley. In 1970 he was elected to the United States Senate and one of the reasons for that victory was an even stronger showing among Irish voters. Buckley opposed liberal Republican incumbent Charles Goodell and liberal Democrat Richard Ottinger in a campaign that was better organized and better funded than in 1968. Buckley received the blessings of the

[4] Curiously, in his 1962 Senate race against Irish Democrat James Donovan, Javits had run slightly better with Irish voters. In Irish precincts, Javits took 42 percent of the vote to Donovan's 58 percent.

White House and although he was running only on the Conservative party line was considered by many voters to be the "legitimate" Republican candidate. His conservative campaign was tailor-made to the issues troubling the New York electorate in 1970. A *New York Times* survey taken late in the campaign indicated that the Irish voters were most worried about student unrest. Twenty-seven percent of the Irish mentioned student troublemakers as the number-one domestic issue, compared to 19 percent of all respondents. Other related factors in the social issue—crime, race relations, drugs—were also frequently mentioned by the Irish voters. Buckley attacked Goodell for failing "to draw any distinction between legitimate dissent and outright burning," and he hinted that Ottinger too was "soft" on the social issue. The *Times* survey found that 60 percent of New York's Irish voters planned to cast their ballots for Buckley. That meant at least a 180,000-vote Irish plurality for the Connecticut carpetbagger, and he won statewide by only 116,000 votes.[5]

The 1970 gubernatorial election mirrored the swing of Irish voters away from the Democratic party. Rockefeller, who had been considered a leading voice of moderate Republicanism, moved to the political Right. He backed President Nixon's war policies, sided with labor unions against black militants seeking to halt government projects until hiring demands were met, and embraced conservative Democrat Mario Procaccino.[6] Rockefeller's "Catholic strategy" also produced a hard line on drug abuse, a program of aid to parochial schools, and criticism of the Democratic party as a haven for "radicals." Goldberg, on the other hand, took an ineffectual liberal line on most issues. His campaign never caught fire, and the electorate in general seemed bored with the former Supreme Court Justice. Conservative Paul Adams was lost in the shuffle. Rockefeller's skillfully managed

---

[5] This Senate seat is quickly becoming reserved for out-of-state residents (Robert Kennedy in 1964 and now Jim Buckley). Perhaps in 1976 the Democrats will tap another out-of-stater to run against Buckley, and maybe John Connally, cast out of Texas for his current Washington flirtation with the Republicans, will be ready to switch back—in New York.

[6] Procaccino has always maintained that his Rockefeller support was not tendered in exchange for a *major* political appointment, should the Governor be reelected. *The New York Times* notwithstanding, he was right—to date.

and exceedingly well-financed campaign buried Goldberg, and the Governor won by more than 730,000 votes—some 120,000 votes of that plurality coming from the Irish. Four years earlier, in 1966, Rockefeller had split the Irish vote with Irish Democrat Frank D. O'Connor. According to a survey taken at the time, Rockefeller and O'Connor each won 44 percent of the Irish vote, with 11 percent going to Conservative Paul Adams and only one percent to Liberal nominee Franklin D. Roosevelt, Jr. But in 1970, Rockefeller improved his Irish showing by half, with 64 percent saying they planned to vote for the Governor.

The Irish again revealed their conservative trend in 1970—this time in the Connecticut senatorial contest. Incumbent Senator Thomas J. Dodd, a conservative Irish Catholic, was running as an Independent, having been denied renomination by the state's Democratic party leaders because of his Congressional improprieties. Most prominent among those leaders was Chairman John Bailey, himself an Irish Catholic. Dodd's Democratic opponent was Joseph Duffey, an Irish Protestant minister and former national chairman of the liberal Americans for Democratic Action. Lowell Weicker, the Republican candidate, a one-term Congressman from Fairfield County, was a moderate. Political experts wondered whether Dodd would win enough votes to keep Duffey from victory. Dodd was the only Catholic in the contest, and that counted heavily in a state which is nearly half Catholic. Duffey campaigned initially as an out-and-out dove, but as the campaign progressed, changed his emphasis to attack Nixon and the Republicans for Connecticut's growing rate of unemployment. Weicker stressed his (limited) legislative experience and claimed he would give "selective support" to the President. On election day, Weicker won by 87,000 votes over Duffey, while Dodd ran third, with more than 267,000 votes. According to a survey taken in early September, Dodd was preferred by 41 percent of the Irish. Weicker was second with 34 percent, and Duffey trailed with 25 percent.

In contrast, the 1970 senatorial election in Illinois showed that it is possible for a liberal Democrat to win Irish votes—if he has the backing of a powerful machine. Adlai Stevenson III, son of the famous liberal statesman, ran against conservative Repub-

lican Ralph Smith, who had been named by Governor Richard
Ogilvie to fill the Senate seat following Everett Dirksen's death.
Smith received major backing from the White House, because he
was among the strongest supporters of the Nixon administration.
He ran on his brief record and accused Stevenson of being "soft"
on hippies and disorder. Stevenson denied the allegations,
claimed that Smith deliberately falsified his position, and put an
American-flag pin in his lapel. Smith lost by 545,000 votes. A
substantial part of Stevenson's plurality came from Irish voters. A
survey taken late in the campaign found Stevenson winning 67
percent of the Irish vote compared to Smith's one third. Given
that lead among Irish voters on election day, Stevenson received
an Irish bonus of more than 150,000 votes. Illinois's Irish voters
were attracted to Stevenson's well-known name and they voted
for him because the Daley machine told them to.[7]

In nearly all the elections just reviewed, Irish voters appeared
to have overwhelmingly favored conservative candidates and
issues. To reconcile this electoral evidence with Father Greeley's
data about the relative liberalism of the American Irish we would
suggest looking at their currently high social status. Most either
are well-paid blue-collar workers or belong to the middle and
upper classes. This degree of social success seems to make the
Irish more "secure" than those other ethnics, particularly the Italians and Slavs, who are still laboring to become middle-class. The
Irish are less worried by the fears which plague other Catholic
ethnics. At the same time, those very conditions of economic and
social well-being which give the Irish moderately liberal attitudes
also encourage them to leave the Democratic party. It is a well-
known axiom of political science that the higher an individual's
social status the more likely he is to vote Republican. The Irish
seem caught between two forces: on the one hand is their long-
standing Democratic heritage; on the other, their increasing economic and social status. These two factors may well work to
create a liberal point of view—and a Republican vote.

[7] It should be remembered that the Daley machine has been helpful to
other liberal Democrats as well. In the 1966 Senate election, for instance,
Daley swung 65 percent of the Irish vote for liberal Democratic incumbent
Paul Douglas over challenger Charles Percy.

THE IRISH AND THE KENNEDYS

The preceding section demonstrated how liberal Democrats do not run well with Irish voters. There is, however, one glaring exception to this rule—the Kennedys. When a Kennedy runs for office all bets are off and records are set.

John Kennedy's Senate term had four years to run when he was elected to the Presidency in 1960. Governor Volpe appointed Ben Smith, a former college roommate of the President, to hold down the seat until the general election of 1962. Edward McCormack, Massachusetts Attorney General and nephew of then House Speaker John McCormack, coveted the Senate seat. Unfortunately for McCormack, a wrinkle named Kennedy appeared. Edward Moore Kennedy, barely old enough to be a Senator, announced his candidacy, saying he wanted to go to Washington to help vote for the New Frontier. In the ensuing bitter primary fight McCormack charged that Kennedy was unqualified since he had never held public office. Flailing wildly, McCormack declared that had Kennedy dispensed with his last name and run as Edward Moore his candidacy would have been a joke.[8] Kennedy liked his name, demonstrated his political acumen by keeping it, and won the primary with 69 percent of the vote. Not to be outdone in the family game, the Republicans chose as their Senate nominee liberal George Lodge, son of Henry Cabot Lodge, former Senator, former U.N. Ambassador and former G.O.P. Vice-Presidential candidate (1960). An element of revenge was undoubtedly present. Exactly ten years earlier Ted Kennedy's brother John had retired George's father from the United States Senate.

Lodge attacked Kennedy's youth and inexperience, but refrained from wondering aloud why a young man who had cheated at Harvard should be elected to the Senate. Kennedy did not answer Lodge directly, but said simply, "I can do more for Massachusetts." The McCormack faction of the Democratic party, still rankled by Kennedy's primary victory, threatened to

---

[8] McCormack also charged that Kennedy had never done an honest day's work in his life. At least one factory employee who worked an honest five-day week (every week) told Kennedy he wasn't missing anything.

sit out the election. But shortly before election day, Edward McCormack grudgingly gave his endorsement to Kennedy and the Youngest Son beat Lodge by 285,000 votes. It was the Boston Irish who elected Kennedy. In Irish precincts, Kennedy won 78 percent of the vote, a plurality of 350,000, or one quarter more than his total statewide margin.

In 1964, with a very prestigious form of public service to his credit, Edward Kennedy's hold on the voters of Massachusetts was even more secure. The Republicans wisely saved for another day and ran only a token opponent in Howard Whitmore, the former mayor of Newton. Kennedy was unable to campaign in person because of a back injury suffered in an airplane crash with Senator Birch Bayh of Indiana. No matter. The tragic death of President Kennedy was fresh in the minds of everyone, and Edward Kennedy could do no wrong. He was reelected by a record 1.1 million votes. In Irish precincts, Kennedy also set a state Democratic record, winning 88 percent of the ballots cast. That was good for almost half of Kennedy's record-breaking statewide plurality, and it meant that Kennedy ran a point or two ahead of Lyndon Johnson's strong Irish showing.

In 1964, another Kennedy was also running for public office. United States Attorney General Robert F. Kennedy, recently rejected with the rest of the Cabinet from consideration as L.B.J.'s Vice-Presidential running mate, opposed incumbent Republican Kenneth B. Keating for the United States Senate seat in New York. It was a rough campaign. Keating accused Kennedy of being a "carpetbagger" and impugned Kennedy's liberal credentials. Kennedy replied that he had lived in the Riverdale section of the Bronx as a young man, and the Kennedy partisans did an equally vicious hatchet job on Keating's record. Kennedy beat Keating by more than 719,000 votes.[9] In Irish precincts the vote split 62 percent for Kennedy and 38 percent for Keating. Kennedy's performance was the decade's highest Irish vote for any Democratic candidate in New York State.

[9] Perhaps to assuage a collective sense of guilt, New Yorkers elected Keating to the state's highest court the following year with the greatest plurality ever given any candidate for a contested office in New York history.

In 1970, Edward Kennedy ran for a full six-year Senate term from Massachusetts. His opponent was Josiah Spaulding, the State G.O.P. Chairman. The only real question was whether Kennedy would equal his record 1964 margin. Six years earlier, with a nation still mourning its late President, Kennedy had substantial sympathy from his constituents. But in 1970 the Senator was laboring under a distinct handicap. The accident at the Chappaquiddick bridge had tarnished his image with large segments of the electorate, and Spaulding campaigned hard. It was a losing cause. On election day Kennedy did not equal his 1964 record, but he did beat Spaulding by a creditable 486,000 votes. And among the Irish? A survey taken shortly after Chappaquiddick found that nationwide the Irish were among the most willing to forgive Kennedy for the accident. Massachusetts Irish were even more forgiving than their ethnic brethren. Kennedy won 79 percent of the Irish vote, just about what he had won in his first race for the Senate. His Irish plurality of 300,000 votes was two thirds of his statewide margin.

What is it about the Kennedys that compels the Irish to vote for them in record numbers? For some Irish—mostly those of the working class—the Kennedy liberalism certainly is attractive. Just as obviously, some of the conservative Irish too vote for the Kennedys. The Kennedys are more than "one of their own"; they are *the* Irish Catholic family in America; they give glamour and social prominence to an ethnic group which has until very recently been denied acceptance in American society. So it was with John and Robert. So it is with Edward.

THE IRISH: A DISAPPEARING MINORITY

Father Andrew Greeley relates a story in his book on the Irish about an academic colleague of his who for years tried unsuccessfully to get federal money for an "Irish studies" program. Finally, the academic went to Washington to confront the bureaucrat in the Office of Education who had been turning down his requests. The somewhat perplexed scholar asked outright, "Why don't you fund an Irish studies program?" Replied the bureaucrat, "Because the Irish don't count."

In one very limited sense, the Washington official was right. Of all the ethnic groups, the Irish are the most assimilated. Entire generations of Irish rejected their ethnic past in an effort to become "good Americans," and they succeeded. Now that it is fashionable and no longer un-American to be proud of one's ethnic roots, it is somewhat ironic that the Irish have lost their Irishness. (Perhaps they will rediscover it.)

Despite their increasing social and economic status, the Irish retain their basic commitment to the Democratic party, a commitment that was made early in their immigrant experience. Of the thirty-six elections in the past ten years for which we have data, twenty-seven of them showed the Irish voting at least a majority for Democratic candidates. In twenty-one of the thirty-six elections the Democratic share of the Irish vote exceeded 60 percent. Outside the sociological madness of New York City the percentage of Irish who vote Democratic is even higher. The Irish of Massachusetts and Illinois rarely give less than three quarters of their votes to the Democrats. In Presidential politics, the Irish in general vote at least two-thirds Democratic. If Edward Kennedy ran for President, the Irish Democratic vote might go considerably higher.

Some Irish voters are political conservatives and Republicans. Unlike the Jews, for whom increased social status does not mean decreased Democratic and liberal loyalty, some Irish are becoming increasingly Republican and conservative. The Irish are the more typical group in this respect. They have no long liberal tradition like that of the Jews, and they are more concerned about adopting the political coloration of the WASP majority.

The American Irish did much to shape the political institutions of this nation. The typical Irish voter, conscientiously supporting these institutions, is no longer much of an ethnic, but more simply an American, whatever that is.

6

The Slavs: Not at All Republican

Vice-President Agnew and Senator John L. McClellan call them "Polacks." Senator McClellan apologizes. The media think of them as hard-hats. Supposedly enlightened people tell tiresome and derogatory jokes about them, and others taunt them with cries of "Hunkie." Both socially and politically, Americans of Slavic descent face ethnic barriers.[1] And until recently Slavic Americans seemed unwilling or unable to do very much about it. They were "represented" by mild-mannered umbrella organizations like the Polish-American Congress, and although politicians always attended Pulaski Day parades, most never seemed to be around when important issues like housing, schools and civil rights were being discussed.

But all that is changing. Slavs are taking positions in the ethnic-power movement. In Baltimore, for example, Barbara Mikulski of the Southeast Community Organization says Slavs are tired of

[1] Throughout this chapter we will use the generic term "Slav" instead of naming a specific nationality group. Poles are the most numerous of all the Slavic-American groups, but there are also Czechs, Slovaks, Ruthenians, Slovenians, Russians, Ukrainians, etc. Hungarians, who are not really Slavs, are included in this grouping; interestingly, the slang term Hunkie, which is used to denigrate all East Europeans, is derived from *Bohunk,* a corruption of *Hungarian.*

140

"phony white liberals, pseudo black militants and patronizing bureaucrats" who make things difficult for the Slavic community. And in Indiana's Lake County, a thousand delegates from church, civic and fraternal organizations met recently to found the Calumet Community Congress with the goal of helping the Slavs living in the industrial towns of Gary, Hammond and South Bend to achieve a better life. In Detroit, black Congressman John Conyers and a Polish priest named Daniel Bogus have started the Black-Polish Conference to help "depolarize" the community. If such efforts are successful, perhaps these natural allies will awaken to their community of ethnic interest. (One is reminded of the recent summit conference of Jewish Defense League and Italian-American Civil Rights League officials; a pattern of ethnic "community" could be emerging.)

Slavic-Americans have much to complain about. For years the power structure ignored them, and now they are blamed for institutional racism. For the distraught Slavic-American one way to do something about all of this is to utilize the political process. Slavs have traditionally voted for Democratic candidates, and they continue to do so. But increasingly, Slavic Democrats are thinking about their vote.

THE POLITICAL DEMOGRAPHY OF SLAVIC AMERICA

In electoral politics, numbers are everything. Politicians pay attention to voters in direct proportion to their real or presumed strength in the electorate. It is not surprising, therefore, to find that spokesmen for ethnic groups often overestimate their group's numerical strength. A check of several different sources disclosed a wide variance of thought regarding Slavic-American numbers. Congressman Dan Rostenkowski of Chicago, a leading Polish-American politician, said there are fifteen million Americans of Polish descent. Professor Joseph Wytrwal estimates the number at ten million. The *Polish-American Journal* put the figure at seven million, and a recent account in *The New York Times* reported that there are six million Polish-Americans. A much lower figure, but one which is at least free from ethnic exaggeration, comes from the U.S. Census Bureau. In its special 1969 survey the Bureau found four million Americans whose families came from Poland. Not all of these four million are Catholic. About one quarter of America's Poles are Jewish. So at most, there are 3.2 million Catholic Poles. Added to this 3.2-million figure are some 1.5 million Czechs, Slovaks, Slovenians, Lithuanians, Bohemians, et cetera. In all, then, a fair but conservative estimate would place the total Slavic population of the United States at around five million, or 2.5 percent of the total.

About half of Slavic America lives in the urban centers of the Northeast. New York, Philadelphia, Buffalo, Bridgeport and Pittsburgh, all have sizable Slavic minorities. Most of the rest live in the Midwest. The largest single grouping of Slavs is said to be in Chicago, where there may be as many as 800,000, and there are also substantial Slavic communities in Detroit, Milwaukee and Cleveland.

Of all the white ethnic groups, Slavs are the least assimilated. They tend to live together in "Little Polands," read Polish newspapers—of which there are five dailies—and celebrate Slavic holidays together. They maintain many of the "old ways" long after arriving in the United States. A survey reports that in two thirds of Polish families, the Polish language is spoken by the children, and other studies have found substantial numbers of third-generation Slavs still fluent in their grandparents' language. A Catholic education, and particularly a Catholic ethnic education, is also important to Slavic-Americans. There are, for instance, more than six hundred Polish parochial schools, and nearly ten thousand fraternal, social and athletic clubs based on ties to the old country. One organization alone, the Polish National Alliance, has more than 300,000 members.

Poles are second only to Italians in the percentage who own their own homes, and those homes are likely to be neat, spotlessly kept small houses found in areas like Cleveland's "Buckeye Road" and Southside Milwaukee. As with Italians, Slavs normally live close to friends and relatives, are extremely conscious of property values, and outsiders, be they white or black, are generally not welcome on the block.

By most measures, Slavs are at the bottom of white urban

society. Father Greeley reports that only one out of six Poles holds a "prestige" job, and a survey of Slavs in Connecticut found three quarters were blue-collar workers. Approximately 40 percent belong to labor unions. Nationally, less than one out of every five Poles earned more than $14,000 a year in 1963, and in Connecticut only one out of five earned more than $10,000 a year in 1968; one reason for these low income figures is that less than half of Slavic America has graduated from high school.

The relatively low social status indicated by these statistical measures yields powerful political and sociological implications. Slavs are strongly attached to the Democratic party for economic reasons; but, being only one rung ahead of blacks on the economic ladder, they often find themselves competing with blacks for jobs and housing. The politicians say this leads to the Republican party. But apparently no one has told the Slavs that their "numbers" mandate a political switch. They remain Democrats.

SLAVIC VOTERS: THE "TWO THIRDS" DEMOCRATS

Of all the white ethnics, Slavs are most likely to consider themselves Democrats. According to Father Greeley, 77 percent of all Poles say they belong to the Democratic party; and the figure is even higher in the Midwest, where eight out of ten Poles identified with the Democrats. This high level of Democratic party identification is reflected at the polls.

Slavs showed a remarkably consistent record of support for the Democrats through the 1964 election. In 54 of 57 elections for senator, governor and President from 1958 through 1964, the Democratic percentage was at least 65 percent of the vote. In 19 of these elections (one third of the total), the Slavs' Democratic vote exceeded 80 percent.

Since 1964, Democratic candidates have consistently carried the Slavic vote, but have been unable to maintain the extraordinary pre-1964 pluralities. In 37 of 40 races for senator, governor and President since 1964, Democratic candidates won a clear majority. The Democratic vote was greater than 65 percent in 29 of 40 elections, or nearly three quarters, yet surpassed 80 percent only twice.

The post-1964 returns certainly represent a plurality decline for the Democrats among Slavs. However, there is no pattern in the 1966, 1968 and 1970 election returns to suggest a steadily eroding Democratic base, nor is there any suggestion other than that the average Democratic candidate should expect two thirds of the Slavic vote. Republicans who win more than one third of the Slavic vote are exceptions to the rule.

What is happening to the Slavic vote? In places like Gary, Indiana, and Cicero, Illinois, there are Slavic voters so beset by racial worries that they do vote a backlash ticket for Republican candidates. But Slavs in cities like Buffalo, Youngstown, Hartford and South Bend remain staunchly Democratic. These working-class Slavs may be troubled by racial problems, but they seem to vote their class interests; and they perceive those interests as dictating a vote for the Democrat. At the same time, Slavic voters in other cities, like Chicago, Milwaukee and Hamtramck, Michigan, continue to vote Democratic, but in slowly declining numbers.

PRESIDENTIAL POLITICS

In 1960 John Kennedy won 82 percent of the vote cast in predominantly Slavic precincts. In Buffalo, where Kennedy campaigned with his wife's brother-in-law, Prince Stanislas Radziwill, Kennedy took more than five out of every six Slavic votes. In two states—Ohio and Maryland—Kennedy's Slavic vote exceeded 85 percent, and in Michigan he won a phenomenal nine out of every ten votes cast in Slavic neighborhoods. New Jersey's Slavic voters gave Kennedy a plurality of 70,000 votes over Nixon, and J.F.K. carried New Jersey by only 22,000 votes. Slavic voters also played an important role in Kennedy's victories in Pennsylvania and Illinois. In Pennsylvania, Kennedy came out of Philadelphia and the coal country with a lead of 110,000 Slavic votes; he carried the state by 116,000. The pattern was extended in Illinois, where Kennedy carried the state by only 9,000 votes, but led Nixon in the Slavic precincts of Chicago's "Polish Corridor" by more than 100,000.

The Senator's Slavic support was generally strong throughout the nation.[2] Apparently, his appeal to Slavic voters was based on three factors: the Kennedy family was well known for its interest in Poland and Polish charities, the Senator's economic liberalism appealed to the blue-collar interests of Slavic Americans, and Slavic voters took pleasure in voting for Kennedy because he shared their religion.

What is most noteworthy about the 1964 Slavic Presidential vote is just how little movement to the G.O.P. actually occurred. Numerous pundits expected Goldwater's candidacy to draw a fairly substantial backlash vote from the Slavs. Generally, no such pro-Goldwater support appeared, and Lyndon Johnson won 80 percent of the vote in Slavic precincts, an insignificant decline from the 1960 Kennedy total.

Improvement in the Republican vote from 1960 to 1964 was the exception rather than the rule. In Cleveland, which was beginning to have serious racial problems, the President won nearly four out of five Slavic votes, and in Detroit, L.B.J.'s Slavic strength equaled John Kennedy's of four years before. In the industrial center of Youngstown, Ohio, Slavs gave Johnson a remarkable 93 percent of their votes and both in Hartford, Connecticut, and in Milwaukee, Wisconsin, Johnson received 85 percent in primarily blue-collar Slavic districts.

The Republican pickup that did materialize was not substantial. Senator Goldwater's best gains were less than 10 percentage points better than Nixon's 1960 performance, and for the most part these advances came in the more traditionally Republican, yet racially troubled areas. In Cicero, where the blue-collar suburbanites feared black disturbances, and Republicans had fared well for years, Goldwater won 40 percent of the vote, a 7-percentage-point gain over the 1960 G.O.P. showing. In Gary, Indiana, where the black population was nearing 50 percent, Slavic voters gave 45 percent of their votes to the Arizona Senator. Again, these Republican Slavic totals were the exception, not the rule.

[2] Only in one city, Cicero, did Kennedy's Slavic vote drop below 70 percent, and there it was still two thirds for J.F.K. Cicero has been a Republican town since before the days when Al Capone made his peace with the local G.O.P. leaders. The work of the local Republican machine and historic voting patterns probably explain this slightly depressed Kennedy vote.

CHART 1: SLAVIC VOTERS
PRESIDENT, 1964
SELECTED CITIES

	Percent Johnson	Percent Goldwater	Percent GOP Change from 1960
Youngstown, Ohio	93	7	−4
Detroit	89	11	+1
Milwaukee	85	15	−1
Buffalo, N.Y.	85	15	−2
Cleveland	80	20	+6
South Bend, Ind.	77	23	+2
Philadelphia	69	31	−2
Chicago	67	33	+7
Cicero, Ill.	60	40	+7
Gary, Ind.	55	45	*
Nation	80	20	+2

SOURCE: Institute of American Research; NBC News.
* Insufficient data in 1960 for comparison.

Four hundred thousand Slavs who voted for John Kennedy in 1960 deserted his fellow Democrat Hubert Humphrey eight years later. Most of these Democratic defectors supported Wallace, but the Alabama governor's percentage among Slavs was only slightly higher than his non-South average. Nixon gained an insubstantial seven percentage points over his 1960 run among Slavic voters, but the plurality loss for Humphrey was quite significant.

The fall-off in the Democratic Slavic vote hurt Humphrey in two key states, New Jersey and Ohio. In New Jersey, where one occasionally finds persuasive evidence of an emerging Republican statewide majority, the Vice-President just about won a majority in Slavic precincts. His Slavic plurality of 15,000 votes trailed Kennedy's 1960 total by 75,000, and the Vice-President accordingly lost the state. Had he run as well as Kennedy, Humphrey would have carried New Jersey by 10,000 or 15,000 votes. Slavic voters in Ohio too let Humphrey down. In Youngstown the Vice-President managed a respectable three quarters of the Slavic vote, but in Cleveland he captured only 57 percent in Slavic neighborhoods. Ohio's Slavs gave Humphrey nearly

100,000 votes more than they gave Nixon; but again, had he run as well as J.F.K. ran in 1960, Humphrey would have added an additional 60,000 votes, and with only 30,000 more, he would have taken Ohio.

The effect of these minor Nixon gains and Wallace inroads was to cut the Democratic plurality from its previous high of 60 percent to a respectable but much less substantial 40 percent plurality. And had it not been for Humphrey's Polish running mate, Edmund S. Muskie (whose family name was originally Marcisaewski), the Democratic portion might well have fallen below 65 percent of the Slavic vote.

Wallace's unimpressive showing simply reinforces the notion that the Slavs are a good deal more liberal than some conservatives would like to believe. Even in racially troubled cities, Slavic voters did not buy Wallace's brand of segregationist populism in wholesale numbers. In Milwaukee, for example, where Father Groppi had led two hundred straight nights of civil-rights marches, Wallace won only 13 percent of the vote. And in Cleveland, which had experienced a bloody riot, only 22 percent

CHART 2: SLAVIC VOTERS
PRESIDENT, 1968
SELECTED CITIES

	Percent Humphrey	Percent Nixon	Percent Wallace	Percent Change in Nixon Vote from 1960
Detroit	77	11	12	+1
Youngstown, Ohio	76	11	13	0
Buffalo, N.Y.	72	18	10	+1
Milwaukee	69	18	13	+2
South Bend, Ind.	58	23	15	+2
Cleveland	57	21	22	+7
Philadelphia	57	30	13	+5
Chicago	50	36	14	+10
Cicero, Ill.	35	43	22	+10
Gary, Ind.	35	47	18	*
Nation	64	24	12	+6

SOURCE: Institute of American Research; NBC News.
* Insufficient data in 1960 for comparison.

of Slavs voted for Wallace. Twenty-two percent of Cicero's presumably conservative Slavs also cast their ballots for Wallace, and in Gary, which had a black mayor, only 18 percent of the supposedly "backlashing" Slavic community voted for Wallace.

A hard core of roughly two thirds of Slavic voters remains loyal to the Democratic presidential party. An Ed Muskie candidacy could well bring the Slavic vote back to its 1960 levels, and even beyond, as Slavs rally to support one of their own. But the era of an automatic 80 percent Slavic support of the Democratic Presidential candidate appears gone forever.

SLAVS, BLACKS AND THE MAYOR GAME

Slavic-Americans are city-dwellers. They find themselves battling with white technocrats who want to bulldoze their neighborhoods in the name of urban renewal and with blacks who want to move onto the Slavic turf to escape the ghetto. Slavic-Americans—like most of us—are afraid of crime in the streets and are anxious to protect their property values.[3] According to Father Greeley's survey, almost half of all Poles would object if blacks moved onto their block, and more than one third believed that blacks shoud go to separate schools. These deeply held beliefs surface in elections, and particularly as more cities become black and more blacks run for office, often against Slavs.

In 1969, Carl Stokes, Cleveland's first black mayor, was challenged by Cuyahoga County Auditor Ralph Perk, a Czech. Perk ran a tough law-and-order campaign, and accused Stokes of interfering with the work of the police department. About 40 percent of Cleveland's population is Slavic, and Perk expected a substantial vote from these so-called "Cosmo" voters. He wasn't disappointed. On election day, Perk won 85 percent of the vote in Cosmo precincts, but that wasn't quite enough, as Stokes com-

---

[3] These twin issues can be clearly seen in the 1971 Chicago mayoral election. Mayor Daley spoke to a dinner dance of the local Polish-American Democratic Club, and received a tumultuous ovation when he was introduced as the man "who doesn't want public housing in white neighborhoods" and the man who issued the "shoot to kill" order against arsonists and looters.

bined a large and united black vote with just enough liberal white ballots to win.[4]

In the 1969 Detroit mayoral election, Wayne County Sheriff Roman Gribbs, a Pole, was opposed by Richard Austin, a moderate black, and Mary Beck, a Polish councilwoman who promised to "sweep the streets clean of crime, corruption and every form of pollution." Gribbs took a hard line on law and order too, but tempered his stand with appeals for understanding between the races. In the primary, Austin received a nearly unanimous black vote which put him in first place with 38 percent of the total. Sheriff Gribbs was second with 32 percent, and Miss Beck trailed with 21 percent. (The rest of the votes were scattered among several minor candidates.) Austin led because of the split in the Slavic vote; Gribbs had won a majority and Miss Beck nearly all the remainder. Had the Slavic vote not split between two Slavic candidates, Gribbs could have won outright. The inevitable result was merely delayed. In the runoff, Gribbs nosed out Austin by 6,000 votes, a major reason being Gribbs's newly united Slavic support. Turnout rose substantially in Slavic areas for the runoff, and Gribbs won five out of every six votes cast there.

In the 1969 Buffalo, New York, mayoral contest incumbent Democrat Frank Sedita, an Italian, was challenged by Alfreda Slominski, a Polish Republican-Conservative city councilwoman, and Ambrose Lane, a black antipoverty official. Sedita ran on his record, taking credit for Buffalo's relatively turmoil-free years. Lane campaigned against Sedita's record, blamed him for the strained relations between Buffalo's blacks and the police, and said something had to be done about substandard housing. Mrs. Slominski's was a more conservatively positioned campaign. She opposed busing of children to integrate the schools and blamed Sedita for the rising crime rate. But none of the challengers' maneuvering made any difference as Mayor Sedita was reelected with 54 percent of the vote. Mrs. Slominski ran second with 41 percent, and Lane trailed far behind with only 5 percent. In Slavic neighborhoods, Mrs. Slominski ran very well, as those voters responded both to her stand on the issues and to her Slavic

[4] In 1971, Perk won two thirds of the "Cosmo" vote against black Arnold Pinkney and white, Irish James Carney.

name; she won better than seven out of every ten Slavic votes. And in some precincts, Mrs. Slominski outpolled Mayor Sedita by three and a half to one. Only the fierce Democratic party identification of Buffalo's Slavs prevented Mrs. Slominski from carrying the day.

In each of these three elections—Cleveland, Detroit and Buffalo—we have seen that Slavic voters will unite behind a white candidate who happens to be Slavic and is opposed by a black. But in 1971, Slavic voters in Gary, Indiana, actually voted overwhelmingly for a black mayoral candidate. In a way, of course, they didn't have much of a choice. The two major candidates in the primary—incumbent Richard Hatcher and his challenger Dr. Alexander Williams—were black. But Gary's Slavic voters despised Hatcher to such a degree that they were willing to take the black candidate dictated to them by the all-white Democratic machine. In Slavic precincts, Williams won almost all the votes. Turnout was down compared with black neighborhoods, but it was at least as good as in the election of 1967. Hatcher won a comfortable victory largely because of his black support, but the message from Gary's Slavic voters was clear: given a chance to oust Hatcher, the black man's black candidate, they would try to do so even if it meant voting for another black.

America's cities will grow ever more black in the years ahead. Many Slavs will be unable or unwilling to leave the neighborhoods in which they grew up, and will find themselves in increasing contact with blacks. Slavic voters now make up the core support of white Slavic candidates. A test of ethnic politics in these cities will be their ability to produce candidates, either black or white, who can attract support from both blacks and Slavs. At least for the office of mayor, our evidence suggests, this task will not be easy.

SLAVIC VOTERS AND LIBERAL DEMOCRATS

Ask the average politician, and he will probably tell you that Slavic voters are tending to become conservative and Republican. It's a foregone conclusion in some circles that liberal Democrats don't stand a chance with Slavs. This simply is not true. When

Robert Kennedy ran for the Senate from New York in 1964, he swamped moderate Republican Kenneth Keating by nearly three quarters of a million votes. Certainly Kennedy had a liberal image, he was closely associated with the New Frontier social programs of his brother. But Kennedy also had two other things going for him: he was Catholic and he had a reputation for being a tough Attorney General. Both of these factors helped him with New York's Slavic voters, and Kennedy won nearly eight out of ten Slavic votes against Keating, or more Slavic votes than any Democratic candidate for statewide office won during the sixties in New York.[5]

In 1968, Indiana's Slavic voters helped reelect liberal Birch Bayh to the United States Senate. Bayh was opposed by William Ruckelshaus, who claimed that the Senator was not conservative enough for most Hoosiers. These charges failed to persuade many of Indiana's Slavic voters, and they gave 71 percent of their votes to Bayh, 20,000 votes of his statewide margin of 70,000.

The 1970 Senate contest in Illinois was a classic confrontation between a liberal Democrat and a conservative Republican. Democrat Adlai Stevenson III opposed the A.B.M. and called for federal programs to help the cities. His opponent, Ralph Smith, who had been appointed to fill the vacancy caused by the death of Everett McKinley Dirksen, attacked Stevenson as an ultra-liberal who was "soft" on dissident students and hippies. Stevenson stuck an American flag in his lapel and hired the prosecutor of the Chicago Seven to run his campaign. Probably what helped Stevenson the most though, were his family name and his liberal credentials. In Chicago, the Daley machine cranked out better than 70 percent of the Slavic vote for Stevenson. He did almost as well statewide, winning more than 60 percent of the Slavic vote, a showing that was better than the Democratic polling of either Governor Otto Kerner in 1964 or Senator Paul Douglas in 1966.

[5] Kennedy's hold on the Slavs was not quite so strong outside New York, however. In the 1968 Presidential primary in Indiana, Kennedy won only 44 percent of the vote in Slavic precincts along Lake Michigan, while Eugene McCarthy, the Left Democratic candidate, won 30 percent. Indiana's Governor Roger D. Branigin took the rest. What is interesting about the Indiana Slavic vote is that three quarters of it went to two very liberal Democrats.

Another Midwestern Senator, Philip A. Hart of Michigan, ran even better with the Slavic voters of his state than did Adlai III in Illinois. In 1970, Senator Hart was opposed by Mrs. Lenore Romney, wife of George Romney, a former Michigan governor and now Nixon's Secretary of Housing and Urban Development. Mrs. Romney attacked Hart for failing to support the Nixon administration's legislative program, while Hart traded on his long-time interest in programs for Michigan's large blue-collar population. The state's G.O.P. failed to unite behind Mrs. Romney, and she lost some support, particularly among white Catholics, when H.U.D. pushed its plans to integrate the Detroit suburb of Warren. Hart won an easy victory of more than 66 percent. A survey taken in mid-September showed that among Slavic voters, Hart was running 10 percentage points ahead of his statewide average. Assuming that the vote on election day reflected the earlier poll—and it most likely did—Hart received nearly three quarters of the Slavic vote.

The preceding elections clearly demonstrate that Slavic voters are not turned off by liberal Democrats. Some liberals like Robert Kennedy won Slavic votes through a unique combination of issues and political "magic," but others without the Kennedy mystique, like Stevenson, Bayh and Hart, win Slavic votes because Slavs believe these liberal Democrats represent their best interests.

SLAVIC VOTERS AND JEWISH CANDIDATES

A Polish-American businessman ran an advertisement in two Detroit newspapers in the fall of 1970, trying to drum up trade with Poland. Part of the advertisement read, "Seven centuries ago, a Polish king knew that men could differ and yet live productively and did something about it." The ad cited the Edict of Kalisz, signed in 1264, and continued, "For the first time in Christian civilization, a Government granted equal protection under the law to Jews." The advertisement was particularly interesting because it chose to deal directly with a controversial subject, Polish anti-Semitism. Despite the Edict of Kalisz, Jews in Poland historically have had a very difficult time with the Polish people.

The list of pogroms and injustices is a long one. What is pertinent today, however, are the attitudes of American Slavs toward American Jews; research indicates that the carry-over from the old country is startling.

Father Greeley found that of all the white Catholics, Poles are most likely to be highly anti-Semitic. The data shows that 53 percent of first- and second-generation Poles score high on sociological tests of prejudice against Jews. Most significantly, this anti-Semitism is not limited to the immigrant generation or its children; just as many third-generation Poles held strongly anti-Semitic views, according to the survey.

All of this does not usually result in anti-Semitic voting. In 1962, Abraham Ribicoff, a liberal Jew, who had been Kennedy's Secretary of Health, Education and Welfare, and Connecticut's governor before that, barely defeated veteran Republican Congressman Horace Seely Brown for a seat in the United States Senate. Ribicoff ran on a very liberal platform and stressed his ties to the Kennedy administration, while Brown strove to be considered as a militant anti-Communist who wanted to temper the social legislation of the New Frontier. Slavic voters were distinctly pro-Ribicoff, with two thirds voting for the Democrat in Hartford and Bridgeport. His margin over Brown was 20,000 votes in Slavic precincts, and he won statewide by only 26,000.

Ribicoff ran again, in 1968, this time against Edwin May, Jr., a moderate Republican and former Congressman. The Senator was a controversial figure in 1968 following his shouting match at the Democratic national convention with Mayor Daley. May attacked Ribicoff for his dovelike stance on the Indochina war and for siding with "ultraliberal dissent groups." Remarkably, Ribicoff won an easy victory, with 54 percent of the vote. Ribicoff's Slavic vote actually increased slightly from six years before to nearly 70 percent.

In the 1968 Illinois gubernatorial election, Democrat Samuel Shapiro, a liberal and a Jew, lost by 127,000 votes to Republican Richard Ogilvie, a law-and-order Republican from Cook County. But the Slavic vote held for Shapiro. Slavic voters in some "machine" precincts of Chicago voted better than two to one for Shapiro, and overall the Democrat won 57 percent of the Slavic vote. That was just about as well as Otto Kerner did in 1964 and as Paul Douglas did in 1966.

And in Pennsylvania Slavic voters had little difficulty voting for liberal, Jewish Democrat Milton Shapp. In 1966, when Shapp lost to moderate Republican Raymond P. Shafer, he nevertheless won 64 percent of the Slavic vote or just about what senatorial and gubernatorial Democrats were accustomed to winning in Pennsylvania. In 1970, Shapp defeated Republican Raymond J. Broderick by a half million votes. According to a survey taken in early fall, in Slavic precincts Shapp was running ten to fifteen points ahead of his statewide percentage. Assuming that there was no fall-off in Shapp's Slavic support as the campaign progressed, he probably captured at least two thirds of the Slavic vote in 1970 as well.

The pattern does break down, but only slightly, and the Democrat still receives a substantial majority of the Slavic vote. In the Michigan gubernatorial election of 1970, liberal Democrat Sander Levin, a young Jewish state senator, lost to Republican incumbent William Milliken, one of the nation's most progressive Republican governors. Milliken had proposed a sweeping program of state aid to parochial schools, a measure which was warmly received in the Slavic community. Levin opposed the Parochiaid plan. Milliken started far ahead of Levin, but the Democrat fought hard and lost by only 44,000 votes. One of the reasons Milliken won was Slavic defections from Levin to the G.O.P. Levin did win a majority of the Slavic vote, about 58 percent, but that was the lowest Slavic tabulation any Michigan Democrat had received in years. Had Levin run as well with Slavs as liberal Neil Staebler did in 1964 against George Romney, or Zoltan Ferency did against Romney in 1966, he would have wiped out Milliken's lead and won. Slavic voters did not vote against Levin because he was Jewish, but Levin's social philosophy led him to oppose Parochiaid—and that cost him Slavic votes.

In Ohio too, the Slavic vote cut against another liberal Jewish Democrat, Howard Metzenbaum, and he lost to Robert A. Taft, Jr., by 70,000 votes. Metzenbaum's share of the Slavic vote was a reasonably good 66 percent. But in some Slavic precincts of

Cleveland, Taft won clear majorities. And while Metzenbaum was getting about two thirds of the Slavic vote, the liberal Democratic candidate for governor, John J. Gilligan, was running ten to twenty points better with the same voters.[6] At least 25,000 Slavic voters who cast ballots for Gilligan did not vote for Metzenbaum. It is not clear whether it was Metzenbaum *qua* Jew who lost votes with Cleveland's Slavs, or whether it was more directly Metzenbaum's liberal style. Whatever the reason, Metzenbaum did not get his full share of the white Catholic vote and it hurt him.

In New York Arthur Goldberg failed to run as well as he might have with Slavic voters. No survey taken during the campaign found anti-Semitic feelings toward Goldberg on the part of Slavic voters, but still the former United States Supreme Court Justice won only 58 percent of the Slavic vote. In Buffalo, where the political machine of "Boss" Joe Crangle was in good working order, Goldberg beat Rockefeller by two to one in some Slavic precincts. Outside of Buffalo, however, Goldberg and Rockefeller ran neck and neck with Slavs. Overall, Rockefeller won 36 percent of the Slavic vote and the Conservative gubernatorial candidate Paul Adams, who really wasn't a factor in the race, won only 6 percent. Slavic voters were not impressed with either Goldberg's credentials or his liberal political philosophy. Rockefeller courted the Slavic vote. He ran full-page advertisements in the Slavic-language press for weeks before the election, and his aid-for-parochial-schools plan was welcomed in the Slavic community. In all, Rockefeller simply outperformed Goldberg, and it was therefore not surprising that the Democratic share of the New York Slavic vote was so low.

Even though many Slavic voters hold highly unfavorable attitudes toward Jews in general, they appear quite willing to leave their prejudices outside the voting booth. When the Slavic vote declines from its normal Democratic percentages because a Jew is running, other factors—the social issues, a strong G.O.P. candidate, and parochial-school aid—seem at least partially to explain

[6] In 1968, too, when he lost to William Saxbe, Gilligan won 76 percent of the Slavic vote.

the fall-off. As we have seen, liberal Democrats and even *Jewish* liberal Democrats often run quite well with Slavic voters.

If Slavic voters are to be considered part of any emerging Republican majority, they should be giving a substantial portion of their votes to Republican candidates for statewide office. They don't.

First, the rule: Republican candidates do not win a sizable Slavic vote. Thus, George Romney, in three winning races for governor of Michigan, never received as much as 30 percent of the Slavic ballots. Nelson Rockefeller won less than a quarter of the Slavic vote in 1962 and 1966, and barely more than one third in Slavic precincts in his 1970 landslide victory over Arthur Goldberg. William Saxbe took only a quarter of the Slavic vote in Ohio in 1968 while defeating John Gilligan for the Senate, and Warren Knowles never carried more than 25 percent of the Slavic vote in his three successful Wisconsin gubernatorial campaigns. Even Jacob Javits failed to crack the Slavic vote in 1962 when he beat James Donovan by more than 980,000 votes, losing the Slavic vote to Donovan by two to one. Against ultraliberal Paul O'Dwyer six years later the Senator improved his Slavic vote— but insignificantly.

The worst Slavic-Republican showing in any statewide election since 1964 was recorded by Spiro Agnew. In the 1966 Maryland gubernatorial election, the present Vice-President of the United States beat Democrat George Mahoney and Independent Hyman Pressman, but lost the Slavic vote. For the Slavic voters of east Baltimore, there could not have been a more crucial issue than open housing (opposed by Mahoney and favored by Agnew). They feared the encroaching black ghetto, and they voted their fears. It would have been hard for them to vote Republican under any circumstances, but the coincidence of Democratic party loyalty and the race issue made it an easy choice. Mahoney won nearly five out of every six votes in Slavic precincts, or twice his statewide percentage. Agnew, the liberal in the race, took only about 10 percent of the Slavic vote, and Pressman won what was left. It was not a very impressive start for "Agnew the ethnic-vote-getter."

In view of this performance it should not be surprising that Agnew's endorsement was of little help to the successful Conservative senatorial candidacy of James L. Buckley in New York in 1970. Prior to that election, Buckley had taken only 7 percent of the Slavic vote in 1968, when he pulled a million votes against Jacob Javits and Paul O'Dwyer. In 1970 Buckley captured only 22 percent of the Slavic vote, an improvement over 1968, but considerably lower than his statewide portion of 37 percent, and hardly a very conservative showing by the ethnic group widely thought to be a mainstay of independent conservative movements.

And the exception: The most successful Republican candidates among Slavs are either moderate or liberal Republicans.

In New Jersey, liberal Republican Senator Clifford Case did very well with Slavic voters when he last ran for office in 1966, winning 49 percent of the Slavic vote against Democratic liberal Warren Wilentz, the son of the Middlesex County Democratic boss. (Interestingly, Case won better than 60 percent of the vote in the Slavic precincts of Middlesex County.) The Senator's low-key Republicanism, his support for the Johnson administration war policies, and his higher public recognition factor, all added to an easy statewide Case victory.

Another liberal Republican who runs well with Slavic voters is Charles Percy of Illinois. When Percy lost to incumbent Otto Kerner for governor in 1964, he won three out of seven Slavic votes. Although not a majority, it was the best that any G.O.P. candidate for governor would do in the sixties. And in 1966, when Percy beat liberal hawk Senator Paul Douglas, he carried nearly a majority of the Slavic vote. Overall he captured 49 percent and in some sections of Southside Chicago, Percy took almost 60 percent of the Slavic vote.

The first and so far the only Republican to win a clear majority of the Slavic vote statewide is William T. Cahill of New Jersey. In the gubernatorial election of 1969 Cahill ran against former

Governor Robert B. Meyner.[7] Both Cahill and Meyner spoke out against rising crime and student unrest, but apparently New Jersey's Slavs were not moved by Meyner's tired campaign rhetoric, and they found former F.B.I. agent Cahill's straight talk appealing; he won 54 percent of the vote in Slavic precincts and in some Slavic areas of Middlesex County captured more than 60 percent.

The New Jersey Slavic Republican majority did not last long, however. In the senatorial election of 1970, Republican candidate Nelson G. Gross ran against incumbent liberal Democrat Harrison A. Williams, Jr. Gross tried to convince New Jersey's voters that he could do more for them in Washington and President Nixon went out of his way to stump for Gross. Williams countered by stressing his seniority on the important Senate Labor Committee, and apparently New Jersey's voters in general, and Slavic voters in particular, were more impressed with Williams' actual power than Gross's potential clout. Gross lost by 250,000 votes statewide, and he won only one third of the Slavic vote.

With the exception of one candidate, moderate Governor Cahill of New Jersey, none of the Republican office seekers whose races we've outlined won a Slavic majority. The most conservative candidate, James Buckley, managed a dismal 22 percent, while the two Republicans who came closest to winning Slavic majorities were liberals Case and Percy. The Republicans still have a long way to go in turning Slavic voters into members of the G.O.P., and those Republicans who stand the best chance of doing it are moderates or liberals.

Whatever the intelligence both major parties may glean from present-day Slavic voting, one conclusion is readily apparent: the Slavic voter can no longer be taken for granted by the Democrats or ignored by the Republicans as unimportant to their coalition. The Slavic voter is more discriminating than ever, and the politician who forgets this political axiom does so at his peril.

[7] Meyner had beaten five other candidates including Bergen County Congressman Henry Helstoski to win the nomination. However, Slavic voters showed their loyalty to a fellow ethnic (and a Kennedy-McCarthy–type Democrat) and in the primary Helstoski won 45 percent of the Slavic vote, compared to 32 percent for Meyner, with the rest scattered.

7

The Italians: More Democratic Than Not

There in the space of four hours was so much of what it means to be an Italian-American today. Manhattan's Columbus Circle was decked out for the occasion. Red-white-and-green plastic streamers, forty feet long, stretched from the top of the statue of the continent's discoverer to the plaza it graces below. Two hundred thousand sandwiches and four hundred thousand drinks were on hand. Italian tricolor shopping bags were distributed to all; they boasted: "I attended Unity Day, June 26, 1971. Sponsored by the Italian-American Civil Rights League, Inc."

Sadly and ironically those shopping bags quickly achieved collector's-item status. For shortly before the rally began Joseph Colombo, Sr., the League's founder and, according to the F.B.I. at least, a Mafia chieftain, was shot down. A black man was the would-be assassin. While surgeons probed Colombo's wounds, the rally went on. There were speeches, prayers for Colombo, and entertainment. Politicians were there: a Borough President, two Congressmen, the Democratic leader of Brooklyn, and some lesser political lights. Congressman Mario Biaggi, a Democrat-*Conservative* from the Bronx, got a big hand when he hinted that black revolutionaries were responsible for the shooting. And Anthony Imperiale, the karate-chopping, vigilante councilman from Newark, drew a burst of applause from the restless crowd when he told them "the blood of Roman gladiators flows in your veins." During the three hours of speeches, there were occasional outbreaks of violence. Several blacks who unwisely lingered in the crowd were attacked by men wearing "Italian Power" buttons. At 3 P.M. the League's president, Natale Marcone[1] ended the rally, saying: "Go home, but never forget. Be proud to be an Italian, all the time." Unity Day, 1971, was a microcosm of the world of Italian-Americans.

If the day became tragic before it even began, 100,000 Italian-Americans (not all of whom, presumably, were coerced into attending by Mafia pressure), and $450,000 raised seven months earlier in Madison Square Garden, certainly provide ample evidence of a new awareness of Italian ethnicity and its potential power. The desire for unity so obvious on that hot June day, if sustained, can easily create a vulcanizing political force. With prospects so bright in 1971, the dismal failure of the Italian-American Anti-Defamation League only a few years back is a reminder of just how far the Italians have come, and how quickly.

To achieve the voice they so desperately covet this decade will almost certainly require some change and intensification in the elements crucial to the Italian-American consciousness.

The Mafia: The Civil Rights League says use of the term "Mafia" or its substitute "Cosa Nostra" defames all Italian-Americans. A published poll shows that 70 percent of Americans believe that the Mafia exists (but only 24 percent think it's run exclusively by Italians). Experts such as Harvard sociologist David Bell and Australian criminologist Gordon Hawkins doubt the Mafia's existence. And in the 1950s the Kefauver Committee drew its conclusions of Mafia presence from a good deal of evidence that would be ruled hearsay in a court of law. Fascinating though it is for novelists and the general public, the question of the Mafia will probably never be answered to everyone's satisfaction. No matter. Joseph Colombo's reputed underworld leadership did not keep Italian-Americans from associating with his

[1] Colombo had installed his son, Anthony, as vice-president, freely used the title "Founder," and of course reserved all the power for himself.

League and from demonstrating for recognition in 1971. As with the blacks, any vehicle offering a reasonable chance for success will be utilized; the question of Mafia dominance then pales accordingly and is likely to be forgotten.

Blacks and Violence: Italian-Americans are on the front lines of the blue-collar revolt against radical rhetoric, black-power demands, and crime in the streets. At least some blacks are no less kindly disposed to the more suspect elements of the Italian community. Indicting the Mafia for continual trouble in black neighborhoods, black nationalists cried in 1966 that "the Cosa Nostra is flooding our communities with narcotics, destroying our children and families and getting rich at the same time. . . . They are keeping us out of many unions. . . . They have chased decent black numbers bankers from Harlem and [are] using the profits formerly staying in the community to finance Las Vegas, prostitution, loan-sharking and dope." It is interesting that a similar thought was expressed by the black leader Booker T. Washington sixty years earlier as he promulgated the myth of the Italian as an undesirable immigrant. After his visit to Italy the black leader wrote: "It is from these parts [the south] of Italy, where there are the greatest poverty, crime and ignorance, that the largest number of emigrants go out to America."

Present Italian attitudes toward blacks are an apparent reversal from Civil War days, when in 1861 Garibaldi championed abolition, and even refused a commission to command a Union force, because President Lincoln was not yet ready to emancipate America's slaves.

Italian Pride: The Unity Day rally itself indicates a rebirth of Italian activity. Before the immigration waves began in 1880, America's Italian population of 40,000, almost exclusively from northern Italy, had often organized to realize goals perceived as common to the community. In San Francisco the Italian Mutual Aid Society, founded in 1858, established education programs and hired a physician to care full time for the indigent Italian sick. A year before, in New York, the Society of Italian Union and Fraternity was founded and shortly thereafter was able to create a library and night school for adults. Financial aid was given to Italians widowed during the Civil War, and by 1880 all widowed members received one hundred dollars to defray burial expenses. Interestingly this pre-immigration period revealed a great lack of Catholic Church involvement in the problems of the Italian community. Largely populated in its upper echelons by the Irish, the Church claimed fewer than two hundred Italian-American priests throughout the United States in 1870.

Today, in the early 1970s, for the first time since their mass arrival in America from southern Italy almost a hundred years ago, Italian-Americans are coming to grips with their ethnic heritage.

Little is known of the past political and social landscape of Italian America. *L'Eco d'Italia,* the influential New York Italian-language daily founded in 1849 by Secchi de Casali, supported the Whigs and later the Republicans. In 1876 the paper reported the reelection to the Texas House of Representatives of two Italian-Americans, one of whom had served under Garibaldi in 1848. Four years earlier *L'Eco* endorsed General Grant for the Presidency, and in an 1872 statement more prescient than real for that year, claimed that Italians were being sought by politicians who had previously thought their vote would be of little or no political significance.

The Panic of 1873 and the prolonged Depression saw Italian fortunes fall with the rest of the nation's. Secchi de Casali urged a free labor bureau for Italians, but none was created until the twentieth century. During this period many Italians left the country for Italy and South America. Ethnic tension was common. Those leaving California unswervingly blamed the Chinese immigrants for lowering the working standards in that area. Great friction also appeared among the Irish and Italian unskilled laborers in the Northeast, and in 1873 New York's Aldermen requested the Commissioner of Police to justify the hiring of Italian immigrants in place of Irish-Americans for public-works projects.

The assumption of Italian criminal endeavors that persists to this day had its genesis in newspaper accounts in 1880 claiming evidence proving that the Italian government regularly sent its criminals to the United States. *L'Eco* responded saying New York's jails housed mostly Irish and Americans, rather than Italians. So it went, charge and countercharge, slur and denial.

The large-scale immigration of southern Italians began at this time, and whenever possible the northern Italians sought to distinguish themselves from the newly landing immigrants.[2] Secchi de Casali joined the black and German-Jewish leaders of New York in urging the southerners to begin farming in this country,[3] and he aided in the creation of an Italian agricultural colony near Vineland, New Jersey.

As the historian Robert Foerster has noted, the crucial focus of Italian immigration was the making of money. Political activity comparable to the earlier involvement of northern Italians did not exist during these years.

Perhaps desirous of suppressing their true condition, the new Italians continually emphasized their good fortune in being in America in the first place. The pages of *Il Progresso* and other Italian newspapers were filled with news of festivals, rather than indignation at the atrocious housing conditions in the inner cities.

But the Haymarket Riot of 1886 fueled widespread Anglo suspicions of the immigrants.[4] And by 1890 *Il Progresso* was

[2] Echoing his less scholarly countrymen, Allan McLaughlin, in 1904, had this to say about the northern and southern Italians: ". . . in considering Italian immigrants it is necessary to recognize the differences existing between northern and southern Italians. The northern Italian is taller, often of lighter complexion, and is usually in a more prosperous condition than his brother from the south. The northern Italian is intelligent, can nearly always read and write, and very often is skilled in some trade or occupation. He compares favorably with the Scandinavian or German, and his desirability as an immigrant is seldom questioned. On the other hand, the southern Italian, short of stature, very dark in complexion, usually lands here almost destitute."

[3] Over 80 percent of the people of Italy were engaged in agriculture at this time. Those leaving the country did so primarily because of widespread Italian agricultural and economic problems. Booker T. Washington wrote that the southern Italian cities had more people living in "dirt, degradation, and ignorance at the bottom of society" than any other area he was able to visit.

[4] The police chief of New Orleans was murdered in March of 1890. Sicilian Italians were suspected, and an overreaction appeared everywhere. Said *The New York Times:* "These sneaking and cowardly Sicilians, the descendants of bandits and assassins, who had transported to this country

urging its alien readership to seek American citizenship and to participate politically. "It is our vote that must count," the newspaper declared.

Not until the progressive era of the early twentieth century did Italians finally begin banding together again. By 1912 there were 258 mutual aid societies in New York City alone (the societies always being an important indication of Italian community). Elective progress came later; during the years between the two World Wars three Italian judges served on the New York Supreme Court (elective offices) and Angelo Rossi, Fiorello La Guardia and Robert S. Maestri were the mayors of San Francisco, New York and New Orleans.

The scattered political beginnings of this middle decade are today yielding a new Italian political awareness. The sons (and daughters) of Italy have already decided numerous electoral contests. Organized effectively and mindful of its own interests, Italian political clout can only continue and expand. The mass Italian arrests of the 1919 "Red Scare" need never recur, and the pride of heritage that Bartolomeo Vanzetti so courageously exhibited after learning that he was to be executed in 1927 can have a new meaning for his ethnic brothers.

A ROMAN PROFILE

Late in the 1971 Unity Day program, a speaker proudly told the dwindling crowd that there are *34 million* Italian-Americans. The 34-million figure probably didn't mean much to anyone who was listening. But it certainly would have seemed out of line to anyone who ever studied the demography of Italian-Americans. Ethnic hyperbole aside, it is highly unlikely that there are that many Americans who can trace their ancestry back to Italy. Having said that, it is not so easy to find out just how many Italian-Americans there actually are. Two Italian-language newspapers, *Il Popolo Italiano* (of Philadelphia) and *Fra Noi* (of Chicago), estimate the number at 21½ million. A scholarly study in the *International Migration Review* puts the number between

---

the lawless passions, the cutthroat practices, the oath-bound societies of their native country, are to us a pest without mitigation."

15 and 16 million. The most recent and most reliable estimate, however, comes from a special survey conducted by the U.S. Census Bureau. When asked about their family origins 7.2 million people claimed they were Italian-Americans—about 3⅓ percent of the total United States population.

Demographers say that three quarters of America's Italians live in the Northeast. One third of all Italian-Americans live within the Greater New York area, and sizable Italian populations are found in Philadelphia, Boston, Pittsburgh, Buffalo and Providence. Approximately one out of every seven Italians lives in Midwestern states like Illinois, Ohio and Wisconsin; California has a large Italian population, centered around Los Angeles—Long Beach and San Francisco–Oakland. There are few Italians in the South.[5]

Most of the four million Italians who came to the United States between 1890 and 1921 settled in cities, and their descendants move out of these "Little Italys" only with the greatest reluctance.[6] In New York City, for example, 40 percent of Italians continue to live in the same neighborhoods as their parents. Generally Italians are two to three times more likely to be found in neighborhoods of original settlement than either Jews or the Irish. By and large, Italian-Americans have not been caught up in the postwar move to the suburbs, but of course there are exceptions. Italians make up a substantial portion of the population in Nassau and Suffolk counties outside New York City, and Melrose Park is a thriving blue-collar Italian community in suburban Cook County, Illinois. But most Italians appear to linger in the city because urban neighborhoods are considered more congenial to the Italian life style: owning your own small home, living close to friends and relatives, knowing your place in a well-ordered society.

[5] Some of the original Italian immigrants went south to work as laborers and to establish farming communities. They did not receive a very warm welcome. In 1891, for instance, eleven Italians were lynched in New Orleans, and between 1874 and 1915 three dozen Italians were killed by mob violence.

[6] With the easing of restrictive immigration laws in 1965, Italian immigration to the United States picked up again. Between 1965 and 1970, Italian migration grew from 10,800 to 24,000. Most of these new arrivals settled in established Italian neighborhoods in center cities.

Nevertheless, living in the cities presents special problems for Italians, as they increasingly find themselves caught between the bulldozers of urban renewal and the encroaching territorial demands of the black ghetto.

Of all the white ethnics, Italians are second only to Polish Catholics in the percentage who belong to the working class. According to the Census, almost two thirds of Italian-Americans hold blue-collar jobs, and about 40 percent of Italian workingmen belong to unions. In 1969, the average Italian family earned about $8,800 a year, a very modest working-class income.

Very few Italians have made it out of the blue-collar ranks. Only one third of Italians are white-collar workers, and many of them have routine jobs. In fact, only one out of seven Italian-Americans holds a "prestige" job, according to Father Andrew Greeley of the National Opinion Research Center.

There is some difference in the political attitudes of blue-collar and white-collar Italians. A survey in Connecticut showed that 60 percent of Italians with white-collar jobs say they are Democrats, compared to 80 percent of the state's blue-collar Italians. Father Greeley found evidence that better-off Italian-Americans were less likely to belong to the Democratic party. He reports that of Italian-Americans who have graduated from college, just as many say they are Republicans as say they are Democrats. Still, only 7 percent of Italians over the age of twenty-five have been to college, and as we have already seen, less than one third of Italians are in white-collar jobs. On balance, two thirds of Italian-Americans say they are Democrats.

These differences in education and occupation also affect the rate at which Italian-Americans vote. Gallup shows that, in general, Italians turn out in slightly smaller percentages than the population at large. A Columbia Public Health Survey in New York City corroborates this national finding. The survey reports that 59 percent of all New Yorkers vote in almost every election, as opposed to only 56 percent of Italians. New York Italians without a high-school diploma had the poorest voting record of any white Catholic group in the city; only 48 percent said they almost always vote. Italians with a high-school diploma, on the other hand, turn out quite often. Seventy-two percent of these New York Italians said they voted in nearly every election (higher than the average for the city as a whole).

A POLITICAL OVERVIEW

We will be considering how Italian-Americans voted in nine states for President, governor and United States Senator in the 1960s—85 electoral contests in all. The Republican candidate carried the Italian-American vote in only eight of these 85 elections; once in 25 instances of Presidential voting (Nixon in New York in 1968), seven times in 25 gubernatorial elections (Volpe in Massachusetts in 1960, 1962 and 1966, Rockefeller in New York in 1970, Cahill in New Jersey in 1969, and John H. Chafee in Rhode Island in 1964 and 1966), and not once in 35 senatorial contests. It is interesting to note that all four Republican gubernatorial candidates who were successful statewide were from the G.O.P.'s "moderate" wing. There surely is more than one definition of a Republican or Democratic voting bloc (just ask the respective party chairmen), but whatever the definition, a group that supports Republican candidates in only 9 percent of statewide elections can hardly be considered Republican.

Few of the elections considered show startling totals for the Democratic candidates; the Democrat scored over 80 percent in only 5 Presidential, 5 senatorial and one gubernatorial contests. But in three out of five elections the Democratic nominee won by more than two to one. All of which says a great deal for existing Democratic majorities, whatever other observers may claim to be emerging for the Republicans.

In addition to a general pattern of Democratic victories among Italian-American voters, there is a sense of a base—or irreducible-minimum—Democratic vote. The Democratic candidate received less than 40 percent of the Italian vote in only 3 of the 85 electoral contests studied. Two of those Democrats were New York Jews (Richard Ottinger and Arthur Goldberg), and the other was unfortunate enough to run against Republican Italian John Volpe in Massachusetts in 1966 (Francis X. Bellotti). The irreducible Democratic base suggests that any Republican trend among Italian-Americans will stop far short of a convincing majority.

Italians have been becoming "Presidential Republicans" for years—or so it seems—without ever getting there. In the 1950s, political commentators examined the Eisenhower vote and proclaimed, "Italians are moving into the G.O.P." In 1960, when John Kennedy recouped much of the Catholic vote, some conservative columnists still found Republican trends for Nixon. The election of 1964 was the first time we heard of "backlash," and Italians were supposed to have been among the "backlashiest." And the 1968 and 1970 elections also were interpreted as signs that Italians are deserting the party of F.D.R. for the party of Nixon.

Our data suggest that all these commentators were wrong. If Italians were moving to the G.O.P. in 1952 and 1956, they certainly moved back again to the Democrats by 1960. The backlash vote for Goldwater was more noticeable for the cities in which it did not materialize than for those in which it did. And George Wallace ended up doing just about as well among the Italian-Americans, trumpeted by many as his natural supporters, as he did in the North.

In the course of the decade, the Italian vote for Democratic Presidential candidates declined from more than 75 percent for Kennedy and 77 percent for Johnson to only 50 percent for Humphrey. On its face, this indicates an important shift to the Republicans. But to measure a shift you need a base line. From the best available sources, it is possible to estimate Eisenhower's Italian vote at approximately 50 percent.[7] Eisenhower may not have carried the Italian vote, and so far, neither has Richard Nixon. More than a political generation after Eisenhower, Republican

[7] Gallup surveys taken in 1952 and 1956 showed Eisenhower winning less than half of the Catholic vote. Vincent Tortora, writing in *The Nation* of October 24, 1953, says the vote in Italian wards of major cities was running then just under 50 percent Republican.

Presidential candidates do not run even as well as Ike.[8]

In 1960, Nixon won about 25 percent of the votes in predominantly Italian precincts. Goldwater's 1964 portion slipped slightly to 23 percent, but in 1968 Nixon rebounded to take 40 percent of the votes in Italian neighborhoods; Hubert Humphrey just barely managed to win a majority, and George Wallace received 10 percent.

CHART 1: ITALIAN PRESIDENTIAL VOTE, 1956–1968

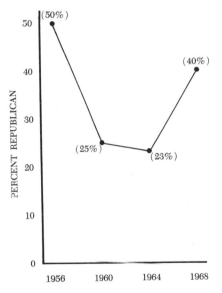

SOURCE: Institute of American Research; NBC News.

John Kennedy's candidacy meant a great deal to all Catholics, not just the Irish. For Italians, who always seemed to lag a politi-

[8] At the time of the 1968 Republican national convention, many "insiders" in the Nixon camp expected Nixon to choose then Governor John Volpe as his running mate. Volpe was said to be in line for the spot because Nixon felt that Volpe would bring additional white Catholic voters into the G.O.P. A similar move might be to the Republicans' advantage in 1972, as we discuss in Chapter 8.

cal generation or two behind the Irish, Kennedy's success offered the dream that perhaps one day even an Italian-American could be President. In four states—Massachusetts, Rhode Island, Ohio and Illinois—Kennedy won upwards of 80 percent of the Italian vote. In three states—Maryland, Pennsylvania and Connecticut— J.F.K.'s Italian vote helped swing the state into the Democratic column for the first time since 1944. Kennedy's Italian vote fell significantly below his national Italian average in only one state, New York, where he still won nearly two thirds of the vote. The Senator's vote in working-class Italian precincts in Buffalo and Syracuse ran as high as 75 percent, but in the Bay Ridge section of Brooklyn Kennedy's vote fell 15 to 20 points off his national showing. Bay Ridge is different. Its Italians are among the most well-to-do of all in New York City. Many live in large single-family homes or luxury apartment buildings; and, sensing a sympathetic constituency, the Republicans began to organize in Bay Ridge shortly after World War II. Today, the section's Italians are quite conservative and they were obviously not attracted by Kennedy's liberalism, even ten years ago. Still, in 1960, Bay Ridge was the exception. Most Italians gave a strong vote to their coreligionist Kennedy.

CHART 2:   NEW YORK ITALIANS
PRESIDENTIAL VOTE, 1960

	Kennedy	Nixon
All Italians	64%	36%
Brooklyn	56%	44%
Upstate	74%	26%

SOURCE: Institute of American Research; NBC News.

Lyndon Johnson did better in Italian precincts than Kennedy had done four years earlier. Between 1960 and 1964, the civil-rights movement had dominated the domestic headlines. Politicians counted the votes for Louise Day Hicks in her race for Boston school board, saw how well George Wallace ran in the Maryland Presidential primary, and expected a considerable backlash of white ethnic voters to Goldwater. Ethnic voters, the politicians said, were going to take revenge on the Democratic party for its aid to Black America. The politicians were wrong. L.B.J. won better than three out of every four votes cast by Italian-Americans. Some signs of backlash were noticed, in racially troubled communities like Newark and Cleveland, but on the whole, Italian voters in important industrial centers rejected the Republican party.

CHART 3: ITALIAN VOTERS
PRESIDENTIAL VOTE, 1964

	Johnson	Goldwater	Change in GOP from 1960
Chicago	85%	15%	−2%
Bay Ridge, Brooklyn	54%	46%	−5%
Hartford, Conn.	82%	18%	−6%
Buffalo, N.Y.	85%	15%	−12%
Newark, N.J.	65%	35%	+1%
Cleveland	66%	34%	+16%

SOURCE: Institute of American Research; NBC News.

What Goldwater gained in blue-collar backlash, he lost in middle-class Italian precincts. His vote in Brooklyn's Bay Ridge, for instance, fell by five percentage points compared to Nixon's 1960 showing. The 1964 Goldwater vote demonstrated that, faced with a choice between pocketbook issues and "the race question," most Italian voters, like most other workingmen, will vote pocketbook. Goldwater marked the decade's low in Republican fortunes, both nationally and with the Italian voter.

In 1968 Nixon did not win a majority of Italian votes. But he did recover from the Goldwater showing to take four out of every ten votes cast in Italian neighborhoods, and he gained substantially on his own 1960 vote as well. We estimate that nearly three quarters of a million Italians who voted for John Kennedy in 1960 did not vote for Hubert Humphrey in 1968.

Many of the Italian votes lost by Humphrey in states such as New Jersey went to George Wallace—but not nearly as many as some commentators predicted. Most political experts expected Wallace to do very well with Italian voters. But on November 5,

1968, Wallace actually ran only as well with Italians as he did outside the South. The Alabama governor won 8 percent of the non-Southern vote, but his share in Italian precincts was only ten percent. In Boston, Wallace could barely muster one out of every fourteen votes cast in the Italian North End. He fared only slightly better in small industrial cities like Erie, Pennsylvania, Rockford, Illinois, and Youngstown, Ohio; and Chicago's Italian Democrats gave Wallace only one out of every eleven votes.

The picture was considerably different for Wallace however, in those racially troubled neighborhoods which showed an inclination to vote for Goldwater and Nixon. In Newark, Wallace won more than 20 percent of the vote in North Ward Italian precincts, and he captured almost 30 percent of the vote in Italian neighborhoods of Cleveland. Nevertheless, Italian voters in general would have little to do with the governor of Alabama. What real movement did take place was to Nixon.

Nowhere was this shift more important than in New Jersey. In 1960, Nixon won 31 percent of the New Jersey Italian vote. John Kennedy recorded a 125,000-vote plurality in Italian precincts, and only carried New Jersey by 22,000 votes. Therefore, the New Jersey Italian vote gave Kennedy the state. But in 1968, Nixon's Italian share jumped to 40 percent. (Humphrey took 42 percent, and Wallace won 18 percent.) Humphrey lost New Jersey by 61,000 votes, a margin that could have been erased had he held Kennedy's 1960 Italian support.

Nixon's gain from 1960 was smallest in the traditionally Democratic Italian areas of Chicago, Boston and upstate New York. His greatest increase came in areas which had shown a Republican trend in the Goldwater election: racially tense neighborhoods in Newark, Cleveland and Philadelphia. The Republican-leaning middle-class precincts of Italian Brooklyn, which had snubbed Goldwater, also came back for Nixon.

If Nixon runs again and improves his showing with Italians it will help him in crucial states like New Jersey and Illinois. For the time being, though, Italians remain an important plus for the Democrats. And until a Republican Presidential candidate can win in Italian neighborhoods by four or five to one, it is premature indeed to read Italian voters out of the Democratic coalition.

CHART 4: ITALIAN VOTERS
PRESIDENTIAL VOTE, 1968

	Humphrey	Nixon	Wallace	Nixon's Gain from 1960
Chicago	72%	19%	9%	+2%
Boston	76%	17%	7%	+3%
Brooklyn	34%	56%	10%	+13%
Newark	31%	48%	21%	+15%
Cleveland	44%	27%	29%	+10%
Philadelphia	44%	45%	11%	+22%

SOURCE: Institute of American Research; NBC News.

ITALIAN VOTERS AND BLACK AMERICA

About a year ago *Variety*, "the show business bible," carried one of its periodic reports that NBC censors had "blipped" a word from a *Tonight Show* program. But the word which the censors deleted wasn't an obscenity. According to *Variety*, a member of the song-and-dance team of Hines, Hines and Dad was being interviewed by Johnny Carson. The black performer said that his new baby's hair was straight instead of kinky, and he attributed that to the fact that his wife was an (*blip*). Then the viewing audience heard him say, "That's the closest I could get to my color." The word that NBC had "blipped" out was "Italian."

Just how sensitive are Italians to racial questions? Father Greeley recently surveyed the racial attitudes of white Catholic Americans and asked them to tell him how strongly they agreed or disagreed with statements like: "Negroes shouldn't push themselves where they are not wanted"; "White people have a right to live in an all-white neighborhood if they want"; "Negroes would be satisfied if it were not for a few people who stir up trouble." The results showed that Italians were second only to Polish-Americans in their dislike for blacks. In fact, more than half of the Italian-Americans interviewed scored high on sociological scales designed to measure racism.

Five elections illustrate how these attitudes affect Italian voting patterns. The first demonstrates how a classic sociological fact can influence an election.

Of all the ethnics, Italians are most likely to own their own small homes. For them a home, however small and crowded, is still the center of family life, where relatives and neighbors come to visit, a symbol of core values in the Italian heritage. Father Greeley found that 70 percent of Italians would object if a black family moved into their neighborhood, the highest rate of opposition to neighborhood integration of any Catholic group and half again as strong as the national average. The 1966 election for governor of Maryland was tailor-made to evoke an antiblack vote from Italians. Spiro Agnew, who was everybody's favorite liberal of the time, won, but to the row-house-owning, marble-step-washing Italians of east Baltimore, Agnew was the devil incarnate. Democrat George P. Mahoney won almost three quarters of their votes. For Baltimore's Italians, their home was indeed their castle and they voted to protect it.

Another bit of sociological insight, fraught with political impact: of all white ethnics, Italians are least favorably disposed to political militancy. In fact, a NORC survey showed that Italians are less sympathetic to protestors than the general population of the United States.[9] This dislike of radical and racial protest showed up clearly in the 1966 Civilian Review Board vote in New York City. As we have already seen, the Review Board vote split New Yorkers into two deeply antagonistic camps. All New Yorkers, white and black, were against militants and muggers, but Italian-Americans voted even more strongly for "law and order" against some ill-defined fear of disorder. A survey conducted for the American Jewish Committee showed that an astounding 87 percent of Italian voters opposed the Review Board.

A desire to protect social turf and a dislike for black militants combined to influence the 1969 municipal elections in Newark, New Jersey. About half of Newark's voters are black. Of whites, about three fifths are Italians, most of them living in the North

[9] Of course, Italians think it's all right to demonstrate for their own causes. In 1971, 69 Italian homeowners in the Corona section of Queens fought a Lindsay administration order which would have torn down their homes to build a school. Hundreds of speeches were made and demonstrations were held. A bill was introduced into the state legislature. And finally, the Mayor gave in and agreed to move their homes, piece by piece, to city-owned land in the same neighborhood.

Ward. Seven candidates ran for the mayoralty, including the incumbent Hugh J. Addonizio (the first Italian mayor in Newark history), Kenneth A. Gibson (a black highway engineer who was born in Enterprise, Alabama), and City Councilman Anthony Imperiale from the North Ward. The memory of the 1967 riots was still fresh in the minds of all Newark voters. Mayor Addonizio, who was then under federal indictment, said he alone could end the racial polarization in Newark. Gibson realized that he had few votes to win in Italian neighborhoods and restricted his campaigning almost exclusively to the black wards and some selected middle-income white precincts. Imperiale, meanwhile, attacked Addonizio for being too lenient toward black "troublemakers" and blasted Gibson as the captive of that "foul-mouthed little pipsqueak, LeRoi Jones." On election day, the vote broke along racial lines. Gibson ran very well in the black community and led with 43 percent citywide. Addonizio showed some black strength—about 8 percent—and substantial white support. He was second with a total of 20 percent, and Imperiale trailed with 16 percent of the vote. Most of Imperiale's total came from Italian precincts, where he won about 44 percent of the vote. But Addonizio won about one third of the Italian ballots, and that kept Imperiale from running second citywide.

Since no candidate won a majority, Gibson and Addonizio, the two front runners, faced each other in a runoff several weeks later. Between the first election and the runoff, Gibson changed his tactics. He campaigned more in white neighborhoods and he promised to be "the mayor of all Newarkers, not just blacks." LeRoi Jones was kept under wraps for the remainder of the campaign, and Gibson won, ending the short-lived Italian control of Newark's city hall. But Addonizio still captured seven out of every eight votes cast in Italian neighborhoods (picking up Imperiale's Italian strength). By and large, Newark's Italians were more willing to trust one of their own, even if he was a crook,[10] than to vote for a black man.[11] Italians were frightened by Newark's shifting racial balance, and their vote showed it.

[10] Addonizio has since been convicted of extortion.
[11] Italians have maintained a majority of 6 to 3 on the City Council, but the Board of Education, which is appointed by the mayor, is now dominated

The Italian dislike for black candidates also shows up in some primary contests. In 1970, considerable pressure was brought to bear on the New York Democratic party to name a black candidate to the state ticket. After a bitter convention struggle, the state committee designated Basil Paterson, a black state senator from Harlem, to run for lieutenant governor along with Arthur Goldberg.[12] But in the June primary, the state committee's decision was challenged by Jerome Ambro, a town official from suburban Suffolk County and an Italian. Ambro campaigned vigorously. He denied that he was antiblack, but said it was political folly to run a Jew and a black for the two top state offices. Ambro claimed that the ticket needed to be balanced with a Catholic. What he really meant was an Italian; Paterson is a Catholic graduate of St. John's Law School. Paterson won the primary easily, but was edged by Ambro in Italian precincts. The Italian vote reveals an interesting split. Upstate in Italian areas Paterson beat Ambro handily. Party leaders in Buffalo and Syracuse held Italian voters in line for the official party designee, but in New York City, Ambro ran significantly ahead of Paterson, despite the Senator's having been endorsed by most important city Democratic leaders. Obviously the New York City Democratic leadership could not deliver votes for Paterson.

Ambro's strong Italian vote can be explained, *in part*, by the fact that he is Italian and has an Italian-sounding name. Italian voters may also have been reacting against the ethnically unbalanced ticket the state committee had put together. But Basil Paterson is black, and that seems to have occupied the minds of many Italians.

Big-city Italians who are being crowded out of their old neighborhoods by blacks certainly have shown a reluctance to vote for

---

by a six-man black and Puerto Rican majority. Both Italian and black Democratic clubs coexist peacefully in Newark. "Big Pangy" Raimo distinguishes the two political organizations this way: "We're different from those black clubs where all they do is drink. We're Italians. We prefer eating."

12 Under New York election law, the nominees for governor and lieutenant governor run paired on the November ballot. A vote for governor carries with it an automatic vote for lieutenant governor.

CHART 5: ITALIAN VOTERS
NEW YORK, PRIMARY FOR
LIEUTENANT GOVERNOR, 1970

	Paterson	Ambro
All Italians	47%	53%
New York City	36%	64%
Upstate	58%	42%

SOURCE: Institute of American Research;
NBC News.

black candidates. But Italians who are less pressured look more favorably on black candidacies.

In 1966, Edward W. Brooke, a black Republican with a white, Italian wife, was elected to the United States Senate from Massachusetts. Thus, Massachusetts became the first state to send a black to the Senate since Reconstruction, even though only 3 percent of its population is black. Part of the reason Brooke won was that he cut into the normally Democratic Italian senatorial vote. He captured three out of seven votes in Italian neighborhoods, not a majority, but enough so that his opponent Endicott Peabody ran less well with Italian voters than any other Democratic Senate candidate in the sixties. Brooke's Italian vote was down a few points in Boston's North End, but that can be explained as much by the North End's strong Democratic heritage as by any antiblack sentiments. And Brooke's vote rose slightly in Italian precincts of the smaller industrial cities outside Boston.

Some will say that the Italian vote for Brooke was a fluke, that it came on the coattails of his fellow Republican John Volpe, who ran 20 and 30 points better in the same precincts on the same day. But the truth of the matter is that Brooke was well known as a black man, and still more Italians voted for him than for Richard Nixon both in 1960 and in 1968. Brooke's 40-plus percent of the Italian vote is one of the best recent showings by *any* Republican senatorial candidate anywhere, black or white. Brooke himself explained his strong vote among whites as the "Captain-of-the-ship phenomenon." He said white voters would be hostile to having a black in an executive office like governor, but in the Senate, he wryly added, ninety-nine colleagues would keep him in his place.

Italians are strongly antiblack in the abstract, and like everyone else, their racism has a high symbolic content. Political circumstances apparently determine whether this carries over in antiblack voting. A poll taken in 1968 shows that Italians are just as willing as the next guy to support government programs to help blacks achieve social and economic equality. But when black actions and demands run contrary to deeply felt Italian interests, the Italian-American will protect those interests, and the result is often an antiblack vote.

ITALIANS AND ITALIANS: OR THE IMPORTANCE
OF A FINAL VOWEL

Political rewards have been slow in coming to America's Italians in recent years. The first Italian member of the Cabinet wasn't appointed until 1962, when John Kennedy named Anthony Celebrese to be Secretary of Health, Education and Welfare. Rhode Island, one of the most Italian states in the nation, didn't send an Italian to the United States Senate until 1950, when John Pastore was elected, and Pastore was the first Italian-American ever to serve in the Senate. As Joseph Carlino, a former Speaker of the New York Assembly puts it, "For most Italian-Americans it's a big thing to get elected to some office, like the state legislature. A young, attractive Italian-American thinks he's reached the millennium when he becomes an assemblyman. And what does he want next? What does he dream of? A judgeship!"

Therefore, when an Italian politician tries for a major office, it may be an important event in the Italian community. The political career of John Volpe in Massachusetts is a good example. When Volpe ran for governor in 1960, Democratic Italians of Massachusetts were proud that one of their own was running, even as a Republican. In that Presidential year more than 85 percent of Italians in Massachusetts voted for Democrat John Kennedy, but more than 50 percent crossed over to the Republican line for Volpe. In 1962, Volpe ran for a second term and lost by 5,000 votes to Endicott Peabody, a very proper Bostonian. Italian turnout was down in the off year, and Volpe's share of the Italian vote dropped proportionately. If Volpe had run as well with the Italians in 1962 as he did in 1960, he would have edged Peabody. Volpe tried again in 1964, with the Democrats themselves nominating an Italian named Francis Bellotti. Volpe won by 23,000 votes, but his share of the Italian vote fell to its lowest point—one third. In 1964, given a choice between a Republican Italian and a Democratic one, Italian voters found Democratic party loyalties stronger than their admiration for Volpe.

The Governor ran once more in 1966, and with House Speaker John McCormack's nephew Edward as his opponent, he won by more than 525,000 votes, a record for the postwar years. Volpe's showing in Italian precincts also set a record as he won nearly two out of every three votes. To be sure, part of this phenomenal vote came because of anti-Irish sentiments among Massachusetts Italians.[13] But Volpe's Italian support was more than an "anti" vote, it was a reaffirmation of old-style ethnic politics.

CHART 6: ITALIAN VOTERS
MASSACHUSETTS GOVERNOR 1960–1966

1960	Volpe	54%	Ward	46%
1962	Volpe	51%	Peabody	49%
1964	Volpe	33%	Bellotti	67%
1966	Volpe	66%	McCormack	34%

SOURCE: Institute of American Research; NBC News.

13 This historic tension lingers on even today in Massachusetts. In the 1970 election for governor, Republican incumbent Francis W. Sargent, a Protestant Republican, handily defeated Democrat Kevin H. White, the Irish mayor of Boston. Among Massachusetts' Italians, Sargent won 49 percent of the vote. White took a dismal 51 percent. In some Boston precincts the vote ran two to one for Sargent. Even in White's best precincts—the Italian neighborhoods of Everett and Lawrence—he barely managed to win more than 55 percent of the vote. Given the choice between a liberal Irish Democrat and a somewhat-less-than-liberal Protestant Republican, the Italians voted against their traditional ethnic rival. At least one source, the Boston Italian newspaper *Post Gazette*, attributed the Sargent victory statewide to Italian support. The paper also appeared to gloat over White's dismal showing in Boston. The Mayor lost his own city by 17,000 votes, while his fellow Democrat Senator Edward Kennedy (always an exception) carried Boston by a 70,000-vote margin.

Remarkable as it may seem, Mario Procaccino—perhaps the most visible Italian of 1969—was almost sidetracked early in his political career because he couldn't carry the Italian vote. In New York City, it is no novelty to find an Italian running for a major office, so it often takes more than an Italian name to win Italian votes. New Yorkers have already had two Italian-American mayors, LaGuardia and Impelliteri, and it is not uncommon for Italians to hold important city jobs. In the 1965 Democratic primary for City Comptroller, Procaccino, then a relatively unknown judge from the Bronx, ran against three others, including Orin Lehman, nephew of the famous Senator and Governor Herbert H. Lehman.

Procaccino, who was born in Bisaccia, Italy, just barely won the nomination. Part of his problem was losing the Italian vote to the Jewish candidate Lehman with Italian voters accounting for approximately one sixth of the primary vote. In Italian neighborhoods, Paul Screvane (who headed the slate Lehman ran on) won almost 60 percent of the vote, and Lehman, who was not far behind with 50 percent, came out of the Italian precincts with a 7,000-vote lead over Procaccino. Perhaps it was Screvane's coattails that pulled Lehman through,[14] and those coattails may have been strengthened by Screvane's Italian contacts. Ironically it was only Procaccino's strong showing in Jewish precincts that gave him the nomination. (He went on to win the general election.)

By 1969, Procaccino was already a serious contender for the Democratic nomination for mayor. He seemed to express the outrage of many of New York's blue-collar workers—Italians and non-Italians. He spoke of the good family people who were trapped in changing neighborhoods, whose two-job incomes were being pinched by inflation, and who bitterly resented blacks and Puerto Ricans who seemed to be getting all the breaks. In the mayoral primary, Procaccino had four opponents, but there was no problem now with the Italian vote, and he managed to capture

[14] In the same primary, Screvane's Italian coattails also helped his candidate for City Council, an Irish Catholic named Daniel P. Moynihan. Moynihan carried the Italian precincts by 9 percent over his nearest rival, Frank D. O'Connor, also Irish Catholic.

more than three quarters of those ballots. Former Mayor Robert Wagner, who had been the early favorite, was second, but won only slightly more than one out of ten Italian votes. Curiously, Herman Badillo, the first Puerto Rican to run for mayor, did almost as well as Wagner with Italians, perhaps because they thought he was one of their own. Procaccino carried Italian neighborhoods by more than 45,000 votes, while beating Wagner citywide by only 31,000. For Procaccino, Italians supplied the vital margin.

Italians played an even more striking role in the 1969 New York Republican primaries. In the mayoral primary, incumbent John Lindsay was challenged in his own party's contest by John Marchi, a conservative state senator from Staten Island. Marchi campaigned hard against Lindsay's liberal approach to government. He appealed to the small homeowners outside Manhattan who were turned off by "Fun City" and by the Mayor's concern for blacks and Puerto Ricans. Marchi was endorsed by the official Republican organizations in Staten Island and the Bronx, and he had considerable grass-roots support in Queens and Brooklyn. Lindsay countered by charging that Marchi was a hopeless reactionary who could not win in November. But Lindsay knew he was more liberal than most city Republicans and he trimmed his sails accordingly. He tried to convince Republican voters in general, and Italians in particular, that he too cared about crime in the streets and the little man. It didn't work, and Lindsay lost the Republican nomination.

A major factor in Lindsay's defeat was the Italian voter. In Italian precincts, Marchi, whose ancestors lived in Lucca in northern Italy, outpolled Lindsay by three to one.[15] The strongest votes against Lindsay—ten and twelve to one—came in the Republican-leaning Italian neighborhoods in Bay Ridge and Bensonhurst. Lindsay ran best in Italian areas of Manhattan and the Bronx. But even in these relatively pro-Lindsay precincts, the

[15] Almost all of New York's Italians come from three impoverished provinces of southern Italy: Calabria, Apulia, and Sicily. We have already mentioned the antagonism between northern and southern Italians, but in this primary, at least, southern Italians seemed quite willing to support Marchi.

Mayor did not even come close to winning a majority. In all, Italian voters gave Marchi a 30,000-vote plurality over Lindsay, and he won the nomination by only 8,000 votes. (Of course, Lindsay was still in the general election picture, since he already had the Liberal party's nomination.)

In the Republican primary for Comptroller, Italians had the luxury of choosing between two of their own. A handsome bachelor named Fioravante G. Perrotta, the City Finance Administrator, convinced Lindsay strategists he would add strength with Italian voters (who constituted about one quarter of the Republican primary vote) and won a spot on the Lindsay ticket.[16] Perrotta was opposed by Vito Battista, another Italian and a colorful conservative state senator from a changing neighborhood in Brooklyn. Battista was widely known, since he had been running for mayor before Marchi induced him to join his ticket with Marchi at the top.

How much Perrotta, who ran very much in the Mayor's shadow, helped Lindsay among Italian voters is difficult to determine. Certainly Lindsay could not have run much worse in Bay Ridge whoever his ticket-mates might have been. But Perrotta certainly helped himself among Italians. By winning nearly 40 percent of the Italian vote, Perrotta cut his plurality loss among Italians to 10,000 votes, enough to win a narrow victory citywide over Battista.

In the general election, Lindsay had the advantage of running against two Italians at once, an advantage he had sought in the Republican primary, but had been denied when Battista joined the Marchi ticket. Having to write off the Italian vote must have been painful for Lindsay—and a rude awakening. In 1965, he had carried the Italian vote with the then highest-ever Republican percentage of the Italian electorate (43 percent). In the 1969 general election, both Democrat Procaccino and Republican

[16] In 1968, Perrotta had been named City Finance Administrator by Lindsay. At a news conference to introduce the new appointee, Mario Procaccino, who was then City Comptroller, said he was pleased that Lindsay had finally appointed someone whose name ended in a vowel. Perrotta replied, "Mr. Procaccino, *both* my names end in a vowel." In the general election, though, Perrotta preferred to be called Fred.

Marchi campaigned strongly on the themes of crime and disorder. Procaccino charged that Lindsay handcuffed the police, put "known criminals" on the city payroll and fomented divisions between the city's ethnic groups. Marchi echoed Procaccino's attacks in his own low-key, sardonic fashion. Italian voters had little trouble deciding whom they did not wish to vote for, but their indecision between the two Italian candidates helped Lindsay to his 100,000-vote reelection plurality. Procaccino won more than four out of seven Italian votes. Marchi took two out of seven, and Lindsay polled only one seventh of the vote in Italian precincts. New York's Italian voters gave Procaccino more than an 180,000-vote plurality over Lindsay. Had Marchi not been on the ballot, Procaccino certainly would have run considerably stronger. In a head-to-head contest with Lindsay, Procaccino could have won an ethnic bonus of more than a quarter million Italian votes, which would have gone a long way toward improving the credibility of his challenge to Lindsay.

ITALIANS AND JEWS

During that ill-fated Italian "Unity Day" rally in Columbus Circle, Rabbi Meir Kahane of the Jewish Defense League spoke to the crowd about the alliance between the J.D.L. and the Italian-American Civil Rights League. Rabbi Kahane said that he was proud that the J.D.L. was associated with the Italian organization because both were fighting for the same goals. One woman wearing a red-white-and-green "Italian Power" button turned to her companion and said loudly, "Just what we need, a Jewish Italian." There may not have been any hostility in her remark, but sociologists *have* reported some disturbing evidence about Italian attitudes toward Jews. Father Greeley asked a sample of white Catholics to say how strongly they agreed or disagreed with questions like "Do Jews have too much power in the United States?" and "Are Jewish businessmen about as honest as other businessmen?" He rated their responses and found that more than three out of seven Italian-Americans scored high on an anti-Semitism index. More than half the Italians who did not graduate from high school were highly anti-Semitic, while among Italian high-school graduates only one third were strongly prejudiced against Jews.

And the influence of these attitudes on the way Italians vote? In Pennsylvania, the present governor, Milton Shapp, a Jewish self-made millionaire, has run twice. In 1966, as the first Jewish gubernatorial candidate in the state's history, he lost to Raymond P. Shafer, the hand-picked successor of the popular Governor William W. Scranton. In 1970 Shapp ran again and beat Raymond J. Broderick, Shafer's lieutenant governor and an Irish Catholic. In 1966, Shapp won 58 percent of the vote in Italian precincts, and in 1970 52 percent, not a very impressive share for a Democrat. Or is it? Hubert Humphrey won only 57 percent of Italian votes and in the entire decade no Democratic candidate for governor or senator in Pennsylvania ever won more than 65 percent of the Italian vote. So, by Pennsylvania standards at least, Shapp did just about as well as could be expected.

Illinois conforms to the Pennsylvania example. We've already seen how strongly Democratic Illinois Italians are. In 1968, Samuel H. Shapiro, an Estonian-born Jew, ran for a full four-year term,[17] with the full blessings of Mayor Daley and campaigned for a statewide open housing law. Shapiro lost to Republican Richard Ogilvie, a former Cook County sheriff, who ran a hard-nosed conservative campaign. Italian voters who might have been attracted to Ogilvie's conservatism and who might have found it hard to vote for a liberal Jewish Democrat, gave Shapiro better than four out of every five votes. In fact, Shapiro did better with Italians than either Hubert Humphrey or John Kennedy.

Howard Metzenbaum's 1970 senatorial race in Ohio reveals a different inclination among Italians. Metzenbaum, a wealthy businessman, lawyer and publisher, beat Astronaut John Glenn with an expensive media-blitzing primary campaign. In the fall he faced the son of "Mr. Republican," Robert A. Taft, Jr. The contrast between Taft and Metzenbaum could not have been sharper. One local newspaper columnist summed it up: "Moder-

[17] He had been lieutenant governor and was briefly governor when Otto Kerner resigned to become a federal judge.

ate vs. Liberal. Classic Republican vs. Classic Democrat. Support
for Nixon vs. Disdain for Nixon. Establishment Background vs.
Nouveau Riche . . . Episcopalian vs. Jew." In its 167 years of
statehood, Ohio has elected only one Jew to statewide office.
True to form, Metzenbaum lost to Taft, but by only 70,000 votes.
In Italian precincts of Cleveland and Youngstown, Metzenbaum
barely edged Taft, winning a fraction over half the Italian vote.
But on the same day, Democrat John Gilligan, an Irish Catholic
who was just as liberal as Metzenbaum, won two thirds of the
vote in the same precincts. If Metzenbaum had run as well as
Gilligan—and two thirds of the Italian vote is low for most Democratic senatorial candidates in Ohio—he would have wiped out
Taft's statewide plurality. Admittedly it is very difficult to know
whether Ohio's Italians were repelled by Metzenbaum because
he was a Jew, whether they voted against him because of his
personal style, or whether Italian voters simply knew Taft better.
It is clear, however, that Ohio's Italians felt perfectly comfortable
voting for Gilligan, an aloof and sometimes pompous liberal, and
couldn't support an equally liberal candidate who was Jewish.

The 1970 New York gubernatorial election offers one more
example of just how hard it can be for a liberal Jewish candidate
to run well with Italian voters. Arthur Goldberg, whose impressive record in public office seemed to make him a perfect candidate, lost to Nelson Rockefeller by almost three quarters of a
million votes. It was Rockefeller's greatest victory in four elections and the largest plurality for any Republican gubernatorial
candidate in New York's postwar history. Rockefeller's victory
margin came from many sources, but his most dramatic showing
came among New York's Italian voters. In 1962, the Governor
managed three sevenths of the vote in Italian districts against
Robert Morgenthau, who like Goldberg was a Jew with a fine
record of public service. Against Frank O'Connor in 1966, Rockefeller's Italian vote dropped to about one third. But against
Goldberg, Rockefeller's vote in Italian precincts reached an all-
time high. He won a clear majority, more than five out of every
eight votes. In Italian neighborhoods of Brooklyn, he won better
than 80 percent of the vote, and even in the Italian Democratic
strongholds upstate Rockefeller nearly won majorities.

CHART 7:   ITALIAN VOTERS
NEW YORK GOVERNOR 1962–1970

1962		1966		1970	
Rockefeller	42%	Rockefeller	34%	Rockefeller	65%
Morgenthau	58%	O'Connor	50%	Goldberg	33%
		Roosevelt	5%	Adams	2%
		Adams	11%		

SOURCE: Institute of American Research; NBC News.

It would be unfair to state that Italians boycotted Goldberg simply because he was Jewish. At times during the campaign it appeared that Goldberg was deliberately trying to snub the 13 percent of the electorate which is Italian. He rarely went into Italian neighborhoods and once, while speaking to an Italian audience, reprimanded them in his most judicial manner for demanding that they receive special treatment as an ethnic bloc. Rockefeller, on the other hand, went out of his way to appeal to Italian voters. He ate pizza, accepted an honorary membership in the Italian-American Civil Rights League, and was endorsed by every important Italian politician in New York, including Mario Procaccino.[18] Goldberg should have done far better with Italian voters, half of whom are registered Democrats, according to a *New York Times* survey. He didn't—in part, because of the way he campaigned; and in part, because of Rockefeller's extraordinary campaign. Goldberg didn't know how to handle the interrelated issues of law and order and social unrest, and that hurt him also. His was a decidedly inept campaign.

ITALIANS, REPUBLICANS AND THE "NIXON COALITION"

Even those Republicans who do well with the Italian vote, lose it; and more often than not these creditable performances come from candidates identified with the liberal wing of the G.O.P.

[18] Procaccino was still smarting from Goldberg's endorsement of Lindsay in the 1969 New York mayoral election. Procaccino once said, "Goldberg just didn't want to see an Italian become mayor of New York."

In 1962, New York's liberal Jewish Republican Jacob Javits beat Democrat James Donovan by almost one million votes. Javits did not carry the state's Italian precincts; they went sixty-forty for Donovan. Even so, Javits won more Italian votes on the G.O.P. line than any other Republican candidate from 1958 through 1970.[19]

In the Pennsylvania senatorial election of 1968, local experts expected incumbent Democrat Joseph Clark to lose badly in Italian precincts. Clark, a liberal, patrician reformer, had been roughed up in the primary by an Italian-American Congressman, John Dent. During the primary Dent had accused Clark of making intemperate remarks about a state court justice, Michael Musmanno, a popular Italian figure. Although losing in November, Clark carried many Italian neighborhoods and won five out of every nine Italian votes. His Republican opponent, Richard S. Schweiker, a liberal Congressman from suburban Philadelphia, took 40-plus percent of the Italian vote, no better and no worse than Republican senatorial candidates were accustomed to winning from Pennsylvania's Italian electorate.

Another Republican politician who proves it is possible to be liberal and still win Italian votes is New Jersey's scholarly senior Senator, Clifford P. Case. New Jersey is very much a swing state and Republicans often win statewide office there. The Italian homeowners of Passaic, Essex and Bergen counties make up the backbone of New Jersey's Republican party. In 1960, while Richard Nixon was winning only three out of ten Italian votes in New Jersey, Case outpolled him by at least five points per precinct. Case's most impressive Italian vote came in 1966, when he was opposed by Warren Wilentz, the politically naïve son of a Jewish Democratic boss. Statewide, Case came close to beating Wilentz among Italians, and in the Italian communities of North Bergen, Paterson and Fairview, Case won clear majorities.

In contrast, one liberal Republican who proved how difficult it

---

[19] Javits' vote in Italian precincts dropped slightly in 1968, despite his landslide victory over Democrat Paul O'Dwyer and Conservative party candidate James Buckley. Most of Javits' Italian loss went to Buckley, who won one quarter of the votes cast in Italian precincts. O'Dwyer won 39 percent of the Italian vote.

can be to win Italian votes is Senator Charles E. Goodell of New York. In the 1970 election, Goodell, an outspoken critic of the Indochina war, won only one out of five votes in Italian precincts. It was the worst Italian showing of any Republican candidate for any major New York office during the entire decade. Goodell's Italian vote was even 10 points lower than Goldwater's remarkably poor performance in 1964. The candidate who benefited most directly from Goodell's misfortune was Conservative James Buckley, a fervid supporter of the Nixon administration. Forty-two percent of New York's Italians voted for Buckley, twice Goodell's showing, and a handful more than his liberal Democratic opponent, Richard Ottinger. In the Bay Ridge and Benson-hurst sections of Brooklyn and in the Corona neighborhood of Queens, Buckley won clear majorities. Ottinger's Italian vote in this three-way race was reduced to the hard-core Democrats, the same people who voted for Hubert Humphrey and Paul O'Dwyer. Because Buckley and Ottinger ran even among Italian voters, neither candidate gained a plurality advantage. Had Ottinger run as well with New York's Italian voters as even James Donovan in his poor showing of 1962, he would have erased 90,000 votes from Buckley's winning plurality of 117,000.

A little help from the White House is often a boon to a state-wide candidacy. The 1969 New Jersey gubernatorial race is a case in point. William T. Cahill, a thoroughly unexciting Republican Congressman from Camden, beat a tired old Democratic warhorse, former Governor Robert Meyner. Cahill thereby became the first Republican governor of New Jersey in sixteen years. During the campaign, he stressed his close ties to Washington, and President Nixon made two campaign appearances in his behalf. This "intervention" apparently paid off. New Jersey Italians had been trending Republican for a decade, but no Republican candidate, not even Nixon or Case, had been able to win a statewide Italian majority. In 1969 the Italians finally made the break, giving Cahill 57 percent of their votes. In some Italian districts in Newark, Cahill's vote reached two thirds.

Despite Cahill's inroads with Italian voters, the Republican Italian majority in New Jersey was short-lived. Nelson Gross, who ran on the G.O.P. ticket for senator in 1970, did not run well against the liberal Democratic incumbent, Harrison Williams. Whatever else it may have done, a Presidential campaign visit did not help Gross with Italians; he garnered only three out of every ten of their votes. Gross won one third fewer Italian ballots than Richard Nixon picked up in 1968. New Jersey's blue-collar Italians seemed more interested in Senator Williams' important position on the Senate Labor Committee than in Nelson Gross's friend in the White House.

Are Italians becoming Republicans? Will they form an important part of the emerging Republican majority? Has the black revolution driven Italian voters from the Democratic party forever?

Today, the Italian vote is in a state of flux, and there are many routes to winning that vote. But Italian-Americans remain very much blue-collar workers, and that in itself will keep them thinking like Democrats. On the state level, Italian voters are not giving Republican candidates consistent majorities, let alone the bloc support that would allow them to be called Republicans. And in Presidential politics, Italian voters have come full circle. They vote just about as Republican now as they did in the Eisenhower elections, but they still do not give the G.O.P. majority support. Fundamentally, Italian-Americans are still Democrats.

Italians are beginning to recognize the political muscle inherent in the elections just reviewed. They are openly following the black lead, organizing unabashedly through whatever vehicle is most readily available, regardless of the efforts of "outsiders" to taint those organizations, and generally preparing to emerge not as Republicans, and perhaps not even as Democrats, but surely as a cohesive ethnic political force, a force no politician will be able to ignore safely.

In a beautiful song about a WASP woman (Mrs. Robinson), Paul Simon wonders what became of an ethnic (Joe DiMaggio). For those who want to know, and don't, the Yankee Clipper is a successful San Francisco restaurateur. But there is another answer. The song asks where have all the heroes gone—in politics as well as in baseball, where are those American symbols of group identity? Italian-Americans, like other ethnics, are finding those symbols in their own heritage and are redefining American politics in the process.

8

The Ethnics and Winning the Presidency

Analyzing election trends is more often a pastime of political scientists than of politicians. The latter are concerned with only one question, and for many reasons it is the only relevant one— what does it all mean for the upcoming election? Summarizing any political analysis to highlight implications for future electoral contests is of necessity a patchwork of predictions and accompanying qualifications. And our most certain prediction is that events will prove some of our predictions wrong. But if only in the spirit of fostering political dialogue, we will predict.

First, we are concerned with the most telling impact each of our six ethnic groups can have on the 1972 Presidential race; second, we view the states which will be the ethnic battlegrounds of the 1972 election and the prospects for the various candidates therein; and third, we offer some observations regarding an issue with which a candidate might reach across individual groups to build a winning coalition. We assume a familiarity with the group analyses presented in earlier chapters.

A Serious Independent Black Presidential Candidacy Will Insure Democratic Defeat

A medallion of Machiavelli—the authors' highest political award—will undoubtedly go to that Republican who makes the first substantial cash contribution to an independent black Presidential candidate. For there is no better way to insure Republican victory in 1972 than to place a highly visible independent black candidate on the ballot.

Such an independent black Presidential candidacy is by no means unlikely. (Even if a black candidacy is not launched in 1972, the threat of such a candidacy will remain a bargaining tool through the decade.) The groundwork has been laid through a series of meetings of key black elected officials. Several visible black leaders have publicly expressed interest in such a bid— Congressman William Clay of Missouri and Congresswoman Shirley Chisholm of Brooklyn among them. The experience of independent black candidacies in the South, in gubernatorial and senatorial elections, has been encouraging. Skilled black field forces exist in many states and the proper combination of money and charm can mold those forces into the beginnings of a regional machine.

Money is apparently not a problem. Whatever support is needed beyond that offered by the quickly growing and increasingly proud black upper class will probably be funneled through Republican contributors doing their best to remain anonymous. But black financial support should be substantial in its own right. Black money as displayed at an event like the Muhammad Ali–Joe Frazier prizefight can afford to finance more than a few posters in black (and white) neighborhoods.

That the blacks would be willing to break with the Democratic party should not come as a great surprise. What better warning to the American political structure of black political clout than desertion of the Democratic party's nominee in a campaign likely to be closely contested?

A scenario for black political separatism is not difficult to construct. First, all-black delegations fight for seating privileges at the 1972 Democratic convention at the expense of white delegates, mostly from the South. In an attempt to prevent an imminent Wallace or black walkout, the convention at large compromises the issue, leaving both groups unhappy.

Whatever the outcome of the seating and credentials challenges, blacks, or white liberals on their behalf, will come to the convention floor with their "demands": among them a $6,400 annual income (perhaps by that time with a cost-of-living escalator), an end to political trials, and a "something" that legitimizes radical black political action. The convention will probably be faced with the unhappy choice of catering to black demands or risking a black walkout from the convention. Of course, the Democrats will be spared this particularly thorny dilemma should blacks elect to nominate their own candidate in advance of the major party gatherings.

If an independent black Presidential candidate can carry between 20 and 30 percent of the black vote, it will be virtually impossible for the Democratic nominee (whoever he might be) to carry nineteen states representing 285 electoral votes. These nineteen—all states in which black voters play a key role—account for more than half the nation's 538 electoral votes. Thus even if the Democratic nominee could win all thirty-one remaining states (among them the staunchly Republican bastions of the Midwest), he would fall short of an electoral majority. Of course a strong Wallace candidacy leaves open the possibility of an electoral stalemate and ensuing Democratic victory in the House of Representatives, regardless of the popular vote.[1]

An independent black candidacy will depress the Democratic vote below its already depressed levels in the Deep South. In 1968 Hubert Humphrey won roughly one quarter of the votes cast in Alabama, Arkansas, Georgia, Louisiana, Mississippi and South Carolina. A substantial majority of the Humphrey vote came from black voters. An independent black candidate who polls 20 percent of the black vote will likely force the Democratic portion below 25 percent in each of the six states.

Of course these six Deep South states do not necessarily represent an electoral-vote loss to the Democrats. In 1968, George Wallace carried all but South Carolina, which was preserved for Nixon by Strom Thurmond. All but Arkansas voted for Goldwater over Johnson in 1964. A black candidacy simply assures

[1] When voting for President in the House, each state has one vote. The Democrats currently control more state Congressional delegations and, assuming party solidarity, would be able to elect the Democratic nominee. John Quincy Adams was thus elected President in 1824 when neither he nor either of his opponents, Henry Clay and Andrew Jackson, received a majority in the Electoral College.

CHART 1: STATES WITH SIGNIFICANT BLACK ELECTORATES
IN WHICH DEMOCRATIC VICTORY BECOMES IMPOSSIBLE IN THE
EVENT OF AN INDEPENDENT BLACK PRESIDENTIAL CANDIDACY

	Electoral Vote 1972	Democratic % 1968	Nixon plurality over Democrat 1968 %	Blacks as % of electorate
Alabama	9	18.7	*	21
Arkansas	6	30.4	*	14
Florida	17	30.9	9.6	12
Georgia	12	26.8	*	20
Louisiana	10	28.2	*	24
Mississippi	7	23.0	*	25
North Carolina	13	29.2	10.3	16
Tennessee	10	28.1	9.7	12
Virginia	12	32.5	10.9	13

* Carried by Wallace in 1968.
Note: The average vote for Humphrey among blacks in these nine states was 94.5 percent.
SOURCE: Institute of American Research; NBC News.

that the Democrats will be many years returning to the 1960 performance of John Kennedy, when all six Deep South states voted Democratic.

Further, an independent black candidacy will disintegrate Democratic chances to recapture Arkansas, Georgia and South Carolina, where new-breed Democratic governors (all elected in 1970) have attempted with some success to build black-and-white coalitions. Given the substantial strides in black registration and turnout, a Democrat with united black support should come very close to defeating Wallace in those three states. However, in Alabama and Mississippi, the 1968 total major-party vote hovered at little more than one third of the total votes cast. The Democratic nominee, and even his G.O.P. opponent assuming a conservative, Wallace-type candidacy, seems quite dead there, with or without black competition.

Losses of potential in the Deep South become critical losses of base Democratic support outside the South, in the event of an independent black Presidential candidacy. In both 1960 and 1968, the Democrat carried Texas by the narrowest of margins. Black defections as seemingly insignificant as 20 percent in the absence of an upsurge of Chicano voting will push Texas and its

26 electoral votes into the Republican column in 1972. Any chance the Democrat had of reclaiming the always hotly contested states of Kentucky and Missouri evaporates as well with an independent black candidacy.

CHART 2: POTENTIAL DEMOCRATIC GAINS MADE
NEARLY IMPOSSIBLE BY INDEPENDENT BLACK PRESIDENTIAL
CANDIDACY

	Electoral Vote 1972	Democratic % 1968	Nixon plurality over Democrat 1968 %	Blacks as % of electorate
California	45	44.7	3.1	4
Illinois	26	44.2	2.9	9
Kentucky	9	37.6	6.2	7
Missouri	12	43.7	1.2	9
New Jersey	17	44.0	2.1	7
Ohio	25	42.9	2.3	5
Wisconsin	11	44.3	3.6	4

Note: The average vote for Humphrey among blacks in these seven states was 91.4 percent.
SOURCE: Institute of American Research; NBC News.

CHART 3: LIKELY DEMOCRATIC LOSSES IF
INDEPENDENT BLACK CANDIDACY MATERIALIZES

	Electoral vote 1972	Democratic % 1968	Humphrey plurality over Nixon 1968	Blacks as % of electorate
Maryland	10	43.6	1.7	11
Texas	26	41.1	1.2	9

Note: The average vote for Humphrey among blacks in these two states was 95.5 percent.
SOURCE: Institute of American Research; NBC News.

Curiously, in three states an independent black candidacy may help the Democrat albeit at the expense of electoral stability for the country. One likely effect of an independent black candidacy is that the Democratic nominee will be forced to make open appeals for black support throughout the South. This in turn will simplify Wallace's task of appealing to the fears of white Southern voters. One result may be Wallace victories in Florida, North Carolina and Tennessee, states he nearly carried in 1968. Had

Wallace carried these three states in that year, the election would have been thrown into the House of Representatives. All of this suggests that an independent black candidacy may encourage the Democratic nominee to maximize the Wallace vote in the Border States. This strategy would deprive Nixon of the electoral votes needed to win an outright victory.

In five non-Southern states, an independent black candidacy would solidify Nixon's narrow 1968 margins, and in two states would offer Nixon an opportunity to gain ground over 1968. For a Democrat to win in 1972, one of his prime targets must be states with reasonably large electoral votes which were carried narrowly by Nixon in 1968. These states include California, Illinois, New Jersey, Ohio and Wisconsin, where in 1968 Nixon won, on average, less than 48 percent of the vote and scored a plurality of no more than three percentage points. At stake in these five states are 124 electoral votes in 1972. An independent black candidacy is likely to give Nixon an extra 3 percentage points in California and New Jersey, and an extra one percentage point in Ohio and Wisconsin. These are the kinds of advantages successful competition does not give to an incumbent President.

An independent black candidate could pick up electoral votes for Nixon in Maryland and Pennsylvania. Humphrey's 2-percentage-point margin in Maryland can easily be overcome by black defections. Humphrey's Pennsylvania margin of just less than 4 percentage points is safer in the face of a 7 percent black electorate, but by no means secure.

Although the dimensions of their potential importance may be unknown to them at this moment, black voters are in an enviable position for 1972. The Democratic nominee cannot expect to win without the black vote, so he must attempt to stop any movement for an independent black candidacy. Yet the Democratic nominee cannot expect to win if he is forced to focus his campaign on black voters. The American electorate generally and the Democratic electorate as well, is overwhelmingly white and sensitive to racially based appeals. The black voter is clearly in a position to make life very miserable for the 1972 Democratic nominee. And the black voter may be so inclined. On the other hand the black leadership's opportunity to extract promises and commitments from the Democrats has never been better. The Democrats smell victory, and the blacks, if they wish, can stand in the way.

MEXICAN-AMERICANS CAN DETERMINE
THE OUTCOME IN CALIFORNIA AND TEXAS

The Chicano voter is trying hard to make himself irrelevant to the 1972 campaign. Nothing breeds political inattentiveness better than declining registration totals. The Chicanos seem bent on disappearing from the voter rolls altogether in every state except Texas. However, in their unregistered numbers, the Chicanos present real opportunities to the major political parties. The ultimate winner of California's 45 electoral votes, or Texas' 26, can be determined by which major political party is able to capitalize on this Chicano opportunity.

New Chicano votes can neutralize the effect of an independent black candidacy in Texas, and possibly save the state for the Democrats. Texas Chicanos are the best registered in the nation, just as Texas blacks were among the first of their group to flex their political muscles. Yet there is substantial room for improvement in registration. Texas and Illinois illustrate the problem. In 1972 they will have identical electoral vote totals of 26, but dramatically different total votes—4.6 million people voted in Illinois in 1968, while only 3.1 million voted in Texas. Texas turnout increased during the 1960s—from 42 percent of eligibles voting in 1960 to nearly 50 percent voting in 1968. Nevertheless, Texas fell far short of the 1968 national average of 62 percent. Much of the Texas underregistration is a reflection of large black and Mexican-American populations.

Even where Chicano registration is relatively good, it is bad. Thus in Texas, where Chicano registration is high (when compared with Chicano registration in other states), the total registration picture is rather dismal. Chicanos outnumber blacks in Texas by more than three to two. This gives Chicanos the leverage to deflate any independent black political movement. In fact, our data suggest that given the undifferentiated Democratic propensities of Texas Chicanos, each 10-percentage-point gain in Chicano registration will offset an 18-percentage-point showing by an independent black Presidential candidate. Since the Democrats and their union supporters may find it easier to register Chicanos on their home turf than to steal the constituency of a national black candidacy, the political message for Texas Democrats seems clear: the only good bet against an independent black candidacy is a serious Chicano registration drive.

Several recent developments greatly enhance the prospects for success of a Chicano voter drive. The eighteen-year-old vote brings eligibility to proportionately larger numbers of Chicanos than Anglos. The relaxation of residency requirements simplifies many of the logistical complications of a voter drive and increases the likelihood that some groups of farm laborers can be registered. And the ban on literacy tests both eases any Mexican-American fear of voting registrars and greatly reduces rejection rates for those Mexican-Americans who do appear to enroll.

While in Texas the Mexican-American voter drive would basically be a holding action by Democrats determined to maintain the narrow victory margins of 1960 and 1968, a California surge in Mexican-American turnout could put 45 electoral votes into the Democratic column. Chicano voting totals have been cooling steadily in California since 1960, and the participation level of that year was still substantially below that of California's other voter groups. Also, California's Mexican-Americans have been less unified in their support of Democratic candidacies than their brethren in Texas.

The combination of declining Mexican-American registration and mild Republican inroads suggests that opportunities in California lie in both party camps. A selective Republican drive, targeted at maximizing Mexican-American affiliation with the Republicans, can greatly dilute the impact of any large-scale Democratic drive. Even if Republicans can attract only three out of every ten new Chicano registrants, the Republican leverage will be impressive. (Ronald Reagan has won two in ten Chicano votes statewide.) For if three of every ten new registrants are Republican, only four new Democratic votes are produced for every ten Mexican-Americans registered (seven Democrats minus three Republicans equals four net Democratic votes). In Texas, where Democratic proportions are often well above 90 percent, ten new registrants could produce at least eight Democratic votes. Thus, if the Republicans do their job in California, the Democrats will have to register double the number of Chicanos they would have to register in Texas to produce the same gain in Democratic votes. By making the job of the Democrats twice as hard as it otherwise would be, the Republicans may just save their 3-percentage-point margin in the California vote. The argument for Democratic registration of Chicanos in Texas is overwhelming. The same is true for the Republicans in California. But Democratic Chicano registration in California must be balanced against the campaign's resources.

With or without increased registration, Chicano voters are unlikely to influence the outcome in Arizona, Colorado and New Mexico. The traditional Republican Presidential pluralities are large enough, and the Mexican-American population small enough, to insure Republican victories in these states unless there is a dramatic and largely unexpected shift in the Anglo vote. The already significant Republican inroads in New Mexico make it likely that voter drives there can solidify the Republican grip, and strengthen G.O.P. chances in local elections.

The Spanish-speaking impact on the nation's second-largest state is hardly as dramatic as the electoral sweepstakes in California, but New York's Puerto Ricans are in a position in 1972 to be a much greater help to the Democratic nominee than they normally are. In 1964, a large-scale New York City voter drive kept Puerto Rican registration from declining below its 1960 levels. Despite a voter drive in 1968, and the citywide candidacy of Herman Badillo in 1969, Puerto Rican registration appears to have declined below 30 percent of eligibles. Humphrey's 5 percent margin in New York is by no means insurmountable, and a Puerto Rican voter drive could net the Democrats six or seven new votes for every ten Puerto Ricans registered.

JEWS—TROUBLE FOR THE DEMOCRATS IF THERE IS A LIBERAL FOURTH PARTY

The most certain element about Jewish voting behavior is the act of voting itself; Jews vote. That vote has been overwhelmingly Democratic in the past three Presidential elections and as a result has helped the Democrat especially in New York (where

an estimated 14 percent of the electorate is Jewish) and somewhat in California (3 percent), Florida (2 percent), Illinois (3
percent), Maryland (4 percent), Massachusetts (5 percent),
Ohio (2 percent) and Pennsylvania (4 percent). It is easy to say
simply that Jews will vote for the Democrat again in 1972 and
leave it at that. However, the same liberal sentiment which
helped Henry Wallace in 1948, and today supports the Liberal
party in New York, makes the Jewish vote a questionable com-
modity in 1972 in the event of a liberal fourth-party candidacy.

Whether George Wallace runs in 1972 will have little effect on
the Jewish vote, except to the extent that appeals to potential
Wallace defectors by either major party turn off Jewish voters. An
independent black candidacy would attract some Jewish support,
but probably a good deal less than many people might think.
Many of the black supporters of independent candidacies have
associated themselves with the Arabs in the Middle East, not a
notably popular view among Jews. Jewish voters have less reason
to vote for "black pride" than do blacks themselves, and Jews will
probably not be anxious to help a Republican carry New York,
the likely outcome of heavy Jewish defections from the Democrat.

A coalition between the independent black candidacy and
disenchanted white liberal Democrats would make a more attractive ticket for Jewish voters than a black ticket alone. However,
it is difficult to see an independently backed black candidate
settling for a Vice-Presidential spot on a white man's ticket, and
harder still to see a major white antiwar figure taking the second
spot on a black ticket. Whatever else Gene McCarthy may be
interested in doing, he is probably not very anxious to become
Shirley Chisholm's running mate.

But Jewish voters are susceptible to an independent Presidential candidacy built on the Democratic left. Such a candidacy by
Henry Wallace helped Republican Thomas Dewey carry New
York in 1948. Of course, Dewey had the advantage of being a
native son—he had been (and was still to be) a popular governor. The absence of that advantage has been quite evident in
the unimpressive voter response to Richard Nixon in New York.
Parties on the left generally recruit more Democrats than Repub-

licans, and thus it is all to the Republicans' advantage to encourage either a splinter Democratic effort or a race built on coalitions "above politics."

In California, Florida, Illinois and Ohio an independent liberal candidacy will draw votes (among them many Jewish votes) from an underdog Democratic nominee. With Jewish voters no more than 3 percent of the electorate in any of these states, the damage that can be done to the Democrat by Jews is somewhat minimized. But the losses, though minimal, can be critical for a Democratic candidate desperately in need of states with large electoral votes currently in the Republican column. The Democrats would do well to avoid, and the Republicans to provide, any potential obstacles in states as crucial as these to the Democratic nominee.

In Maryland and Pennsylvania, Jewish defections from the Democrat could squander already scarce Democratic electoral votes. In 1968, Humphrey carried Maryland by fewer than 2 percentage points, and Pennsylvania by fewer than 4. Since Jews make up 4 percent of the electorate in each state and vote nearly unanimously for the Democrat, any serious defections will cut into already thin Democratic pluralities. In this regard, the role of the two Jewish Democratic governors—Milton Shapp of Pennsylvania and Marvin Mandel of Maryland—can be critical. Their defection from the Democratic standard-bearer could be a death blow to the candidate in their respective states.

Curiously, in the states in which Jews are most numerous, it will take large-scale defections to affect the outcome. In Massachusetts, the Democrat has been winning by an average of 30 percentage points. For the Jewish 5 percent of the Massachusetts electorate to take the state out of the Democratic column, there will have to be a good many companion Irish recruits to an independent candidacy. In New York, nearly 40 percent of all Jews would have to defect to a liberal candidacy before the Democrat would be in serious danger of losing the state. The thought of losing New York's 41 electoral votes will probably be so terrifying for the Democratic nominee, that he will do whatever he can to dissuade an independent candidacy.

THE CASE FOR AN ITALIAN VICE-PRESIDENT

Politicians look to the bloc vote. Nothing warms a candidate's heart like a group whose members are more than 80 percent in support of his candidacy. Then campaign appearances are a pleasure, registration drives a lively interest, and the assemblage of the total number of votes necessary to win a simpler task. The thorn in a candidate's side is a group ambiguous about its feelings. At least an opposition group can either be avoided completely or wooed with the knowledge that there's nothing to lose. A group divided in its feelings will be courted only if there appears to be a way to unite its sentiments. Italians show signs of dividing their Presidential vote between the major parties. The nomination by either party of an Italian for Vice-President can reunify the Italian vote.[2]

Italian switches would affect the outcome in at least four states—Illinois, New Jersey, New York and Pennsylvania—with a total of 111 electoral votes. These states run the gamut of Italian voting behavior. In 1968, Illinois Italians behaved as most of the nation's Italians behaved in 1960, and Hubert Humphrey carried the state's Italians by nearly 58 percentage points with 75 percent of the Italian vote. Pennsylvania showed the more typical Italian erosion as Humphrey won by 23 percentage points (half his Illinois margin) with 57 percent of the Italian vote. New Jersey Italians gave Humphrey a bare 2-percentage-point plurality, and only 42 percent of the Italian vote. And in New York, Nixon carried the Italian vote by 7 percentage points and left Humphrey with 42 percent.

 [2] Every Italian vote won from the opposition is worth two votes in plurality terms. The theory of registration, as applied chiefly to unified groups, is simply to expand the voter pool. Thus 1,000 new registrants (by definition, nonparticipants in the previous campaign) brings the underdog 1,000 votes closer (assuming all vote) to the leader. A campaign to switch votes, if successful, has a much more devastating effect. One thousand new Italian Republican votes (i.e. votes which were formerly Democratic) brings the Republican 2,000 votes closer to the Democrat—the 1,000 votes the Republican gains plus the 1,000 votes the Democrat loses: It is not surprising then that candidates are always trying to spot groups with high switch potential.

The Wallace vote among Italians was volatile as well. Wallace was at or below his statewide average in Illinois and Pennsylvania, yet scored nearly double his statewide average among Italians in New Jersey and New York. All in all, this split-voting pattern spells opportunity for massive Italian switches toward either party in 1972.

CHART 4: ITALIAN VOTING—1968

	Humphrey %	Nixon %	Wallace %	Statewide Voting Plurality %	Italians as % of electorate
Illinois	75	17	8	2.9 R	3
New Jersey	42	40	18	2.1 R	9
New York	42	49	9	5.4 D	9
Pennsylvania	57	34	9	3.6 D	5

SOURCE: *Statistical Abstract* (U.S. Department of Commerce); Institute of American Research; NBC News.

The nomination of an Italian like John Volpe for Vice-President could make the Republican ticket unbeatable in Illinois and New Jersey, and put the Democrat in serious trouble in New York and Pennsylvania. If Volpe can add 30 percent of the Illinois Italian vote to the Republican column, the plurality gain statewide would be better than 2 percent, a comforting addition to the 3 percent plurality of 1968. New Jersey Italians are more numerous than their Illinois brethren, but Italian statewide candidacies are just as scarce. If Volpe can add 25 percent of New Jersey's Italians to the Republican column (or in other words, run only 8 percentage points better with Italians than did William Cahill in 1969), the G.O.P. can count on a full 4-percentage-point addition to their base 1968 plurality of two percentage points.

Should Volpe add 20 percent of Italian New Yorkers to the Republican column over the 1968 showing, the Republican statewide percentage would pick up nearly four percentage points. Volpe would have to push the ticket 4 percent ahead of Nelson Rockefeller's admittedly strong showing in 1970. Success of the Volpe appeal to Italians would greatly enhance Republican opportunities to carry New York. The same is true of Pennsylvania, where a 2 percent Republican statewide gain can be fashioned from a 20-percentage-point switch in the Italian vote.

John Volpe's record in Massachusetts suggests that his appeal to Italian voters is formidable. Italian voters who generally gave less than 20 percent of their votes to Republican Presidential and senatorial candidates gave Volpe a majority of their votes in three of his four gubernatorial races. Volpe's margin fell off only when he faced another Italian in 1964. The attractiveness of a first-time national candidacy of "one of their own" should be substantial for Italian voters.

Should the Democrats nominate a Catholic for President, or an Italian for Vice-President (for example, Senator John O. Pastore of Rhode Island), the impact of a Volpe Vice-Presidential candidacy would be diluted. However, Ed Muskie as a Catholic Vice-Presidential candidate in 1968 apparently did not do much to head off Republican inroads among Italians.[3] Muskie did help hold the Slavs in line. The same could be said for promoting John Pastore for Vice-President. He might hold the Italians in line in Pennsylvania, Illinois and New York, and win enough new Italian votes in New Jersey to swing that key state into the Democratic column. Unfortunately for the Democrats, Italian voters are concentrated in states the Democrat carried in 1968. A result is that the Democrats would be forced to preserve their strength when they would much prefer to increase their electoral vote.

THE SLAVS: MUSKIE AND WALLACE: PRIDE AND PREJUDICE

Slavic voters may not swing many states in 1972, but they are likely to make their voices heard clearly before the campaign is over. Basically, there are two Slavic votes in 1972—one if Ed Muskie is the Democratic nominee, and the other if Muskie is *not* the nominee and George Wallace is in the race. It is hard to see

---

[3] It should be noted that Spiro Agnew's presence on the Republican ticket did not prevent the Republicans from losing Maryland. And Agnew's strongest ethnic vote as governor in Maryland came from the blacks. He lost the Italians.

the Slavs deserting one of their own in a race for the Presidency, even if his ideology and policy positions are not exactly to their liking. As Humphrey's running mate in 1968, Muskie unquestionably helped cut down on Slavic defections from the Democrats.[4]

At the top of the ticket in 1972, Muskie would in all likelihood reclaim Slavic votes both from the Republicans and from Wallace.

The chief impact of a Muskie candidacy on Slavic voters would be to solidify Democratic margins in Connecticut, Michigan, New York and Pennsylvania, and to enhance Democratic prospects in Illinois, Indiana, New Jersey, Ohio, Wisconsin and Michigan. Slavs in Michigan gave three quarters of their votes to Humphrey in 1968. That doesn't leave much room for improvement, but a Muskie performance as strong as John Kennedy's 90 percent in 1960 would net an additional one-percentage-point plurality for the Democrat in Michigan. Similarly in Pennsylvania an improvement to the Kennedy level would net an additional one-percentage-point plurality for the Democrat statewide. The same situation exists in New York and Connecticut. Although these single-percentage-point gains are not momentous, they are important in the context of traditionally narrow Democratic victory margins in these states.

The best opportunity for a payoff from Muskie's Slavic identification lies in Illinois. Republican inroads have been substantial at all levels of office-seeking among the Slavic 7 percent of the Illinois electorate. Only in 1960 did Slavic voters in Illinois give more than 70 percent of their ballots to the Democratic nominee for President, governor or senator. Humphrey's plurality among Slavic voters was cut to fifteen percentage points over Nixon in 1968. If Muskie can corral the votes of between 70 and 80 percent of his fellow Slavs, his net statewide plurality gain will be in the neighborhood of 4 percentage points, more than enough to close the 1968 Republican victory margin of 3 percentage points.

Any Muskie gains among Slavic voters will assist, but not

assure, Democratic victories in Indiana, New Jersey, Ohio and Wisconsin. In Indiana, it would take a yeoman's showing among the Slavic-for-Muskie 3 percent of the electorate to pick up one percentage point statewide. And that leaves Muskie 11 percentage points short of Nixon's 1968 statewide margin. Due to the already high Democratic percentage among Slavs in Ohio and Wisconsin (Humphrey picked up two thirds of the vote in each state in 1968), Muskie's potential gains are limited to little more than one percentage point in those states. More than two thirds of Nixon's 1968 victory margin would remain intact. In New Jersey, minimum Republican votes suggest that Muskie would do well to carry 70 percent of the state's Slavs. That would about halve Nixon's 1968 victory margin.

If Muskie fails to win the nomination and George Wallace elects to run, the Slavic vote picture becomes quite complicated. The 1968 Wallace vote among Slavs can be read as low or high, depending on your perspective. The Wallace Slavic vote is certainly not high when compared with Wallace's national percentage. Four of the eight states with significant Slavic voting blocs had Slavic percentages for Wallace below the national Wallace percentage. However, when the Wallace percentage among Slavs is compared state by state with his statewide percentages, the Wallace inroads are more visible. Wallace nearly doubled his statewide percentage among Slavs in Illinois and Wisconsin, and did nearly 50 percent better than his statewide percentage among Slavs in Indiana, New Jersey, New York and Ohio. On the average, Wallace ran 50 percent better than his statewide percentage among Slavs—averaging just under 9 percent statewide and just over 13 percent among Slavs. The unanswerable question is just how large or significant a 13 percent Slavic vote for Wallace would be in the context of the 1972 election.

Wallace inroads among Slavic voters, even in the absence of Muskie, are unlikely to tip any state to the Republicans. Wallace inroads could add one percentage point to Democratic difficulties in Illinois, New Jersey, Ohio and Wisconsin, all closely competitive states. But Wallace inroads among Slavs should not cut too heavily into existing Democratic pluralities in Michigan, New York and Pennsylvania. The Slavs just don't seem ripe for large-

CHART 5:   WALLACE AND THE
SLAVS—1968

	Statewide Wallace %	Slavic Wallace %
Illinois	8.5	16
Indiana	11.4	16
Michigan	10.0	13
New Jersey	9.1	14
New York	5.3	9
Ohio	11.8	17
Pennsylvania	8.0	9
Wisconsin	7.6	13

SOURCE: Institute of American Research;
NBC News.

scale Democratic desertions, and they are positioned in such a
way that desertions must be substantial indeed to start costing
the Democrat electoral votes.

IRISH—ALL-AMERICAN

The Irish voter in 1972 will be pretty much like most of the
people who vote in American elections: white, high-school
graduate, middle-class, predominantly Democratic in party affiliation, and wedded to the two-party political system. In one sense,
then, the Irish are afield from ethnic strategies—a Wallace candidacy will almost certainly leave them cold, an independent black
candidacy will make hardly a ripple, and a liberal fourth-party
candidacy (even if led by the O'Dwyers and the McCarthys)
will attract very few of the brethren.

One candidacy would make a very special difference to the
Irish—a Presidential race by Ted Kennedy. All indications are
that whatever the problems Kennedy might encounter with various blocs of the electorate, the least of those will be with the
Irish. Kennedy's Irish appeal would minimize Republican
chances in New York, where Republicans and Conservatives alike
have been pulling many Irish votes out of the Democratic
column. Massachusetts would be untouchable for the Republican, but that is likely to be the case with any Democratic

nominee. It is Illinois where Kennedy's Irish associations might make a difference. If Kennedy could push the Democratic percentage of the Illinois Irish up toward 85 percent (about a 20-percentage-point gain over the normal showing), it would be worth at least 3 percentage points statewide in closing the small 1968 Republican lead.

No Republican strategy is likely to unify the Irish vote against any particular Democratic nominee. The Irish of Massachusetts have shown themselves a hard bunch to move from the Democrats. New York Irish have already dallied with Republicans, and we can expect any additional Republican gains to be so small that the significant Democratic plurality statewide remains unchallenged. The Irish of Illinois seem frozen at a minimum of 65 percent Democratic, even in the face of expensively launched "social issue" appeal, as in Ralph Smith's race for the Senate in 1970. The Republicans will not triumph in 1972 because of anything special they might do with, or to, the Irish vote.

Appeals to the Irish in 1972 will most probably resemble general-electorate strategy, rather than the efforts directed at the other five ethnic groups. This is just another way of saying that ethnicity has become less important to the Irish, and general issues of the day more important. Conceivably, the bloody exchanges in Northern Ireland could have a strong effect on American-Irish politics. However, the trouble in Northern Ireland is more than old enough to have had a shaping effect on the American Irish, and no such effect is visible today. The contrast with American-Jewish political interest in Israel is striking, and a good indication of relative degrees of assimilation as well.

THE BATTLEGROUND STATES:
COALESCING THE ETHNICS

Part of what makes ethnic minorities interesting generally, and particularly interesting to politicians, is that they tend to congregate in the states which decide Presidential elections. States with large electoral votes and traditionally close Presidential contests tend to have large numbers of some or all of our six ethnic groups. If the ethnic groups tended not to concentrate in large cities of big states, an ethnic strategy would hardly make sense. But as the demographic information presented at length throughout indicates, ethnic groups do concentrate in states with large electoral votes. When victory margins in these states start shrinking below 4 percentage points (as they do in all but aberrant elections), it behooves the candidates to take a good long look at the votes of ethnics and the manner in which they can be influenced.

We have chosen in this section not to deal with either the Deep South or the New South. There the story is first of black voting and the possibility of an independent candidacy siphoning off support, and second of George Wallace, whose behavior is unlikely to be influenced by any prediction of ours. And that story has already been told. We pass the states in those groupings with one very important exception—Texas. In 1972, Texas will cast 26 electoral votes. If those votes go to the Republican, he will be a long way toward election as President of the United States. That and the fact that winning Presidential candidates in Texas tend not to win by very much make the state of great interest for its blacks, its Chicanos and its national figures.

A Chicano registration drive can protect Democratic pluralities from the effects of black desertions to an independent black Presidential candidacy. What the local Democratic officials cannot control is the impact on Texas voters of the selection of former Governor, and now Secretary of the Treasury, John Connally as the Vice-Presidential nominee of the Republican party[5]

Evaluating the effect of a Connally candidacy as a Republican in Texas is chancy at best. Lyndon Johnson, certainly a popular

---

[5] It would not be an unprecedented move for a Democrat, even should he remain a Democrat. Andrew Johnson, then a Democrat, was selected as Abraham Lincoln's Vice-Presidential running mate in 1864. As in the case of his namesake one hundred years later, Johnson succeeded to the Presidency after an assassination. Those are two tragic reasons why politicians tend not to turn down an offer of the Vice-Presidency, whatever the local advice. Yet another scenario could find Secretary Connally, triumphant in administering the Nixon economic policy, resigning from the Cabinet in advance of the Democratic convention and being nominated by his old party as it casts for a strong Presidential candidate after a series of inconclusive primaries.

Senator, could produce only a paper-thin margin in 1960 as a
Vice-Presidential *Democrat*. Why a local Democrat running as a
Republican Vice-Presidential nominee should have a more telling
effect on Texas voters is quite difficult to determine, however
popular a governor Connally may have been. (Johnson's average
percentage plurality was a shade lighter than Connally's in three
statewide races.) On paper, John Volpe looks like a candidate
who can contribute more to the Republican cause. On television,
the verdict may be quite a different matter.

Texas is exceptional in that blacks and Mexican-Americans are
the sole influential ethnic groups. Also, one of the major candidates may have his political base in that state. The more general
situation for closely contested, large-electoral-vote states is more
complex interactions among ethnic groups and more subtle relationships with the candidates. California, Illinois, New Jersey,
New York, Ohio and Pennsylvania are illustrative. In 1972, these
six states will cast 181 electoral votes, or two thirds of the electoral total necessary for outright victory. In 1960, Kennedy
carried two thirds, or 120, of the then 177 electoral votes. In 1968,
Humphrey managed 98 of the 181 electoral votes (then differ-
ently distributed). The Democrat must win a significant plurality
of these 181 electoral votes to run close to the Republican in a
national election. Whether the Democrat can gain that goal is
largely a question of the voting behavior of our six ethnic groups.

When Richard Nixon managed a narrow victory in California
in 1960, it was worth 32 electoral votes. Victory in California in
1972, even if by a single vote, will be worth 45 electoral votes,
one sixth of the 280 necessary for victory. The average Democratic Presidential percentage for California blacks, Mexican-
Americans and Jews, in 1960, 1964 and 1968, was 88 percent.
That doesn't leave much room for Democratic improvements in
percentages. However, turnouts in California can vary dramatically, and with more than one third of the Democratic votes
necessary to win California coming from these three groups, a
good deal of attention should be directed to turning out the
vote.

One Republican strategy in California should be to deflect
Democratic attempts to unify and expand black, Chicano and

Jewish votes. Even the strongest Democratic candidate among blacks will falter somewhat in the face of an independent black candidate. It is in the Republican interest to foster such a candidacy. Ted Kennedy is the only Democrat likely to excite Mexican-American voters. It is none too clear that Mexican-Americans vote in large numbers even if excited, but given the choice the Democrats had best pump extra adrenalin into the Chicano part of their equation. The Republicans are well advised to recruit maverick Democrat Los Angeles Mayor Sam Yorty and his earthy Spanish to at least confuse the Chicano voter, if not recruit him for the Republicans. California Jews have generally voted up to 20 percent for Republican candidates. A well-timed administration announcement of jet sales to Israel may both minimize Democratic pluralities and boost the spirits of a sagging California aerospace industry. Of course, the best announcement for the administration would be that of a liberal fourth-party candidate. Most Democratic bloc votes bend a bit in that event.

With the bloc support of blacks, Chicanos and Jews in numbers larger than prior campaigns, the Democrat has the necessary boost to compete with Nixon among all those other Californians he has so assiduously tried to cultivate. Without that bloc support, the Democrat is well advised to pray for selectively heavy rains on election day.

To win the 26 electoral votes of Illinois, the Democrat must mold into one bloc the votes of five ethnic groups. Due to the peculiarly Republican nature of Illinois Slavs, Ed Muskie would appear to be the Democratic nominee best suited to this particular task. Illinois blacks, Italians, Jews and Irish are uniform Presidential Democrats. In the last three Presidential elections, these four groups have averaged better than 83 percent of their ballots for the Democratic nominee. Illinois Slavs have averaged little better than 60 percent Democratic, and Humphrey's 1968 Slavic vote of 49 percent was more than twenty percentage points below the next-lowest Democratic showing in the five groups.

The Republican strategy in Illinois will again seek to dislodge the Democratic bloc. An independent black candidacy will drain some black votes, although the old Dawson Chicago machine (even without its leader) seems to handle competition of any form easily. Giving the Republican Vice-Presidential nod to John Volpe should dislodge quite a few Italian Democrats. A Catholic as Democratic nominee would minimize those defections and help expand the Democratic percentage should Volpe not get the nomination. Mayor Daley's Irish seem comfortably secure in the Democratic column, and Illinois's Jews show few signs indeed of Republican inclinations and unpredictable attitudes toward fourth-party candidates. Republicans should concentrate on the ever-eroding Slavic Democratic vote. However, a Muskie candidacy will make the Slavs indistinguishable from the other largely Democratic ethnic groups of Illinois and take the Republicans' best opportunity away from them.

The ethnic base in Illinois approaches 30 percent of the electorate. A Muskie candidacy without an Italian on the Republican ticket should unite the five ethnic blocs and produce more than half the votes necessary for the Democrat to win. If Republicans can count on eroding the Slavic vote (that is, if Muskie is *not* the nominee) and attack the Italian vote, the Democratic candidate will probably end up thinking that his 1968 losing margin was a good show.

Democratic chances for unifying ethnic blocs do not appear to be nearly as good in New Jersey as they are in California and Illinois. Both New Jersey Italians and Slavs have been trending significantly Republican in recent local elections, and the Democratic losses have shown up as well in Presidential voting patterns. The average Democratic percentage for New Jersey blacks, Italians and Slavs in the past three Presidential elections has been 71 percent. In 1968, Humphrey carried only 42 percent of the Italian vote and 49 percent of the Slavic vote.

In many ways, New Jersey is ethnically the most elusive state for the Democrats. An independent black candidacy, a successful Republican appeal to Italians, either no Muskie or a lukewarm reception of Muskie by Slavs, and the Republicans will have neutralized the entire ethnic bloc, nearly 20 percent of the New Jersey electorate. To build a base plurality which can catapult their candidate into the more Republican parts of the state, the Democrats must block a black candidacy and find a way to recoup Italian and Slavic votes in the face of a concerted Republican attempt to expand already hard-won gains. Success in New Jersey, should it come, augurs success for the Democrat nationwide.

There is a reason people think "New York" when the word ethnic is mentioned, and the reason is that New York just has more ethnics. Although New York's electoral vote has declined from 45 in 1960 to 41 in 1972, it remains the state with the largest and most varied collection of ethnic groups. Even without counting the hard-to-locate Irish, who are certainly present in large numbers, New York finds 44 percent of its electorate composed of our five other ethnic groups. That is nearly half again the national ethnic percentage of 30 to 33 percent.

Not only is New York ethnically the most varied state, but the ethnics it does have vote in more haphazard and unusual patterns than their counterparts around the country. Even the blacks, Puerto Ricans, Slavs and Jews, whose Democratic Presidential percentages have been consistently over 80 percent, show many signs in state and local elections of varying behavior that could hurt the Democratic nominee. Among blacks, Puerto Ricans and Jews, the average New York Democratic vote in the last three Presidential races was 84 percent. Blacks, Jews and Puerto Ricans voted consistently more Democratic in 1968 than they did in 1960. The Democratic problems for 1972 are that black and Puerto Rican turnouts continue to lag, that an independent black candidate can drain already scarce black votes, and that a liberal fourth-party candidacy can deflate Jewish pluralities.[6] A statewide Democratic party forced to welcome Mayor John Lindsay as its leading Democrat has its own internal problems as well.

Republican inroads among Slavs in New York have not been dramatic. If Muskie is not the nominee, Slavs should be a Republican target group. Also, New York's Italians were the only

[6] Alex Rose and his Liberal party may once again become the conduit of an independent candidacy. John Lindsay may end up with the Liberal party line just to convince the national convention of the seriousness of his candidacy. This threat apparently does not impress A.F.L.–C.I.O. President George Meany, who said of Lindsay after the Mayor's party switch, "I think he is the poorest example of a public official I have seen in a long time."

Italians in the country to give Richard Nixon a plurality of their votes in 1968. The Democrats should have a very hard time reversing the flow of Italians to the Republicans. The infatuation of New York's Irish with the "real Republican" ticket of Rockefeller and Buckley in 1970 suggests that the Democrats would do well to break even in 1972. A lot of unfortunate events must occur simultaneously in New York for the Democrat to lose in 1972. But any student of the state's Democratic politics would not hesitate to predict that somehow the party will gravitate to the worst of all possible outcomes.

In Ohio, George Wallace stands in the way of solid Democratic pluralities among Slavs and Italians, and Jews dally impressively with Republican Presidential candidates. In 1968, Wallace totals of 17 percent among Ohio Slavs and 16 percent among Ohio Italians seem to have come directly out of formerly Democratic plurality margins. The Wallace drain among Slavs and Italians accounts for at least half of Humphrey's losing margin in 1968. If Wallace chooses not to run, these Slavic and Italian votes will be fluid, there being no convincing signs of Republican inroads in recent statewide elections. If Muskie is the Democratic candidate, the Slavic voters should come home to roost with the Democrat.

As in other states, Democrats would like to avoid any loss of the black vote (certainly a split among field workers in Cleveland would be disastrous) and to minimize Slavic and Italian movement to Republicans. Since in the last three Presidential elections, the Republicans have never scored higher than 22 percent of the vote among Ohio Slavs or Italians (the Republican average vote was under 17 percent), this task is within reach if Wallace inroads can be controlled. Ohio Democrats have an unusual target group in that Jews have turned in lackadaisical pluralities for the Democratic nominee. The 1970 Democratic ticket of Gilligan and Metzenbaum scored a full 20 percentage points higher among Ohio Jews than had Humphrey in 1968. Ohio is the only state where potential Democratic gains among Jews can be critical in swinging electoral votes to the Democrat.

The options to influence Ohio's 25 electoral votes seem to fall mostly to the Democrats. In 1968 Republicans successfully broke up a unified ethnic-bloc vote. Whether the Democrats can prevent this from happening again among the ethnic 14 percent of the Ohio electorate is the critical question of the 1972 Ohio campaign.

Unlike Ohio, Pennsylvania has a strongly unified black and Jewish voting bloc, with its Slavic and Italian minorities moving more toward the Republicans than toward Wallace. Pennsylvania blacks and Jews have together averaged nearly 87 percent for the Democratic ticket in the last three Presidential campaigns. Statewide elections suggest that Pennsylvania blacks and Jews will be less willing to stray off the Democratic line than, say, the same groups in California or New York. The key to Pennsylvania is the Slavic and Italian vote, together some 12 percent of the electorate.

In 1968, Wallace ethnic strength in Pennsylvania was not extremely impressive, barely one percentage point above his statewide showing of 8 percent. For their part, Republicans achieved decade highs of 26 percent among Slavs and 34 percent among Italians. Republican inroads in local elections have been at least 10 percentage points higher. The Democrat is definitely vulnerable in 1972 among Pennsylvania Slavs and Italians. If Muskie is not on the Democratic ballot to hold the Slavic vote, and Volpe is on the Republican ballot to attract the Italian vote, the G.O.P. can gain enough among Slavs and Italians alone to wipe out the 1968 statewide Democratic plurality of less than four percentage points. Pennsylvania's 27 electoral votes are not the kind of numbers the Democrats can afford to lose. Pennsylvania's Slavs and Italians should be priority targets for the Republicans in 1972.

We have attempted to highlight some of the factors operative for 1972 in large states with relatively large ethnic minorities. From the perspective of today, any of the six states can be won by either of the major-party candidates, and there is enough swing in the votes of ethnic minorities to reverse the 1968 outcomes. But the 1972 election, like most elections of this century, is virtually certain to be closely contested in non-Southern and border states as well. Some of these have significant ethnic minorities, and all are competitive enough for the votes of these ethnic minorities to be critical.

Connecticut and Indiana are two states where Slavic voters
play a major ethnic role, and one party tends to dominate the
outcome. Humphrey carried Connecticut in 1968 by more than 5
percentage points, which in the context of that election for the
Democrats was a fairly comfortable margin. The Slavic minority
and the Catholic majority in Connecticut are still willing to
maintain Democratic voting patterns. It required a serious split
in the Democratic ranks in 1970, and a rather unpopular Democratic governor, to sneak in two Republican officials, Governor
Thomas J. Meskill and Senator Lowell P. Weicker. A Muskie
candidacy would help solidify Catholic and Slavic support for
the Democrat, but any Democratic nominee with a fairly united
party behind him will run strongly for Connecticut's 8 electoral
votes in 1972. It would be demoralizing indeed for the Democrats to lose in Connecticut.

Indiana presents an opposite picture. Although the state is
often regarded as Presidentially competitive, Republican candidates have very rarely had difficulty carrying the state. In 1968,
Indiana gave Richard Nixon a plurality of twelve percentage
points. Slavs are an active ethnic group in Indiana (the steel-
workers of Gary are not simply a creation of the media), but the
state at large more closely resembles a nonethnic farm state, like
Iowa, than its contiguous neighbors, Illinois and Ohio. To make
matters even worse for the Democrat, Indiana Slavs are splitting
both to the Republicans and to Wallace in significant numbers. If
Muskie as a candidate can unite the Slavs and find the same
appeal Senator Birch Bayh has demonstrated in nonurban areas
(or perhaps, find Bayh as his running mate), the Democrats will
have a fighting chance in Indiana. An Indiana Democratic victory
(13 electoral votes) would have the added advantage of stealing
from Republican strength, the best technique for demoralizing
the opposition—and winning an election.

Unlike Connecticut and Indiana, Maryland offers the view of a
Democratic plurality balancing precariously on the backs of
blacks and Jews. Maryland blacks and Jews, together 15 percent
of the electorate, have voted consistently Democratic with the
glaring exception of Spiro Agnew's race for governor in 1966. In
that election one third of Jewish voters supported an indepen-

dent Jewish candidate who had no realistic chance of winning. Similar desertions to a liberal fourth-party candidacy in 1972 could cost the Democrat Maryland's 10 electoral votes. Maryland blacks are less likely to vote off the party line than to simply sit home. The effect on the Democratic vote totals is identical. Black stay-at-homes probably cost Joe Tydings his Senate seat in 1970 and, in the absence of a serious voter drive, will cost the Democrat a Maryland Presidential victory in 1972 as well.

Theoretically, blacks and Jews could desert the Democrat in Massachusetts. But Democratic margins are so substantial that the state can absorb those defections (and more) and still give its 14 electoral votes to the Democrat by a comfortable margin. Humphrey actually ran better in Massachusetts in 1968 than John Kennedy did in 1960. The Vice-President's 30-percentage-point plurality was exceeded only in the District of Columbia. (Nixon lost by more than four to one in the District in 1968.) For Massachusetts to slip from the Democratic grasp in 1972, the worst of everything will have to happen. The blacks will have to vote uniformly for an independent candidate or stay at home. The Jews will have to vote in a bloc for a fourth-party candidacy. The Irish will have to split between independent candidacies and the Republican. The Italians will have to be delivered by John Volpe. The voters who support liberal Republican statewide candidacies will have to troop to Richard Nixon, a candidate they have never before supported. And the Republicans just have to be plain lucky. If this all happens for the G.O.P. in Massachusetts the Democratic candidate's *national* electoral totals are going to end up looking like Alf Landon's in 1936.

The Democratic plurality margin in Michigan is quite a bit smaller than that of Massachusetts. Nevertheless, the stanchly Democratic voting behavior of Michigan blacks and Slavs suggests that overcoming the Democratic lead will be a formidable task. Humphrey carried Michigan in 1968 by nearly seven percentage points. He won a plurality among Slavs of sixty-five percentage points. Assuming a Muskie candidacy capturing the Slavs, and an unsuccessful independent bid for black votes, these two blocs and their 13 percent of the Michigan electorate are secure for the Democrats. Any Republican strategy to break up unified blocs of ethnic minority groups will succeed in a good many other places before succeeding in Michigan.

The last of our highlighted states looks just like Michigan, except that the Democrat is a good bet to lose, because of general Republican tendencies. Wisconsin's 11 electoral votes went to Richard Nixon by nearly four percentage points in 1968 despite a Democratic plurality of eighty-three percentage points among the black 4 percent of the Wisconsin electorate and forty-nine percentage points among the Slavic 5 percent of the Wisconsin electorate. The Republicans may not do much better than they did in 1968 among blacks and Slavs—any gain will be a bonus—but they don't have to do any better to win. The Wisconsin Democratic strategy must look for guidance to successful Democratic appeals in the other largely Republican states of the Midwest. A good ethnic strategy won't be enough to carry Wisconsin. As for a good ethnic strategy plus a good farm strategy—well, that is another question.

REACHING ACROSS ETHNIC MINORITIES—AN ISSUE

We have purposely avoided much issue discussion. Our concern throughout has been to search for underlying trends within groups, between elections. Each election—its personalities, its circumstances—is, and hopefully forever will be, unique. At the same time, it is our thesis that ethnicity breeds a special consanguinity in voting behavior and that an examination of a series of elections for a given group is as good an approach as any to understanding that dynamic.

The election of 1972, like any other, will have unique personalities and unique circumstances, none yet well defined. On these points our data is of little help. Also the issues and programs which most intimately concern ethnics have been proposed and discussed by others, on other occasions.

But another issue is of equal, and perhaps greater, importance. It is largely psychological and reflects our faith in the electoral process.

What is especially intriguing about ethnic politics is the way in which minority Americans, and most notably the blacks, have come, finally, to realize the significance of electoral power. This understanding has been rightly colored by a long history of mistreatment, no treatment, and well-intentioned treatment gone wrong. American liberal history, angry always, has championed the plight of the minority American over many years. Imaginative and far-reaching solutions to many poverty, housing, education, and employment problems have been proposed, and to some extent implemented. But with only a few exceptions these efforts have done little for those they were designed to help, and precisely because of that peculiar method of political genius which results in American government. The very art of compromise, of reasoning together, first urged Biblically and by many since, in addition to the President who so often quoted the challenge, has missed the point.

The concerned American, be he bureaucrat, statesman, politician or political dabbler, has, on behalf of the downtrodden, asked government to *give* something to somebody. And when a government *gives*, it reserves, conditions, or otherwise tempers that aid to a point where a recipient, if he receives at all, is either ungrateful or unwilling to then better his own position. Most often in this century, and particularly with and since the New Deal, aid for the average American (ethnic or WASP) has trickled outward from the center in Washington through an increasingly complicated maze of lower-echelon government structures. All of these, in turn, seek to preserve a measure of control for themselves. They normally succeed, and in so doing rob the "victim" of much of the intended benefit. Of late, much of New Deal liberalism has been fashionably debunked, and the calls for "decentralization" and "community" have received the interested attention of government and, to the pleasure of their advocates, prominent display in the press. But these catchwords and their attendant "solutions" also require *giving* something to somebody. And again the point is missed.

It is unreasonable to assume that a nation born in the ideal of an individual's *taking* for himself what he can will easily adapt to the handout—even if cloaked in the guise of a bureaucracy created at the lowest possible societal level. It is not that government is not capable of removing "strings" (it is, although often, as with O.E.O., it doesn't). Rather, it is that the concept of *giving* itself, while in the interim it may alleviate a particular problem, can never totally eradicate it.

The ballot at least offers a semblance of *taking*. It also, and significantly, ensures that a program won at the polls or extracted from a government because of a realization of electoral power, will more likely be beneficial to those who are to participate in its promise, than a program *given* beneficently out of goodness, or even out of the fear of marches, demonstrations or violence. A program or solution won from a government at the polls is in reality *created* by those who vote for it. It has, to be sure, a better chance of being administered by those who have "elected" it (if that is what they want), but the more important point is that somebody *took* something from someone legitimately and was not given it. The pride inherent in such an assertion can allow a people to comprehend their own worth and to intelligently use their power.

The ethnic Americans have electoral power. They have had it for a long time and can have more. Most have been largely unaware of its existence. To realize that potential is to *take* for oneself. In so doing most if not all of the programs that would be created from such an activity will undoubtedly resemble, or perhaps even be identical with the solutions or programs that others might have advocated, and that government might have given. (Thus, various forms of "decentralization" and "community" might very well characterize twenty-first-century America.) But the *method* is crucial. Taken at the polls, and not given by even a genuinely concerned government, solutions will have a more certain meaning and a more lasting benefit.

The politician (in 1972 and beyond) who can excite a people (especially the ethnics) to an understanding of their own electoral power, and who can suffer the exercise of that power without fear of the consequences, will get, and will deserve, that people's vote. Not incidentally, for those who care about such things, the preeminent distinguishing American characteristic, rule by free election, will be reinvigorated.

By accident of geographical location, the ethnics have within their grasp the political power which can make them responsible for their own destiny. They can take solutions, administer programs, and in so doing need never wonder if a complacent majority will one day rise to trample them, as happened to so many of the ethnics who fled their native lands for the "gold sidewalks" of America.

AFTERWORD

Conventional wisdoms (and there are many) regarding ethnic America are changing. "Rules" once rigid are now fluid, and theories, scenarios, and indices of importance abound.

Within the maze of American ethnic studies most of the thinking, both theoretical and substantive, has been sociological. The old assumptions of assimilation and the melting pot, claiming that American society (particularly through the public school system) would quickly eliminate immigrant differences, have been largely discredited. "Cultural pluralism"—an essentially romantic set of sociological axioms—replaced "assimilation" as the dominant catch phrase for what ethnic America was all about. Out of a nation of immigrants emerged a nation of immigrant groups, a phenomenon that, the pluralists reasoned, would allow for the retention of varying cultural heritages while Americanization proceeded apace.

More recently a dual-assimilation thesis has been propounded. "Cultural assimilation" or "acculturation," the first component, is defined as the act of learning and following society's cues (modes of dress, "acceptable" employment, and so on). The second component, "structural assimilation" (which is really plain, old-fashioned assimilation warmed over), refers to an intermingling of ethic groups and the development of cross-ethnic ties (*i.e.,* friendship and marriage). Those sociologists subscribing to this particular explanation generally concede that acculturation has occurred almost uniformly, but that structural assimilation has not, and that ethnic or religious barriers still inhibit intergroup relationships, particularly intermarriage. This analytical framework offers the added advantage of allowing a hypothesis which sees ethnicity as continuing indefinitely. As long as the outward manifestations of conformity are accepted or performed, social tensions emanating from ethnicity are unlikely.

An especially intriguing thesis (whose prime proponents are Nathan Glazer and Daniel Patrick Moynihan) views ethnic groups as interest groups (like labor unions and professional associations) which exist today as useful vehicles for social, economic and political action. Cultural differences are declining, say these theorists, but the extracultural benefits of ethnic unity are too significant to abandon.

All of this scholarly activity—and more research is being conducted constantly—is interesting and instructive. For implicit in this work is the common notion that ethnicity in America persists —whatever the disparate reasons for that persistence. One gratifying by-product of this viable American ethnicity is that the fear of ethnic identification as bad or divisive in a nation whose motto is "Out of many, one" appears finally to be subsiding.

An integral corollary of the sociological *fact* of ethnicity is the increasing political participation and visibility of ethnic Americans. The United States elected its first Irish Catholic President in 1960. Four years later the G.O.P. nominated a Catholic for Vice-President and chose as its Presidential candidate an Arizona Senator whose immigrant grandfather had been Jewish. The cries of black power that frightened most whites not too long ago are now familiar and accepted; and in the true spirit of American "me-tooism" a host of other ethnic-power chants are being heard everywhere.

But despite the rash of sociological inquiry and the entrance of many ethnics into political races, little is known of the *electoral behavior* of America's ethnics—an unconscionable ignorance, given the exhaustive electoral analyses of the past fifteen years.

Our efforts in this area have yielded the most comprehensive, in-depth study of ethnic voting behavior yet achieved, simply because we took the time and trouble to accumulate the data. But much work remains. Survey analysis of the non-ghettoized ethnics, a costly proposition to be sure, must be undertaken if a complete political profile is to be drawn. And our contribution of course will require expansion and updating. We urge the ethnics themselves and those interested in ethnic Americans to fill this important gap in our electoral knowledge.

Twenty years ago, in *The Future of American Politics*, Samuel Lubell observed: "Those who suffered discrimination in the past—the children of the 'micks,' 'wops,' 'kikes,' 'niggers,' 'polacks,' and other abused groups—at last have the political strength to do something about it." Lubell's prescience is being confirmed—rapidly. Ethnicity is becoming increasingly crucial in our political scheme, and we must strive to understand the dimensions of this reality as completely as possible.

METHODOLOGICAL NOTE

In the 1787 Massachusetts gubernatorial election John Hancock, the Revolutionary War hero, defeated the incumbent Governor James Bowdoin, the suppressor of Shay's Rebellion. Shortly after the election, a Boston newspaper published the following analysis of the vote:

	For Mr. B	For Mr. H
Usurers	28	0
Speculators in Publick Securities	576	0
Stockholders and directors of the M-tts B-k	81	0
Persons under British influence	17	0
Merchants, tradesmen, and other worthy members of society	21	448
Friends to the Revolution	0	327
Wizards	1	0

Hopefully, our analysis has been somewhat less fanciful than this early example of psephology—although equally engaging.

A word is in order concerning our data and methods. Our primary unit of analysis is the precinct. Most of the precinct returns were supplied by NBC News and the remainder by the Institute of American Research. In all, we examined nearly two thousand precincts and more than seven hundred elections. Each precinct was carefully screened to make sure that it contained a very high percentage of a certain type of voter—Italians, Jews, blacks, et cetera.

The maintenance of these unique election-return archives requires the full-time efforts of dozens of people. Vote returns are often hard to come by. Some local officials do not keep complete records; others save only handwritten copies of returns, and then only for a few months after an election. In some jurisdictions, particularly in the South, voting officials are often reluctant to give returns to "outsiders." An official in Mobile, Alabama, for instance, once told us to "get the returns from the goddamn Justice Department, they have all our records anyway." When finally retrieved, the thousands and thousands of individual precinct returns are stored on computer tape.

The NBC Election Unit is quite naturally most concerned with using its data on one night only—election night. The number of precincts collected for any given group in any given state varied from year to year, and often precincts were dropped from the sample because of suspicions that the precinct was no longer "pure" (NBC had no reason to compare precinct returns from year to year).

The Institute of American Research staff developed an analytical package to "mine" the computer tapes. The twofold goal of the package was to permit comparisons of group performances in different elections, and to array all of the data available for any given precinct. The Institute arranged a computer program to meet those goals.

For each ethnic group and for each election in the past decade for which there was data, the precinct returns were rank-ordered by percentage for each of the political parties. This computer processing revealed geographic and socioeconomic patterns within each precinct sample. After the precincts were rank-ordered, they were divided into quartiles. Average party percentages were struck for the highest quartile, the lowest quartile and the aggregation of the middle two quartiles. These percentages were displayed in a table tracing the movement of quartile averages over time. We also looked at individual precinct returns over time, and these were selected so that the population characteristics and boundaries were stable for several elections. This allowed "tracking" of microchanges in party preference and voter turnout down to the precinct level.

We recognize that there are some limitations to election analysis based on precinct-level information rather than survey data. For precinct analysis to work, it is necessary to find ethnic voters who live in large concentrations. The voting habits of these so-called "ghettoized ethnics" may differ somewhat from those of ethnics who, because they are more assimilated into American society, no longer live in the old neighborhoods. A random probability sample would find ethnics wherever they live, but unfortunately, there is no collection of survey data which is detailed enough to allow the level of analysis presented in this book. Even the archives of the Michigan Survey Research Center are limited to Presidential voting and do not have in-depth studies of state and local politics.

But even if survey data did exist, its conclusions would probably not differ greatly from our voter-oriented findings. We have checked, wherever possible, our precinct returns against survey data, and there is considerable coincidence between the results. In the 1964 Presidential election, for example, a Gallup survey found that 24 percent of Catholics said they voted for Goldwater. Our sample precincts for the three groups which comprise most of the Catholic vote—Irish, Slavs, and Italians—gave 20 to 23 percent of their ballots to Goldwater, well within the tolerance limits of the Gallup survey. Certainly our precinct-level analysis is far preferable to the citywide or at best ward-level investigations which have marked most political-science and journalistic accounts in the past.

STATISTICAL APPENDIX

SPANISH-SPEAKING VOTERS
PRESIDENT 1960–1968
(*In Percent*)

| | 1960 | | 1964 | | 1968 | | | |
	Kennedy	*Nixon*	*Johnson*	*Goldwater*	*Humphrey*	*Nixon*	*Wallace*	*Others†*
NATION*	85	15	90	10	87	10	2	1
Arizona	77	23	86	14	81	14	3	2
California	83	17	90	10	87	12	1	1
Colorado	75	25	88	12	75	19	3	3
New Mexico	70	30	77	23	59	38	2	1
New York	77	23	86	14	83	15	2	
Texas	91	9	94	6	93	6	1	

SOURCE: Institute of American Research; NBC News.
* This national figure is for Chicanos only and does not include the vote from New York which is based on Puerto Rican precincts.
† In 1968, the fourth-party Presidential candidates were:
    Arizona—McCarthy (New Party)
    California—Cleaver (Peace and Freedom Party)
    Colorado—Gregory (New Party)
    New Mexico—Chavez (People's Constitutional Party)

BLACK VOTERS
PRESIDENT 1960–1968
(*In Percent*)

| | 1960 | | 1964 | | 1968 | | |
	Kennedy	Nixon	Johnson	Goldwater	Humphrey	Nixon	Wallace
NATION	75	25	97	3	94	5	1
Alabama	68	32	98	2	97	1	2
Arkansas	62	38	98	2	94	4	2
California	86	14	98	2	89	8	3
Connecticut	77	23	95	5	—	–	–
D.C.	—	—	99	1	98	2	0
Florida	76	24	98	2	95	3	2
Georgia	46	54	98	2	97	2	1
Illinois	83	17	98	2	95	5	0
Indiana	78	22	97	3	93	6	1
Kentucky	59	41	95	5	78	19	3
Louisiana	73	26	99	1	96	1	3
Maryland	72	28	96	4	93	4	3
Massachusetts	58	42	97	3	—	–	–
Michigan	89	11	99	1	97	3	0
New Jersey	71	29	95	5	89	10	1
New York	73	27	97	3	94	6	0
North Carolina	85	15	99	1	98	2	0
Ohio	78	22	98	2	90	4	0
Pennsylvania	85	15	97	3	93	7	0
South Carolina	80	20	97	3	95	2	3
Tennessee	72	28	99	1	97	2	1
Texas	84	16	99	1	98	1	1
Virginia	66	34	99	1	97	2	1
Wisconsin	76	24	95	5	91	8	1

SOURCE: Institute of American Research; NBC News.

JEWISH VOTERS
PRESIDENT 1960–1968
(*In Percent*)

| | 1960 | | 1964 | | 1968 | | |
	Kennedy	*Nixon*	*Johnson*	*Goldwater*	*Humphrey*	*Nixon*	*Wallace*
NATION	82	18	90	10	83	15	2
California	83	17	89	11	86	13	1
Illinois	71	29	86	14	82	17	1
Maryland	74	26	84	16	77	20	3
Massachusetts	70	30	90	10	86	13	1
Michigan	75	25	88	12	—	—	—
New York	86	14	92	8	87	12	1
Ohio	63	37	74	26	65	31	3
Pennsylvania	79	21	88	12	80	18	2

SOURCE: Institute of American Research; NBC News.

SLAVIC VOTERS
PRESIDENT 1960–1968
(*In Percent*)

| | 1960 | | 1964 | | 1968 | | |
	Kennedy	*Nixon*	*Johnson*	*Goldwater*	*Humphrey*	*Nixon*	*Wallace*
NATION	82	18	80	20	65	23	12
Connecticut	77	23	82	18	—	—	—
Illinois	73	27	67	33	49	35	16
Indiana	79	21	74	26	57	27	16
Maryland	85	15	75	25	—	—	—
Michigan	90	10	86	14	76	11	13
New Jersey	72	28	75	25	49	37	14
New York	82	18	84	16	71	20	9
Ohio	88	12	86	14	66	17	17
Pennsylvania	78	22	79	21	65	26	9
Wisconsin	83	17	85	15	68	19	13

SOURCE: Institute of American Research; NBC News.

IRISH VOTERS
PRESIDENT 1960–1968
(*In Percent*)

| | 1960 | | 1964 | | 1968* | | |
	Kennedy	*Nixon*	*Johnson*	*Goldwater*	*Humphrey*	*Nixon*	*Wallace*
NATION	75	25	78	22	64	33	3
Illinois	73	27	67	33	–	–	–
Massachusetts	80	20	87	13	–	–	–
New Jersey	–	–	–	–	45	51	4
New York	60	40	64	36	45	48	7
Pennsylvania	–	–	–	–	46	41	13

SOURCE: Institute of American Research; NBC News.
* The 1968 national percentages are based on a NORC postelection survey and the two state percentages are from an Oliver Quayle survey taken in late July and early August of 1968.

ITALIAN VOTERS
PRESIDENT 1960–1968
(*In Percent*)

| | 1960 | | 1964 | | 1968 | | |
	Kennedy	*Nixon*	*Johnson*	*Goldwater*	*Humphrey*	*Nixon*	*Wallace*
NATION	75	25	77	23	50	40	10
Connecticut	72	28	79	21	–	–	–
Illinois	80	20	84	16	75	17	8
Maryland	74	26	73	27	–	–	–
Massachusetts	87	13	89	11	77	16	7
New Jersey	69	31	73	27	42	40	18
New York	64	36	70	30	42	49	9
Ohio	83	17	78	22	65	19	16
Pennsylvania	78	22	72	28	57	34	9
Rhode Island	78	22	87	13	–	–	–

SOURCE: Institute of American Research; NBC News.

SELECTED ETHNIC VOTES STATE BY STATE
GOVERNORS AND SENATORS (*In Percent*)
[Key to party designations on page 241.]

	Italians	*Jews*	*Slavs*	*Blacks*	*Spanish*	*Statewide*
ALABAMA						
1970 Governor						
Wallace (D)				3		75
Cashin (NDPA)				91		15
Others				6		10
1968 Senator						
Allen (D)				7		70
Hooper (R)				6		22
Schwenn (NDPA)				87		8
1966 Governor						
Wallace (D)				43		63
Martin (R)				22		31
Robinson (Ind.)				35		6
1966 Senator						
Sparkman (D)				94		61
Grenier (R)				6		39
ARIZONA						
1970 Governor						
Castro (D)					89	49
Williams (R)					11	51
1970 Senator						
Grossman (D)					85	44
Fannin (R)					15	56
1968 Governor						
Goddard (D)					88	42
Williams (R)					12	58
1968 Senator						
Elson (D)					87	43
Goldwater (R)					13	57
ARKANSAS						
1970 Governor						
Bumpers (D)				11		66
Rockefeller (R)				89		34
1968 Governor						
Crank (D)				8		48
Rockefeller (R)				92		52

	Italians	*Jews*	*Slavs*	*Blacks*	*Spanish*	*Statewide*
1968 Senator						
Fulbright (D)				66		59
Bernard (R)				34		41
1966 Governor						
Johnson (D)				4		46
Rockefeller (R)				96		54
CALIFORNIA						
1970 Governor						
Unruh (D)		82		95	82	45
Reagan (R)		18		3	16	53
Others		—		2	2	2
1970 Senator						
Tunney (D)		85		94	86	54
Murphy (R)		15		3	13	44
Others		—		3	1	2
1968 Senator						
Cranston (D)		86		91	87	52
Rafferty (R)		13		6	12	47
Jacobs (P&F)		1		3	1	1
1966 Governor						
Brown (D)		85		96	80	42
Reagan (R)		15		4	20	58
COLORADO						
1970 Governor						
Hogan (D)					68	45
Love (R)					23	53
Gurule (LRU)					9	2
1968 Senator						
McNichols (D)					75	41
Dominick (R)					25	59
1966 Governor						
Knous (D)					77	45
Love (R)					23	55
1966 Senator						
Romer (D)					76	42
Allott (R)					24	58
CONNECTICUT						
1968 Senator						
Ribicoff (D)			69			54
May (R)			31			46

	Italians	*Jews*	*Slavs*	*Blacks*	*Spanish*	*Statewide*
1966 Governor						
Dempsey (D)	67		73	84		56
Gengras (R)	33		27	16		46
1964 Senator						
Dodd (D)	77		80	93		65
Lodge (R)	23		20	7		35
1962 Governor						
Dempsey (D)	69	70	69	77		53
Alsop (R)	31	30	31	23		47
FLORIDA						
1970 Governor						
Askew (D)				95		57
Kirk (R)				5		43
1970 Senator						
Chiles (D)				94		54
Cramer (R)				6		46
1968 Senator						
Collins (D)		91		96		44
Gurney (R)		9		4		56
1966 Governor						
High (D)		87		94		45
Kirk (R)		13		6		55
GEORGIA						
1970 Governor						
Carter (D)				72		59
Suit (R)				28		41
1968 Senator						
Talmadge (D)				79		78
Patton (R)				21		22
1966 Governor						
Maddox (D)				4		46
Callaway (R)				41		47
Arnall (Ind.)				55		7
ILLINOIS						
1970 Senator						
Stevenson (D)		86	61	95		58
Smith (R)		14	39	5		42
1968 Governor						
Shapiro (D)	82	84	57	93		49
Ogilvie (R)	18	16	43	7		51

	Italians	*Jews*	*Slavs*	*Blacks*	*Spanish*	*Statewide*
1968 Senator						
Clark (D)	80	80	56	95		47
Dirksen (R)	20	20	44	5		53
1964 Governor						
Kerner (D)	83	71	58	94		52
Percy (R)	17	29	42	6		48
INDIANA						
1970 Senator						
Hartke (D)				93		50
Roudebush (R)				7		50
1968 Governor						
Rock (D)			09	94		47
Whitcomb (R)			31	6		53
1968 Senator						
Bayh (D)			71	94		52
Ruckelshaus (R)			29	6		48
1964 Governor						
Branigin (D)			76	94		56
Ristine (R)			24	6		44
KENTUCKY						
1968 Senator						
Peden (D)				74		48
Cook (R)				26		52
1967 Governor						
Ward (D)				68		48
Nunn (R)				32		52
1966 Senator						
Brown (D)				45		36
Cooper (R)				55		64
1963 Governor						
Breathitt (D)				68		51
Nunn (R)				32		49
MARYLAND						
1970 Governor						
Mandel (D)		92		88		66
Blair (R)		6		7		32
Merkle (AIP)		2		5		2
1970 Senator						
Tydings (D)		80		91		48
Beall (R)		20		6		51
Wilder (AIP)		—		3		1

	Italians	*Jews*	*Slavs*	*Blacks*	*Spanish*	*Statewide*
1968 Senator						
Brewster (D)		63		84		39
Mathias (R)		32		14		48
Mahoney (Ind.)		5		2		13
1966 Governor						
Mahoney (D)	73	21	82	5		41
Agnew (R)	15	44	10	85		50
Pressman (Ind.)	12	35	8	10		9
MASSACHUSETTS						
1970 Governor						
White (D)	51	46				43
Sargent (R)	49	54				57
1970 Senator						
Kennedy (D)	79	72				63
Spaulding (R)	21	28				37
1966 Governor						
McCormack (D)	35	42		39		37
Volpe (R)	65	58		61		63
1966 Senator						
Peabody (D)	59	45		10		39
Brooke (R)	41	55		90		61
MICHIGAN						
1970 Governor						
Levin (D)			58	92		49
Milliken (R)			42	8		51
1970 Senator						
Hart (D)				96		67
Romney (R)				4		33
1966 Governor						
Ferency (D)		51	71	84		39
Romney (R)		49	29	16		61
1966 Senator						
Williams (D)		65	78	94		44
Griffin (R)		35	22	6		56
MISSOURI						
1970 Senator						
Symington (D)				92		51
Danforth (R)				8		49
1968 Governor						
Hearnes (D)				84		61
Roos (R)				16		39

	Italians	*Jews*	*Slavs*	*Blacks*	*Spanish*	*Statewide*
1968 Senator						
Eagleton (D)				95		51
Curtis (R)				5		49
1964 Governor						
Hearnes (D)				95		62
Shepley (R)				5		38
NEW JERSEY						
1970 Senator						
Williams (D)	65		66	87		55
Gross (R)	31		34	11		42
Job (Ind.)	4		—	2		3
1969 Governor						
Meyner (D)	43		46	83		39
Cahill (R)	57		54	17		61
1966 Senator						
Wilentz (D)	54		51	64		38
Case (R)	46		49	36		62
1965 Governor						
Hughes (D)	69		68	83		58
Dumont (R)	31		32	17		42
NEW MEXICO						
1970 Governor						
King (D)					69	52
Domenici (R)					30	47
Sedillo (PCP)					1	1
1970 Senator						
Montoya (D)					77	52
Carter (R)					21	47
Higgs (PCP)					2	1
1968 Governor						
Chavez (D)					67	50
Cargo (R)					33	50
1968 Senator						
Anderson (D)					68	53
Carter (R)					32	47
NEW YORK						
1970 Governor						
Goldberg (D-L)	33	75	58	78	71	40
Rockefeller (R)	65	23	36	21	28	53
Adams (Con.)	2	2	6	1	1	7

	Italians	*Jews*	*Slavs*	*Blacks*	*Spanish*	*Statewide*
1970 Senator						
Ottinger (D)	37	67	53	71	70	37
Goodell (R-L)	21	20	25	25	22	24
Buckley (Con.)	42	13	22	4	8	39
1968 Senator						
O'Dwyer (D)	39	35	59	71	71	31
Javits (R-L)	36	60	34	28	27	53
Buckley (Con.)	25	5	7	1	2	16
1966 Governor						
O'Connor (D)	50	49	66	54	71	38
Rockefeller (R)	34	32	21	33	19	45
Roosevelt (L)	5	16	10	12	8	8
Adams (Con.)	11	3	3	1	2	9
NORTH CAROLINA						
1968 Governor						
Scott (D)				99		53
Gardner (R)				1		47
1968 Senator						
Ervin (D)				91		61
Sumers (R)				9		39
1966 Senator						
Jordan (D)				93		56
Shallcross (R)				7		44
1964 Governor						
Moore (D)				90		57
Gavin (R)				10		43
OHIO						
1970 Governor						
Gilligan (D)	69	87	77	88		55
Cloud (R)	31	13	23	12		45
1970 Senator						
Metzenbaum (D)	53	85	66	90		49
Taft, Jr. (R)	47	15	34	10		51
1968 Senator						
Gilligan (D)	65	74	76	88		49
Saxbe (R)	35	26	24	12		51
1966 Governor						
Reams, Jr. (D)	55	40	64	61		38
Rhodes (R)	45	60	36	39		62

	Italians	*Jews*	*Slavs*	*Blacks*	*Spanish*	*Statewide*
PENNSYLVANIA						
1970 Governor						
Shapp (D)	52	85		83		57
Broderick (R)	48	15		17		43
1970 Senator						
Sesler (D)	65	68		89		47
Scott (R)	35	32		11		53
1968 Senator						
Clark (D)	56	73	72	91		46
Schweiker (R)	44	26	26	8		52
Others	—	1	2	1		2
1966 Governor						
Shapp (D)	58	83	64	83		47
Shafer (R)	42	17	36	17		53
SOUTH CAROLINA						
1970 Governor						
West (D)				98		52
Watson (R)				1		46
Bethea (Ind.)				1		2
1968 Senator						
Hollings (D)				97		62
Parker (R)				3		38
1966 Governor						
McNair (D)				98		58
Rogers (R)				2		42
1966 Senator						
Morah (D)				98		38
Thurmond (R)				2		62
TENNESSEE						
1970 Governor						
Hooker, Jr. (D)				98		47
Dunn (R)				2		53
1970 Senator						
Gore (D)				96		48
Brock (R)				4		52
1966 Senator						
Clement (D)				90		44
Baker (R)				10		56

	Italians	Jews	Slavs	Blacks	Spanish	Statewide
1962 Governor						
Clement (D)				90		76
Patty (R)				10		24
TEXAS						
1970 Governor						
Smith (D)				90	77	54
Eggers (R)				10	23	46
1970 Senator						
Bentsen, Jr. (D)				94	83	54
Bush (R)				6	17	46
1968 Governor						
Smith (D)				82	89	57
Eggers (R)				18	11	43
1966 Senator						
Carr (D)				94	82	43
Tower (R)				6	18	57
VIRGINIA						
1970 Senator						
Rawlings (D)				91		31
Garland (R)				7		15
Byrd, Jr. (Ind.)				2		54
1969 Governor						
Battle (D)				61		46
Holton (R)				39		54
1966 Senator						
Spong (D)				89		64
Ould (R)				11		36
1965 Governor						
Godwin (D)				80		56
Holton (R)				20		44
WISCONSIN						
1970 Governor						
Lucey (D)				94		55
Olson (R)				6		45
1970 Senator						
Proxmire (D)				95		71
Erickson (R)				5		29
1968 Governor						
La Follette (D)			75	87		47
Knowles (R)			25	13		53

	Italians	Jews	Slavs	Blacks	Spanish	Statewide
1968 Senator						
Nelson (D)			83	92		62
Leonard (R)			17	8		38

D —Democrat
R —Republican
L —Liberal
Con. —Conservative
Ind. —Independent
AIP —American Independent Party
PCP —People's Constitutional Party
LRU—La Raza Unida
P&F —Peace and Freedom Party
NDPA —National Democratic Party of Alabama

SELECTIVE BIBLIOGRAPHY

Abbott, David W., Gold, Louis H., and Rogowsky, Edward T., *Police, Politics and Race: The New York City Referendum on Civilian Review.* New York and Cambridge, Mass.: The American Jewish Committee and the Joint Center for Urban Studies of M.I.T. and Harvard University, 1969.

Abramson, Harold J., *Ethnic Pluralism in the Connecticut Central City.* Urban Research Report No. 17, August, 1970. Storrs, Connecticut: Institute of Urban Research, University of Connecticut.

Bailey, Harry A., Jr., and Katz, Ellis (eds.), *Ethnic Group Politics.* Columbus, Ohio: Charles E. Merrill Publishing Co., 1969.

Brink, William, and Harris, Louis, *Black and White.* New York: Simon and Schuster, 1967.

Characteristics of the Population by Ethnic Origin: November, 1969. Series P–20, No. 221. Washington, D.C.: U.S. Government Printing Office, 1971.

Davidowicz, Lucy, "Jewish Voting in the 1968 Presidential Election: Preliminary Report." Paper prepared for the American Jewish Committee, Research and Information Services, November 15, 1968.

——— and Goldstein, Leon J., *Politics in a Pluralist Democracy.* New York: Institute of Human Relations Press, 1963.

Elinson, Jack, Haberman, Paul W., and Gell, Cyrille, *Ethnic and Educational Data on Adults in New York City 1963–1964.* New York: School of Public Health and Administration, Columbia University, 1967.

Fitzpatrick, Joseph P., *Puerto Rican Americans: The Meaning of Migration to the Mainland.* Englewood Cliffs, N.J.: Prentice-Hall, 1971.

Fuchs, Lawrence H., *The Political Behavior of American Jews.* Glencoe, Ill.: Free Press, 1956.

———(ed.), *American Ethnic Politics*. New York: Harper and Row, 1968.

Gans, Herbert, *The Urban Villagers*. Glencoe, Ill.: Free Press, 1962.

Goldstein, Sidney, "American Jewry, 1970: A Demographic Profile." Paper prepared for the Task Force on the Future of the Jewish Community in America, American Jewish Committee, New York, September, 1970.

Gordon, Milton M., *Assimilation in American Life*. New York: Oxford University Press, 1964.

Grebler, Leo, Moore, Joan W., and Guzman, Ralph, *The Mexican-American People*. New York: Free Press, 1970.

Greeley, Andrew M., *Why Can't They Be Like Us?* New York: E. P. Dutton, 1971.

———, *That Most Distressful Nation: The Taming of the American Irish*. New York: Quadrangle Books, forthcoming.

———, and Sheatsley, Paul B., "Attitudes Toward Desegregation." *Scientific American* (December, 1971).

Greer, Scott, "Catholic Voters and the Democratic Party." *Public Opinion Quarterly* (Winter, 1961).

Hadden, Jeffrey K., Masotti, Lewis H., and Thiessen, Victor, "The Making of the Negro Mayors 1967." *Transaction* (January–February, 1968).

Hawkins, Brett W., and Lorinskas, Robert A. (eds.), *The Ethnic Factor in American Politics*. Columbus, Ohio: Charles E. Merrill Publishing Co., 1970.

Klebanoff, Arthur, "Is There a Jewish Vote?" *Commentary* (January, 1970).

———, "A Poverty of Politics: Legislative Constituencies and the Borough of Brooklyn 1950–1965." Unpublished Senior Thesis, Yale University, 1969.

LaGumina, Salvatore, "The New York Elections of 1970 and the Italian-American Voter." Paper presented at Conversations in the Discipline, State University of New York at Farmingdale, N.Y., January 23, 1971.

Lemon, Richard, *The Troubled Americans*. New York: Simon and Schuster, 1970.

Levine, Edwin M., *The Irish and Irish Politicians*. Notre Dame, Ind.: Notre Dame Press, 1966.

Lockard, Duane, *New England State Politics*. Princeton, N.J.: Princeton University Press, 1959.

Lopreato, Joseph, *Italian Americans*. New York: Random House, 1970.

Lubell, Samuel, *The Future of American Politics* (third edition, revised). New York: Harper and Row, 1965.

Malzberg, Amy, and Rosenfield, Geraldine, "America Votes, 1970: The Center Holds." Research Report prepared by American Jewish Committee, December, 1970.

Matthews, Donald R., and Prothro, James W., *Negroes and the New Southern Politics.* New York: Harcourt, Brace and World, 1966.

Moynihan, Daniel P., and Glazer, Nathan, *Beyond the Melting Pot* (second edition). Cambridge, Mass.: M.I.T. University Press, 1971.

Parenti, Michael, "Ethnic Politics and the Persistence of Ethnic Identification." *American Political Science Review* (September, 1967).

Persons of Spanish Origin in the United States: November, 1969, Series P–20, No. 213. Washington, D.C.: U.S. Government Printing Office, 1971.

Phillips, Kevin P., *The Emerging Republican Majority.* New Rochelle, N.Y.: Arlington House, 1969.

Scammon, Richard M., and Wattenberg, Ben J., *The Real Majority.* New York: Coward-McCann, 1970.

Schroeder, Richard, "Spanish-Americans: The New Militants." *Editorial Research Reports* (September 25, 1970).

Tomasi, S. M., and Engel, M. H. (eds.), *The Italian Experience in the United States.* Staten Island, N.Y.: Center for Migration Studies, 1970.

Tortora, Vincent, "Italian Americans: Their Swing to the G.O.P." *The Nation* (October 24, 1953).

Velikonja, Joseph, "Italian Immigrants in the United States in the Mid-Sixties." *The International Migration Review* (Summer, 1967).

Voter Participation in November 1968 (*Advance Statistics*). Series P–20, No. 177. Washington, D.C.: U.S. Government Printing Office, 1968.

Wagner, Stanley P., "The Polish-American Vote in 1960." *Polish American Studies* (January–June, 1964).

Wolfinger, Raymond, "The Development and Persistence of Ethnic Voting." *American Political Science Review* (December, 1965).

Wytrwal, Joseph A., *Poles in American History and Tradition.* Detroit: Endurance Press, 1969.

INDEX

245